Spirituality and English Language Teaching

NEW PERSPECTIVES ON LANGUAGE AND EDUCATION

Series Editors: Professor Viv Edwards, *University of Reading, UK* and Professor Phan Le Ha, *University of Hawaii at Manoa, USA*

Two decades of research and development in language and literacy education have yielded a broad, multidisciplinary focus. Yet education systems face constant economic and technological change, with attendant issues of identity and power, community and culture. This series will feature critical and interpretive, disciplinary and multidisciplinary perspectives on teaching and learning, language and literacy in new times.

All books in this series are externally peer-reviewed.

Full details of all the books in this series and of all our other publications can be found on http://www.multilingual-matters.com, or by writing to Multilingual Matters, St Nicholas House, 31–34 High Street, Bristol BS1 2AW, UK.

NEW PERSPECTIVES ON LANGUAGE AND EDUCATION: 60

Spirituality and English Language Teaching

Religious Explorations of Teacher Identity, Pedagogy and Context

Edited by

Mary Shepard Wong and Ahmar Mahboob

MULTILINGUAL MATTERS
Bristol • Blue Ridge Summit

https://doi.org/10.21832/WONG1534
Library of Congress Cataloging in Publication Data
A catalog record for this book is available from the Library of Congress.
Names: Wong, Mary Shepard, editor. | Mahboob, Ahmar, editor.
Title: Spirituality and English Language Teaching: Religious Explorations of Teacher Identity, Pedagogy and Context/Edited by Mary Shepard Wong and Ahmar Mahboob.
Description: Bristol, UK; Blue Ridge Summit, PA: Multilingual Matters, [2018] | Series: New Perspectives on Language and Education: 60 | Includes bibliographical references and index.
Identifiers: LCCN 2018012623| ISBN 9781788921534 (hbk : alk. paper) | ISBN 9781788921527 (pbk : alk. paper) | ISBN 9781788921565 (kindle)
Subjects: LCSH: English language—Study and teaching—Foreign speakers. | English teachers—Religious life. | English language—Religious aspects.
Classification: LCC PE1128.A2 S635 2018 | DDC 428.0071—dc23 LC record available at https://lccn.loc.gov/2018012623

British Library Cataloguing in Publication Data
A catalogue entry for this book is available from the British Library.

ISBN-13: 978-1-78892-153-4 (hbk)
ISBN-13: 978-1-78892-152-7 (pbk)

Multilingual Matters
UK: St Nicholas House, 31–34 High Street, Bristol BS1 2AW, UK.
USA: NBN, Blue Ridge Summit, PA, USA.

Website: www.multilingual-matters.com
Twitter: Multi_Ling_Mat
Facebook: https://www.facebook.com/multilingualmatters
Blog: www.channelviewpublications.wordpress.com

The policy of Multilingual Matters/Channel View Publications is to use papers that are natural, renewable and recyclable products, made from wood grown in sustainable forests. In the manufacturing process of our books, and to further support our policy, preference is given to printers that have FSC and PEFC Chain of Custody certification. The FSC and/or PEFC logos will appear on those books where full certification has been granted to the printer concerned.

Typeset by Nova Techset Private Limited, Bengaluru and Chennai, India.
Printed and bound in the UK by Short Run Press Ltd.
Printed and bound in the US by Thomson-Shore, Inc.

This book is dedicated to our mentors, Tom Scovel and Earl Stevick, who have taught us that the classroom is a sacred place, and to our students, who remind us daily that who we are can be just as important as what we teach.

Contents

Contributors

Deena Boraie is the Dean and Professor of Practice of the School of Continuing Education at the American University in Cairo. She served as President of the TESOL International Association, a large US-based international professional development association for teachers of English to speakers of other languages from 2012 to 2015. Deena is a language testing expert and an assessment and evaluation consultant and trainer. She has published and presented in several countries on topics ranging from assessment literacy, language testing and assessment, teacher beliefs, student and teacher motivation and English as a lingua franca.

Sid Brown has been studying Buddhism since 1982, researching and living in India, Sri Lanka, Japan, Thailand and the United States as she earned her PhD in religious studies. Sid's *The Journey of One Buddhist Nun* explores the life story and meditation experiences of a modern Buddhist nun in Thailand, while her book *A Buddhist in the Classroom* explores ethical quandaries, lived experiences and the intimacy of teaching. She now teaches at the University of the South in Sewanee, TN.

Suresh Canagarajah is Erle Sparks Professor of English and Applied Linguistics at Penn State University. His publication, *Translingual Practice: Global Englishes and Cosmopolitan Relations* (Routledge, 2013), won the best book award from the British Association of Applied Linguistics and the Shaughnessy Award from the Modern Language Association of America.

MaryAnn Christison is a Professor in the Department of Linguistics at the University of Utah. She served on the board of directors of TESOL International Association, including a term as President in 1997–1998. In 2012, MaryAnn received the Alatis Award for Distinguished Service to the Profession, and in 2016, as part of TESOL's 50th anniversary, was recognized with a 'TESOL 50@50 Award' for significant contributions to the TESOL profession through teaching, research and leadership. She is on the Board of Trustees for The International Research Foundation for English Language Education (TIRF).

Eve Courtney is an English language teacher in Sydney. She received the MAK Halliday award for excellence in applied linguistics during her Masters of applied linguistics at Sydney University, and has an interest in research related to English language universities' preparation and support of ESL/EFL students.

Raafat Gabriel works as English instructor in the English Preparation Program, School of Business, American University of the Middle East (AUM). He has been involved in the EFL field as a teacher, teacher trainer and language program administrator for 23 years. He has presented at TESOL International, Nile-TESOL and TESOL Arabia since 2012. Raafat has an MA in TEFL from the American University in Cairo (AUC) and is currently a doctoral student. His publications include a book on EFL for blind learners. His interests are teacher training, EFL professional development, assessment, ESP, EFL instructional technology and EFL educational administration.

Atta Gebril is an Associate Professor in the Department of Applied Linguistics, the American University in Cairo (AUC), Egypt. He obtained his PhD in foreign language and ESL education with a minor in language testing from the University of Iowa. He previously worked for American College Testing (ACT, Inc.), where he was part of the Workkeys assessment team. In addition, Atta has worked as an assessment and evaluation consultant and has participated in a number of test development projects in many parts of the world. His research interests include writing assessment, reading–writing connections, assessment literacy and test validation.

Joel Heng Hartse is a lecturer in the Faculty of Education at Simon Fraser University. He completed his PhD in in TESL at the University of British Columbia. His work in the areas of sociolinguistics, writing and education has appeared in the *Journal of Second Language Writing, Asian Englishes, English Today* and *Composition Studies*, and he is the co-author of *Perspectives on Teaching English at Colleges and Universities in China* (TESOL Press) and co-editor of the *Canadian Journal for Studies in Discourse and Writing/Rédactologie.*

Carolyn Kristjánsson has a PhD in language education and is an Associate Professor of Applied Linguistics at Trinity Western University in Canada where she teaches in the online and resident tracks of the MA TESOL program. Her publications include work on theological influences in Freirian thought, the interconnection of Christian faith and ELT, and research on identity and interpersonal dynamics in church-sponsored language programs and online graduate education.

Ryuko Kubota is Professor in the Department of Language and Literacy Education in the Faculty of Education at University of British Columbia. Her research focuses on critical approaches to culture, race and language education. She is a co-editor of *Race, Culture, and Identities in Second Language Education: Exploring Critically Engaged Practice* (2009) and *Demystifying Career Paths after Graduate School: A Guide for Second Language Professionals in Higher Education* (2012). Ryuko's publications have also appeared in *Applied Linguistics, Critical Inquiry in Language Studies, Journal of Second Language Writing, Journal of Multilingual and Multicultural Development, Linguistics and Education* and *TESOL Quarterly*, among others.

Ahmar Mahboob is Associate Professor of Linguistics at the University of Sydney. He is keenly interested in the application of language sciences to developmental issues, with a particular focus on education. His primary research interest is on an examination of policies, practices and implications of language variation in local and global contexts. In pursuing this goal, he draws from and contributes to a range of linguistics and applied linguistics traditions, theories and methodologies. Some of Ahmar's recent books include *Challenges to Education in GCC during the 21st Century* (2017) with Tariq Elyas, *Genre Pedagogy in Higher Education: The SLATE Project* (2016) with Shooshi Dreyfus, Sally Humphrey and Jim Martin, and *Language and Identity across Modes of Communication* (2015) with Novi Djenar and Ken Cruickshank.

Brian Morgan is an Associate Professor in the Department of English at Glendon College/York University in Toronto, Canada, where he teaches courses in content-based EAP, language teacher education, and graduate courses in Applied Linguistics. His primary research area is in critical theories and their potential implementation across English language teaching contexts. Recently, Brian has collaborated in several projects linking Glendon College with Brazilian universities and scholars. He is also a co-editor (along with Alastair Pennycook and Ryuko Kubota) of the Critical Language and Literacy series published by Multilingual Matters.

Saeed Nazari is a doctoral student and teaching assistant in the Department of Curriculum and Pedagogy at the University of British Columbia where he intends to theorize a learner-centered curriculum in what personalized voices are valued. Previously, he taught English language for over 15 years in Iran at Arsanjan Islamic University and in Canada at Vancouver Georgia College. His work has appeared in the *Journal of the Faculty of Letters and Humanities* and *BC TEAL*. As a Muslim educator, Saeed is interested in interfaith dialogue to bring about mutual understanding for the Abrahamic religions and peace to the world.

Kassim A. Shaaban is Professor of Applied Linguistics in the English Department at the American University of Beirut. His professional experience includes university teaching, research, ESL teacher training, program design and program evaluation, and curriculum development. His research interests cover a wide range of topics: language planning and language policy, ethnolinguistic vitality, multilingualism, attitudes and motivation, assessment and cooperative learning in ESL. Kassim has published numerous articles in international journals and given conference presentations worldwide on these topics. His current focus in research is on language policies in the Arab world and their impact on social, economic and educational development.

Bal Krishna Sharma is an Assistant Professor of English at the University of Idaho, Moscow. His interests include various discourse analytic and qualitative research methods in studying topics of language ideology and identity in sociolinguistics and English pedagogy. His publications have previously appeared in *Classroom Discourse, Linguistics and Education, Language and Linguistics Compass, Multilingua* and *Journal of Sociolinguistics.*

David Smith is Director of Graduate Studies in Education, Professor of Education and Director of the Kuyers Institute for Christian Teaching and Learning at Calvin College. He has published on pedagogy, social justice and intercultural learning and the intersections of Christian practice and educational practice. Some of David's book titles include *Christians and Cultural Diversity* (2016), *Teaching and Christian Imagination* (2016), *Teaching and Christian Practices: Reshaping Faith and Learning* (2011), *Learning from the Stranger: Christian Faith and Cultural Diversity* (2009), *Spirituality, Social Justice and Language Learning* (2007) and *Spirituality, Justice and Pedagogy* (2006).

Stephanie Vandrick is Professor in the Department of Rhetoric and Language at the University of San Francisco. Her research interests include social class and gender issues in second language education, critical and feminist pedagogies, postcolonial theory, and the use of personal narrative in academic research and writing. Stephanie is the author of *Interrogating Privilege*, co-editor of *Writing for Scholarly Publication* and co-author of *Ethical Issues for ESL Faculty*, as well as the author of many journal articles, chapters and conference papers. She serves on the editorial boards of *TESOL Quarterly* and *Critical Inquiry in Language Studies.*

Henry Widdowson has been Professor of Education at the University of London and Professor of Applied Linguistics at the University of Essex. He was a founding editor of the journal *Applied Linguistics* and for 30 years acted as applied linguistics adviser to Oxford University Press.

Henry has lectured and written extensively on applied linguistics, discourse analysis and language teaching. His publications include *Teaching Language as Communication* (1978), *Aspects of Language Teaching* (1990), *Defining Issues in English Language Teaching* (2003), *Text, Context, Pretext* (2004) and *Discourse Analysis* (2007). Now retired, he is Professor Emeritus, University of London and Honorary Professor at the University of Vienna.

Mary Shepard Wong is Professor in the Global Studies, Sociology and TESOL Department at Azusa Pacific University in southern California, where she directs the field-based TESOL program. She has received two Senior Fulbright Awards (Hong Kong 2012–2013 and Myanmar 2015–2016) and served as the principal investigator of two evaluations funded by the Hong Kong Government (2014–2017). Mary is the lead editor of two Routledge anthologies, author of a Cambridge textbook, and has authored several chapters and articles which explore how spiritual, professional and native/non-native teacher identities influence language teaching and learning.

Acknowledgments

We would like to thank the following people who supported us in compiling this volume. I (Mary) would like to thank my provost, dean and chair for encouragement and release time and for the writer retreats in Malibu to work on this book. Thanks, too, to my students in the 'Critical Perspectives' course, for engaging with the readings and each other in deep and difficult ways, allowing your views to be challenged and informed by those who you may at first have disagreed with.

Ahmar would also like to thank his students and colleagues for their support and engagement with his work and projects.

We would also like to thank the contributors to this volume for their patience and willingness to take on such a challenging project. We would especially like to thank Eve Courtney for helping us copyedit and prepare this volume for submission. Special thanks also to our editors at Multilingual Matters who were understanding as contributors joined and left the project and for allowing time for the volume to evolve.

Foreword: Complexifying our Understanding of Spirituality

It is high time religion came out of the closet in language teaching and education. Although spiritual beliefs and experiences have always influenced teaching and scholarship, the modern educational system had not given us a space to talk about them. Education as it was conceived in the Western European enlightenment tradition assumed that religion constituted a form of harmful bias, blind adherence to tradition and unexamined knowledge that needed to be kept out of teaching and scholarship. However, recent philosophical changes suggest the significance of religion and spirituality in education. This book presents for consideration how teachers draw from spiritual experiences in their professional life, enabling us to develop a more critical, reflective and conscious teaching practice.

I wish to outline three reasons why spirituality is becoming important for educators. Firstly, philosophical schools that counter the modernist orientations of positivism temper our belief that reality or truth can be apprehended by a detached, objective and value-free approach. Movements such as social constructionism suggest that human inquiry always draws from our experiences, beliefs and social collaboration. In fact, spiritual commitment can give an enriching perspective on our inquiry. It provides us with certain ethical and moral values which enable us to construct theories and knowledge aimed at furthering quality of life, social justice, environmental sustainability and cultural diversity. From this perspective, the scholarship we develop on education and language teaching comes with a critical edge. It is an attempt to make a better world for all of us. There is no need to pretend that we are engaged in disinterested knowledge.

Secondly, and more directly related to the goals of this book, scholars in teaching and teacher development argue that it is important to engage the identities and beliefs of teachers for more relevant, meaningful and enriching teaching practice. The approach has shifted from earlier models which conceived of teaching as an acquisition of technical skills or certain forms of knowledge. We now hold that teaching is a development of an identity that integrates skills and knowledge in relation to one's overarching sense of beliefs. The skills and knowledge imparted to teachers on effective teaching will be mediated by their beliefs and experiences even if we do not address them in our teacher development courses. The uptake of the skills and knowledge will be considerably motivated by the teacher's beliefs. In addition to religious beliefs, teachers also bring with them beliefs about good teaching that are motivated by their spiritual experiences and values. This realization has motivated teacher development programs to develop more reflective approaches which help make the beliefs of the teachers more explicit and enable them to develop a more coherent practice that integrates their teaching philosophy and professional expertise with their belief systems.

Thirdly, we are also realizing that good language learning involves developing suitable dispositions among students. Here again we have moved beyond earlier language acquisition models which conceived of learning as a behaviorist form of habit formation on grammar use or, contrastingly, a Cartesian mode of cognitive grammatical control. The appreciation that the world is diverse and involves constant interactions with others who do not share our own language norms has made us go beyond conceiving competence as a mastery of grammatical norms. When grammatical norms are diverse and constantly changing (even within the same language, 'English'), we realize that we have to prepare students to be lifelong learners. There is no end point to learning a language (or multiple languages and genres) in order to conduct our social life meaningfully today. This process also involves learning on the spot during an interaction – that is, deciphering the norms and codes of our interlocutors as we interact with them in global contact zones of diversity. For all such purposes, we increasingly realize that the development of suitable dispositions of learning and negotiating are more important than a mechanical mastery of normative grammar. Among such resourceful dispositions are religious beliefs and spiritual experiences that can inculcate tolerance, humility, patience, self-reflection and openness which are important for our students.

The chapters in this book help us sample the teaching practices, professional values and philosophical orientations of spiritually inclined (and in some cases not spiritually inclined) language teachers. I hope that the chapters show us that bringing spirituality into the classroom is not a spontaneous, passive or intuitive practice. It involves a complex negotiation of multiple factors. When there are diverse religions in the classroom, with diverse value systems (some of which are antithetical to religion) and different pedagogical contexts where spiritual experiences will find different manifestation, teachers and students have to negotiate the appropriate representation of religion all the time. The chapters in this book will help us develop a more reflective, analytical and conscious position on how to draw from religion in our teaching.

Furthermore, spirituality doesn't have to be a one-way application of religious beliefs in our professional life. Our professional and scholarly experiences can in turn inform and shape our religious beliefs. The classroom engagement of beliefs is not just good for our teaching; it is good for our spirituality. The challenges we encounter in teaching and scholarship can provide new insights into spirituality. They can help us interrogate how our spirituality can become more relevant to the challenges in our everyday life. They can enrich and complexify our understanding of spirituality.

I pray that this book will motivate us to reflect on more effective ways to draw from our religious beliefs for meaningful education, while probing our beliefs in the light of our professional experiences to deepen our spirituality.

Suresh A. Canagarajah

1 Introduction: Why a Book on Spirituality and Language Teaching?

Mary Shepard Wong

Over the past two decades, there has been a resurgence of interest in exploring the relationship of religious faith and/or spirituality in the process and practices of English language teaching and learning (Edge, 1996, 2003; Johnston, 2017; Johnston & Varghese, 2006; Pennycook & Coutand-Marin, 2003; Smith & Carvill, 2000; Snow, 2001; Stevick, 1997; Varghese & Johnston, 2007; Wong & Canagarajah, 2009; Wong *et al.*, 2013). Canagarajah notes in this volume that recent philosophical changes in human inquiry from positivistic views to social constructivist orientations allow for the consideration of religion and spirituality in language learning and teaching contexts. Moreover, new understandings of teaching and learning as a developmental process value the significance of teacher/student identities. With these changes, the door is now ajar for scholars to explore teacher and student *religious* experiences and *spiritual* identities in second language teaching and learning. This current volume, *Spirituality and English Language Teaching: Religious Explorations of Teacher Identity, Pedagogy and Context*, seeks to make a meaningful contribution by exploring how spirituality affects language teaching and learning.

This is the third book co-edited by Mary Shepard Wong on the topic of faith and English language teaching (ELT); however, it is the first that intentionally seeks out contributions from authors from multiple diverse religious backgrounds. It arises from the discussion in *Christian and Critical English Language Educators in Dialogue: Pedagogical and Ethical Dilemmas* (Wong & Canagarajah, 2009), which sought to establish a dialogue among English language practitioners around the dilemmas of the intersections of religion (mostly Christian) and ELT. It builds on the research in *Christian Faith and English Language Teaching and Learning: Research on the Interrelationship of Religion and ELT* (Wong *et al.*, 2013), which discussed ten empirical studies of the intersections of Christianity and ELT. This present volume enlarges the conversation and includes Muslim, Buddhist, Hindu, Christian, non-religious and other perspectives exploring how religious faith impacts teacher identity and pedagogy and the teaching context.

This anthology contains chapters that describe both data-driven studies and reflective accounts, representing a diversity of experiences and perspectives which develop discussions on the philosophies, purposes, practices, material and theories of the interrelationship of religious faith and language learning and teaching. Chapters are organized into three sections, with a response by an invited author to discuss each section. An Introduction and Conclusion is provided by the co-editors, and noted authors bookend the collection with a Foreword (Suresh Canagarajah) and Afterword (Henry Widdowson). As editors, we are interested in how the spiritual faith and religious beliefs of stakeholders come to bear on the learning and teaching of English and other languages.

In order to address the areas of teacher spiritual identity, the actual classroom experiences and the diversity of language teaching contexts, we grouped the chapters into three sections: religious faith and (1) teacher identity, (2) pedagogical practice and (3) the language learning context. Questions we sought to explore are:

(1) How do teachers' faith beliefs impact their identities, i.e. how do language teachers view themselves and how are they viewed by others?
(2) What common values and practice do teachers from different religious backgrounds share and what can they learn from each other?
(3) How does faith inform their pedagogy and interactions with students in the various contexts in which they teach?
(4) In what ways do religion, faith and other belief systems enter the language classroom and what roles do they play in teaching and learning?
(5) What connections do language teachers with religious convictions make between their faith beliefs and language policies?

Defining Spirituality

The meaning of spirituality varies greatly depending on who you ask, even among those of a similar religious group. Although it may be difficult to arrive at a definition that everyone can agree on, much can be gained from seeking to understand spirituality from multiple perspectives. I became aware of the importance of the distinction between religion and spirituality at a panel I had organized at the TESOL convention in Seattle in 2007 which I had called 'Spiritual Dimensions and Dilemmas of English Teaching'. During my brief introduction, two people suddenly stood up and stormed out, stating 'you should have told us that this was going to be about Christianity and not spirituality!' As the room was packed with people sitting on the floor, their vacated chairs were quickly taken and we continued. But I learned that day that I should not conflate the terms spirituality and Christianity, or assume we all mean the same thing when we speak of spirituality. Although the term 'spirituality' is appropriate for this volume because we address multiple religious and nonreligious viewpoints, it was not an appropriate title for that panel which focused mostly on Christian views. Some would describe spirituality as that which includes a search for what lies beyond ourselves, which may or may not include a belief in God, and which, of course, is not limited to one religion.

Some scholars like to contrast spiritual and religious views. Consider some of these definitions of spiritual versus religion, adapted from the National Center for Cultural Competence (Georgetown University).

Spiritual is:

- 'the experience or expression of the sacred' (Adapted from *The Random House Dictionary of the English Language*, Stein & Urdang, 1967);
- '... the search for transcendent meaning' (Astrow *et al.*, 2001);
- 'individual search for meaning' (Bown & Williams, 1993);
- 'the search for meaning in life events and a yearning for connectedness to the universe' (Coles, 1990);
- 'a person's experience of, or a belief in, a power apart from his or her own existence' (Mohr, 2006);
- 'a quality that goes beyond religious affiliation, that strives for inspiration, reverence, awe, meaning and purpose, even in those who do not believe in God (Murray & Zentner, 1989);
- 'in harmony with the universe, strives for answers about the infinite, and comes essentially into focus in times of emotional stress, physical (and mental) illness, loss, bereavement and death' (Murray & Zentner, 1989);
- 'a broad set of principles that transcend all religions. Spirituality is about the relationship between ourselves and something larger. That something can be the good of the community or the people who are served by your agency or school or with energies greater than ourselves. Spirituality means being in the right relationship with all that is. It is a stance of harmlessness toward all living beings and an understanding of their mutual interdependence' (Kaiser, 2000).

Contrast this with the following definitions of religion.

Religion is:

- 'a set of beliefs and practices related to the issue of what exists beyond the visible world, generally including the idea of the existence of a being, group of beings, an external principle or a transcendent spiritual entity' (Adapted from *The Random House Dictionary of the English Language*, Stein & Urdang, 1967);
- a 'set of beliefs, practices, and language that characterizes a community that is searching for transcendent meaning in a particular way, generally based upon belief in a deity' (Astrow *et al.*, 2001);

- 'formed within the context of practices and rituals shared by a group to provide a framework for connectedness to God' (Davies *et al.*, 2002);
- 'an organized system of practices and beliefs in which people engage ... a platform for the expression of spirituality ...' (Mohr, 2006);
- 'outward practice of a spiritual system of beliefs, values, codes of conduct, and rituals' (Speck, 1998).

It seems from these definitions that the spiritual is a search for transcendence, whereas religion is a set of beliefs and practices that seek to express spirituality or connect a group of people to a transcendent spiritual entity. For this book, the editors use Palmer's (2003: 377) definition that spiritual 'involves the eternal human yearning to be connected with something larger than our own egos', but we acknowledge that each author may use the term in their own ways with various nuances and in some cases the authors use the terms interchangeably. With this in mind, the following overview of the chapters is presented to orient the reader to the volume.

Chapter-by-Chapter Overview

The book begins with a foreword by Suresh Canagarajah, who provides context for the volume and notes the potential it has to make a contribution to the field of second language education (SLE). Canagarajah outlines three reasons why spirituality is important to educators and why it is high time to explore its significance. He contends that recent philosophical changes in the nature of inquiry, current understandings of the developmental learning process and the importance of cultivating dispositions within language learners allow us, if not compel us, to probe 'our beliefs in the light of our professional experiences to deepen our spirituality' (this volume, p. xix).

Part 1: Religious Faith and Teacher Identity

The four chapters of Part 1, as the section title notes, explore religious faith and teacher identity. In Chapter 2, The Dangers and Delights of Teacher Spiritual Identity as Pedagogy, Mary Shepard Wong analyzes the factors one might consider when determining what may or may not be appropriate when it comes to issues of faith and professional practice. Wong discusses the importance of contextualizing an ethical quandary, provides a discussion of the difference between ethics and morals, and lists eight potential sources for teachers to consider when making ethical and moral choices in the classroom. The chapter outlines three dangers and three delights of faith-informed pedagogy and professional practice and concludes with a set of questions and scenarios in which the eight sources of ethical and moral choices can be applied.

In Chapter 3, Buddhist Principles and the Development of Leadership Skills in English Language Program Administration and Teaching, MaryAnn Christison provides a personal account of how she has applied her Buddhist beliefs to her role as a leader within the TESOL organization. The overlapping concern for change and growth in both Buddhism and leadership creates a space for her to apply her spiritual practice in her professional life. In her words, she shows how 'the basic principles of Buddhism can serve as a useful guide when one is working across the international boundaries of language and culture and focused on developing skills as program administrators and leaders' (this volume, p. 33). Christison provides a brief background to Buddhism and then discusses the principles of Buddhism expressed in the Eightfold Path or Middle Way, namely, right understanding, right thought, right speech, right action, right livelihood, right effort, right mindfulness and right concentration. These concepts along with her personal interpretation of the doctrine have contributed to her rewarding and satisfying professional life and serve as an example of how faith can inform practice.

Joel Heng Hartse and Saeed Nazari collaborate in Chapter 4, Attempting Interfaith Dialogue in TESOL: A Duoethnography, to describe a research project that spanned two years in which they set out to explore the common values of their religious faiths – Christianity and Islam. What they found was that the co-exploration of interfaith dialogue led to deeper understandings of how their faiths were constructed, received, contested, expressed, concealed, critiqued, changed and reconceived. The original goal to find a set of common values was eclipsed by the act of 'different individuals trying to make meaning of their life histories and then reconceptualizing those meanings' (Norris *et al.*, 2012: 178). Nazari found himself asking how it is possible to assign a stereotypical label to this dynamic transformation. The chapter concludes with suggestions for further research and the potential that duoethnography has to explore power, inequality and religious difference.

In Chapter 5, Response to Part 1: Possibilities for Nonattachment: Investigating the Affective Dimension of Imposition, Ryuko Kubota provides a response to the chapters by Wong, Christison, and Heng Hartse and Nazari. She asks two overarching questions in her response: How can we come to terms with the problem of imposing one's perspective onto others? How can we deal with our emotional attachment to a certain belief or view, which may conflict with the beliefs and views of others? This process, she contends, requires a deeper engagement with difference, which involves both intellectual and affective domains. Kubota contrasts two approaches that teachers can take when seeking to increase their openness and more profoundly engage with difference: the liberal pluralist approach, often used when teaching controversial issues, and the poststructuralist intellectual approach, used to examine knowledge production. Her personal account of her struggle when dealing with her students' denial of the Nanjing Massacre demonstrates the difficulties teachers can have when seeking a more profound engagement with difference. Her application of concepts of nonattachment and emptiness found in Buddhism, which helped her through this process of hyper-self-reflexivity, further supports her point that religious faith and spirituality play a significant part in our professional lives.

Part 2: Religious Faith and Pedagogical Practice

The four chapters in Part 2, Religious Faith and Pedagogical Practice, written by Sid Brown, Bal Krishna Sharma, Stephanie Vandrick and David I. Smith, are informed by Buddhist, Hindu, non-religious and Christian perspectives. The authors discuss what happens when teachers seek out applications of their religious (and in one case non-religious) beliefs within their classrooms.

Brown, in Chapter 6, A Buddhist in the Classroom Revisited, describes 'daily Buddhist practices and stories and the moment-by-moment transformations of teacher, student and classroom that arise from them, informed by a definition of religion based on how religion functions' (this volume, p. 75). Brown asserts that all teachers have values and that teachers need to be aware of how their values impact their classroom and students. Trained to keep her religious views away from the classroom, she was made to feel her religious practices and views were irrelevant to her teaching. She states:

> I expected students to leave their religious (and anti-religious and non-religious) commitments and questions at the door, until I found that if they did so they could not walk into the room; the experiences and practices that have formed them and their (non- or anti-) religious commitments are how they (and we) are in the world; these commitments and questions form their eyes and move their legs. (This volume, p. 83)

In this chapter Brown demonstrates that her Buddhist practices can be applied to make her more aware and critical and 'awakened' like Buddha to 'see how things actually are' (this volume, p. 76). Her Buddhist practices, such as 'pausing at the door' to reflect on how to cultivate love and attention, help her be more open to the possibility of her awareness of the classroom and reactions to students. She offers her students ways to reflect upon their actions with experiments such as not buying anything for one week and writing 'where I stand' essays to explore their inner convictions. She seeks to live out her Buddhist concepts in the classroom by modeling for students how she deals with the complexities of living in an exceedingly challenging world.

In Chapter 7, The Relevance of Hinduism to English Language Teaching and Learning, Bal Krishna Sharma opens with a scene from a Nepali classroom in which the students respond with polite awkward silence when asked to practice a dialogue about which they prefer, ham or steak. This inappropriate topic, taken straight out of a British textbook, made Sharma realize how important it is to consider students' and teachers' cultural, religious and spiritual traditions and values in language teaching and learning. He began to question the validity of the assertions in his university education in Nepal in which Western 'advanced' theories of education were promoted over 'backward' local pedagogical traditions, and decided to research what the local Hindu spiritual tradition had to offer especially for the Nepali context. What he found was that the traditional Hindu educational ethos and practices found in the Vedic traditions in the Indian subcontinent which included elements of autonomy, debate and discussion are similar to the touted 'Western' pedagogical practices that came much later. Sharma contends that 'understanding Hinduism can help English teachers address some critical issues, such as respect for students as individuals and members of a particular culture/community, peace and social harmony, human relationship with nature and an awareness of environmental crisis, among others' (this volume, p. 87).

In Chapter 8, Multiple, Complex and Fluid Religious and Spiritual Influences on English Language Educators, Stephanie Vandrick describes the findings of a study of her peers. She contends that it is not always one religion but many that might influence teachers, and that these are not static understandings, but changing and complex. To better understand this, she reflects on her own spiritual journey and those of modern authors, and through email correspondence collects the views of ELT colleagues. She frames her discussion of her findings with three assertions: (1) English language educators can be greatly influenced by religion without subscribing to a specific religion; (2) ELT educators can be spiritual without necessarily being religious; and (3) language educators can be ethical without necessarily being religious.

David I. Smith, in Chapter 9, Response to Part 2: 'Religious Faith' and 'Pedagogical Practice' – Extending the Map: A Response to Brown, Sharma and Vandrick, notes that the chapters overlap in five areas, all demonstrating that faith has a role in language classrooms: (1) the texture of the self of the teacher; (2) patterns of interpersonal interaction in the classroom; (3) the teacher's ethical commitments; (4) a broader philosophy of life as it sustains educational engagement; and (5) specific pedagogical practices. Smith concludes, 'As the three essays each show in their different ways, the teacher's lived self, patterns of interaction, ethical commitments and wider worldview all help to shape pedagogical practice, not only through a kind of broad, qualitative contouring, but also in terms of specific interventions' (this volume, p. 123). Smith ends the chapter with the comment that 'The essays and this book as a whole are part of a welcome recovery of an honest naming of the faiths, practices and commitments, including "religious" ones, that inform both scholarly and pedagogical practices. May the recovery continue' (this volume, p. 126). Smith then suggests a number of ways in which we might extend our inquiries to 'enlarge the map'.

Part 3: Religious Faith and the Language Learning Context

Part 3: Religious Faith and the Language Learning Context takes the readers to Lebanon, Egypt and Canada to explore the importance of context in discussions of spirituality and ELT. In Chapter 10, Language and Religion in the Construction of the Lebanese Identity, Kassim Shaaban provides a historical perspective of the role of religious and linguistic affiliation in the formation of a Lebanese national identity. Issues of language policy in relation to communal identity are explored as well as factors that have prevented Lebanese communities from constructing a unifying national identity. Shaaban provides examples from numerous studies to demonstrate the complexity of the role of religion in language choice and use. For example, the chapter states, 'although all groups in Lebanon share a mother tongue, Arabic, each group espouses one or more foreign languages to create its own distinctive identity' (this volume, p. 143), and 'What unifies the Lebanese linguistically is not the Arabic language, but rather multilingualism whose base is Arabic and at least one foreign language, a *multilingualism motivated by political and economic interests*' (this volume, p. 143).

In Chapter 11, Teachers' Perceptions of the Interface between Religious Values and Language Pedagogy in Egypt, three authors, Deena Boraie, Atta Gebril and Raafat Gabriel, provide an insightful study of the relationship between religion and English as a foreign language (EFL) Egyptian teachers' beliefs about English language teaching and learning and attitudes towards Arabic and English. Four Muslim and four Christian teachers attending university were interviewed and an analysis of the data showed a relationship between their religious faith and teaching and learning beliefs and pedagogical practices in the classroom. Both Muslim and Christian teachers viewed Arabic and English as being of importance at personal and professional levels. However, there were some differences with regard to how the spread of English is perceived by both groups. While the Muslim teachers felt that the spread of English is a clear threat to national identity, their Christian counterparts did not. Overall, these results speak to the strong relationship between faith and instructional beliefs and practices in Egypt.

Carolyn Kristjánsson, in Chapter 12, Church-sponsored English as a Second Language in Western Canada: Grassroots Expressions of Spiritual and Social Practice, provides an account of three directors and their reports of program practices. Kristjánsson contends that 'within a sociocultural paradigm, language learning cannot be fully understood apart from the relationships between stakeholders and associated conditions in which learning occurs' (this volume, p. 172). Thus she begins by situating the study in the historical and contemporary Canadian context and then explores the construct of social practice, agency and identity. Based on an analysis of the interview accounts of program providers, she argues that the church-sponsored English as a second language (ESL) programs are mutually constituted expressions of social and spiritual practice. She argues, 'It is a position that challenges the limits of current sociocultural perspectives while opening up a view of the potential for interconnected understandings of social and spiritual agency' (this volume, p. 173).

In Chapter 13, Response to Part 3: Religious Faith and the Language Learning Context: Exploring the 'Interface', Morgan rises to the challenge of examining faith-based influences on language learning across three different settings in three different nation-states. Using Boraie *et al.*'s reference to an 'interface' of sacred and secular activities, Morgan seeks to find a thematic unity in Shabaan's analysis in Lebanon, Boraie *et al.*'s study in Egypt and Kristjánsson's inquiry in Western Canada. Considering both micro and macro influences on the ways in which religious beliefs shape language teaching and the identities of language teachers and students, Morgan discusses inter- and intra-personal aspects of learning, especially one's personal relationship with God/Allah/Yahweh, in the classroom and in the larger contexts of community, city, region and nation-state. Reflecting on his own Insider/Outsider positionings, Morgan discusses the Canadian context in more detail, exploring Kristjánsson's claims in some detail. Although he notes several cautions and critiques of the interface of faith and practice, he concludes by remarking on the 'social importance – i.e. resilience in the face of worldly crises – in being part of a religious community' and notes 'those whose religious convictions motivate and sustain their dedication to language teaching and the building of community should be commended for the resilience they provide students at the spiritual/secular interface' (this volume, p. 204).

In the conclusion, Mahboob and Courtney revisit the five questions that the book sought to explore and propose ideas for future research. They state, 'the individual contributions to the volume provide convincing evidence that teachers' and teacher educators' beliefs can and do influence their practice' (this volume, p. 207), and continue, 'Together the chapters illustrate that religious and/or spiritual beliefs do not remain outside the door when we walk into our professional contexts, but rather they influence our professional identity, our pedagogical practices and the context in which we teach/learn languages' (this volume, p. 207). Some of the themes they highlight are:

- Teachers find satisfaction in teaching in a way that aligns with their spiritual identity.
- Religious and/or spiritual identities are not uniform, and are difficult to separate from culture and other influences.
- There is a need to be aware of contextual factors in relation to content, pedagogy and students' backgrounds and to recognize and not gloss over difference.

- Discussion of religion and values can have a useful role in learning as they help connect with the lives, cultures and identities of students.
- Cultural context is important when making decisions about bringing spirituality into the classroom.

They suggest that future studies might further explore the impact of spirituality on students and also investigate what is being promoted by teachers of faith. For example, in what ways do they promote the dominant beliefs of the community or encourage alternative ways of thinking and being as outlined in the identity management framework?

Finally, Henry Widdowson provides an 'admittedly agnostic, point of view', as he puts it in the Afterword, and points out that the volume extends the scope of teacher cognition research 'by focusing on the influence of spirituality and religious faith on "what teachers know, think, believe and do" – an influence that research on teacher cognition seems hitherto not to have taken into explicit account' (this volume, p. 217). He asks several probing questions such as: How far does religious faith interact with other kinds of belief in shaping the way teachers teach? How is belief in a religion different from a belief in an evolutionary or political or linguistic theory? How do believers act on their beliefs? How far can a belief survive the process of its practical implementation? What is pedagogy that is informed by religious conviction? While leery of the influence of religious faith on teaching, he applauds the influence of spirituality on teachers' assumptions and attitudes.

References

Astrow, A., Pulchalski, C. and Sulmasy, D. (2001) Religion, spirituality, and health care: Social, ethical, and practical considerations. *American Journal of Medicine* 110, 283–287.

Bown, J. and Williams, S. (1993) Spirituality in nursing: A review of the literature. *Journal of Advances in Health and Nursing Care* 2 (4), 41–66.

Coles, R. (1990) *The Spirituality of Children*. Boston, MA: Houghton-Mifflin.

Davies, B., Brenner, P, Orloff, S., Sumner, L. and Worden, W. (2002) Addressing spirituality in pediatric hospice and palliative care. *Journal of Palliative Care* 18, 59–67.

Edge, J. (1996) Keeping the faith. *TESOL Matters* 6 (4), 1, 23.

Edge, J. (2003) Imperial troopers and servants of the Lord: A vision of TESOL for the 21st century. *TESOL Quarterly* 37 (4), 701–709.

Johnston, B. (2017) *English Teaching and Evangelical Missions: The Case of Lighthouse School*. Bristol: Multilingual Matters.

Johnston, B. and Varghese, M. (2006) Neo-imperialism, evangelism, and ELT: Modernist missions and a postmodern profession. In J. Edge (ed.) *(Re)locating TESOL in an Age of Empire*. New York: Palgrave.

Kaiser, L. (2000) Spirituality and the physician executive: Reconciling the inner self and the business of health care. *The Physician Executive* 26 (2), March/April.

Mohr, W. (2006) Spiritual issues in psychiatric care. *Perspectives in Psychiatric Care* 42 (3), 174–183.

Murray, R. and Zentner, J. (1989) *Nursing Concepts for Health Promotion*. London: Prentice-Hall.

Norris, J., Sawyer, R.D. and Lund, D. (eds) (2012) *Duoethnography: Dialogic Methods for Social, Health, and Educational Research.* Walnut Creek, CA: Left Coast Publications.

Palmer, P. (2003) Teaching with heart and soul: Reflections on spirituality in teacher education. *Journal of Teacher Education* 54 (5), 376–385.

Pennycook, A. and Coutand-Marin, S. (2003) Teaching English as a missionary language (TEML). *Discourse: Studies in the Cultural Politics of Education* 24 (3), 337–353.

Smith, D.I. and Carvill, B. (2000) *The Gift of the Stranger: Faith, Hospitality, and Foreign Language Learning.* Grand Rapids, MI: Eerdmans.

Snow, D. (2001) *English Teaching as Christian Mission: An Applied Theology.* Scottsdale, PA: Herald Press.

Speck, P. (1998) The meaning of spirituality in illness. In M. Cobb and V. Robshaw (eds) *The Spiritual Challenge of Healthcare.* London: Churchill Livingstone.

Stein, J. and Urdang, L. (eds) (1967) *The Random House Dictionary of the English Language.* New York: Random House.

Stevick, E. (1997) Response to Julian Edge's 'keeping the faith'. *TESOL Matters* 6 (6), 6.

Varghese, M. and Johnston, B. (2007) Evangelical Christians and English language teaching. *TESOL Quarterly* 41, 5–31.

Wong, M.S. and Canagarajah, S. (eds) (2009) *Christian and Critical English Language Educators in Dialogue: Pedagogical and Ethical Dilemmas.* New York: Routledge.

Wong, M.S., Kristjánsson, C. and Dörnyei, Z. (eds) (2013) *Christian Faith and English Language Teaching and Learning: Research on the Interrelationship of Religion and ELT.* New York: Routledge.

Part 1

Religious Faith and Teacher Identity

2 The Dangers and Delights of Teacher Spiritual Identity as Pedagogy

Mary Shepard Wong

> Teaching has an ethical dimension, for the teacher has the capacity to help or harm others.
> Cahn, 2011: 11

Introduction: Spirituality in Second Language Education

Spirituality: The neglected domain of teacher identity research

Research in second language education (SLE) has examined many types of teacher identities including nativeness and non-nativeness (Braine, 1999, 2010; Mahboob, 2010; Moussu & Llurda, 2008), gender and sexuality (Nelson, 1999), race (Kubota & Lin, 2009), indigenous identities (Hornberger, 2006) and transcultural and transnational identities (Canagarajah, 2011). This scholarship is important because teacher identity can be a valuable 'pedagogical resource' (Morgan, 2004: 174) for teachers. However, a 'blind spot' (Morgan, 2009: 193) and 'neglected' domain (Morgan & Clarke, 2011: 827) in teacher identity scholarship is spirituality and, as Widdowson points out in the Afterword, spirituality is 'an influence that research on teacher cognition seems hitherto not to have taken into explicit account' (this volume, p. 217).

If Morgan and Clarke (2011: 825) are correct in saying that 'the most significant development in language teacher identity research is the turn towards values, morals, and ethics in the work of teachers', then it seems appropriate to explore teachers' spiritual identities. Keeping in mind Foucault's (1983: 231) caution that 'everything is dangerous', along with the historical alignment of missionary work, English teaching and colonialism, concerns regarding teachers drawing from their religious faith to inform pedagogy are not unjustified. This chapter identifies key variables and sources to consider in the deliberation of ethical decisions in the classroom, and contends that teachers' spiritual identities can be a positive motivating factor when teachers approach spiritual identity as pedagogy from an informed critical stance.

Note that the term spirituality is used instead of religion to enlarge the discussion beyond ritual, tradition and the formal and at times oppressive institutional structures associated with organized religion. Palmer's (2003: 377) definition of spirituality will be used here: 'The eternal human yearning to be connected with something larger than our own egos'. When spirituality is discussed from a specific religious viewpoint in this chapter, the term 'faith tradition' or faith is used.

Faith in the classroom: Irrelevant, insensitive or innocuous?

Each year I teach a course called Critical Perspectives of Christianity and ELT as an elective in the MA TESOL program at a Christian university. The course has dozens of readings by evangelicals, atheists and many others from various faith traditions about the dilemmas, tensions and opportunities created around the intersections of religious faith, pedagogy and scholarship (see Wong & Canagarajah, 2009). The majority of my students in this course self-identify as Christians, but there are also students in the classes who are atheists, agnostics, Buddhists, Muslims, spiritualists, non-religious and others. At the end of the course, students are asked to describe which of their beliefs about faith and English language teaching (ELT) were confirmed, which were challenged and which, if any, were changed by engaging with the readings and with their peers.

At the beginning of the course, many students consider the topic of faith and ELT irrelevant and ask: *What does faith have to do with English teaching?* A small minority, who are often non-religious, consider it insensitive, and tend to ask: *Why would anyone discuss anything about religion in a language class?* While still others, often some who are Christian, consider it innocuous and ask: *What harm is there in sharing my faith in class?* After the course, most of the students no longer regard teachers' spiritual identities as totally irrelevant, insensitive or innocuous to teaching. Many of the more religious students concede that what they once thought was harmless needs to be more critically examined. Students who once questioned the relevance of religion or spirituality in SLE now see that it can impact teacher identity and student learning.

While not all students consider faith to be salient to their pedagogical practice, students in the course are exposed to others who view their religious faith as essential to their work, and most students come to understand the perspective that teachers' spiritual identity can provide a sense of calling, purpose, guidance, support and motivation to do one's job with excellence, to connect who one is with what one does and to teach with integrity (Wong, 2012, 2013; Wong *et al.*, 2013). However, there are also dangers to consider related to the ethical concerns of the role of a teacher's faith in the classroom (Wong, 2009), and it is these two sides – the dangers and delights – that this chapter addresses.

This chapter begins with a brief discussion of the importance of context and then considers the difference between morals and ethics. An examination of several sources of ethical principles and moral beliefs is given, followed by the presentation of three delights and three dangers that can emerge when teachers' spiritual identities inform their pedagogical and professional practice. The chapter concludes with implications, including a set of questions and scenarios. Note that the focus of this chapter is *teachers'* spiritual identities. It has been pointed out that a similar singular focus on *students'* spiritual identities in ELT is needed (Vandrick, 2009). Although this chapter does not focus only on students, students' views are included in the discussion, as students' identities must be considered when determining what is appropriate pedagogy.

Identifying and Analyzing Key Variables in the Ethics of Teaching

The importance of context

When determining the limitations and freedoms of a teacher's expression of faith in a classroom, context must be clearly articulated and taken into account. Consider teachers at a Christian university in the United States who are evaluated on 'faith integration' (a term used in Christian higher education to refer to how teachers' religious faith informs teaching and practice and how their discipline informs their faith). Compare that to a foreign teacher in a public elementary school in China, who might be expected to avoid discussions of religion in the classroom. There are several contextual factors to consider when discussing issues of faith and teaching, such as: the nation-state; the community; the institution (public or private, religious or secular); the course content; relevant current events; potential consequences of students discussing their faith; the relationship of the teacher to the students; and several student variables including age, English proficiency level and religious background, just to name a few. With all of these variables in mind, contextualizing all discussions of faith and teaching is important, as context plays a large role in determining what is appropriate or inappropriate.

Ethics and morals

In addition to context, another important factor in the discussion of faith and teaching is the distinction between ethics and morals. Both ethics and morals deal with what is considered to be right or wrong. For the purposes of this chapter, a distinction is made in terms of perspective. Here, ethics is concerned with an *external* evaluation, a set of rules or an ethical code based on professional standards that are consistent within a specific context, but may vary between contexts. Morals are *internal*, individual principles and habits which are usually consistent until one's beliefs change.

Most actions tend to be considered either ethical and moral or unethical and immoral. However, it might be possible for an action to be considered ethical yet immoral and other actions to be considered moral but unethical. Attorneys, doctors, psychologists and teachers, for example, are all required to follow an ethical code of conduct regardless of whether it supports or conflicts with their personal beliefs or morals. Ignoring or violating stated ethical codes can result in the loss of one's job. Violating one's sense of internal morals can result in psychological stress. Thus teachers, like all professionals, need to be familiar with their professional ethical codes of conduct and also cognizant of their own set of moral convictions.

Eight sources influencing ethical and moral decisions in teaching

When resolving ethical dilemmas such as the limits of a teacher's expression of faith in the classroom, how does one determine where 'the line' is that one should not cross? What are the criteria used to determine what is unethical in a given context? How can we sharpen our vision to 'see' this line, but not be so constrained by it that we lose our sense of self and violate our sense of morals? (For a discussion of values and ethics in classroom interaction and ELT, see Buzzilli & Johnston, 2002; Crookes, 2009; Hafernick *et al.*, 2002; Johnston, 2003.)

Determining the sources of our ethical and moral decisions is not easy as they come from many places such as internal influences, including reflections on our: (1) personal experiences; (2) cultural traditions; (3) intellectual justifications; and (4) religious and spiritual beliefs. External influences include: (5) professional guidelines; (6) institutional mission statements and mandates; (7) research guidelines including those used by institutional research boards (IRB); and (8) sacred and/or seminal texts. Examples of each category are provided below. This list is not meant to be exhaustive but rather a place to start when considering the sources of our moral and ethical decisions. The weight or priority that one might give to each of these will vary. Readers should consider how they would rename, reorder, delete or add categories to fit their own value systems and priorities. This is meant as a starting point for reflection, and not a comprehensive framework.

(1) Personal experience

Experience may be one of the most powerful sources one draws from in determining what is ethical or moral. Teachers who extend unwarranted mercy to students, for example, may believe they are drawing from their faith tradition and sacred texts to justify this action, but they may also be allowing an impactful past experience in which they were (or perhaps were not) shown mercy to influence them. Another teacher may decide to withhold mercy to a student based on a different personal experience that emphasizes justice and fairness. This illustrates that in some cases the choice is not between what is right or wrong, but which ethical principle (justice, fairness or beneficence, described further below) will be prioritized in a given context at a given time. The main point here is that teachers may want to consider the extent to which their own personal experiences might be influencing their decisions and how much weight that should have in their decisions.

(2) Cultural traditions

When people are determining what is ethical or moral in a given situation, they will also draw from their cultural traditions. The liberal use of corporal punishment in schools in the United States not long ago was based on both cultural and religious traditions. Today the ban on corporal punishment in schools in the United States is based on these same sources. This demonstrates that cultural and religious traditions can change over time. Being aware of the changes in our understanding of these issues over time might persuade one to be more humble in one's assertions and more careful not to make quick judgments.

(3) Intellectual justification

Reason also plays a role in determining what one considers to be ethical and moral in a given context. When taken together with sacred texts, reason can temper potentially inappropriate responses. For example, an isolated phrase from a sacred text might be taken out of context and applied literally instead of figuratively or vice versa, and thus be misapplied. The application of reason may help to prevent this. For some people, reason might be considered the primary source for ethical and moral decisions, while for others it should be applied in concert with other sources.

(4) Religious traditions

Beliefs about one's faith, religious traditions and spirituality will also impact one's decisions about ethical choices in the classroom. The three examples listed above which demonstrated the application of personal experiences, cultural traditions and intellectual reason also involved religious beliefs, demonstrating that these factors do not occur as isolated influences but interact in complex ways. Consider how a teacher might respond to a student's request to miss a class in order to observe a religious holiday not recognized by the school. Teachers need to consider not only their own religious views, but also those of their students and, as we see in the next factor discussed, the religious policies of their institutions.

(5) Institutional mission

Moving from the more individual or internal sources of reflections on personal, cultural, intellectual and religious traditions to the more external sources, we now consider the ethical obligation of teachers to support the mission statements of the institutions in which they work. If an institution's mission statement includes spiritual or moral development, it stands to reason that teachers have the responsibility to support that mission. If, however, spiritual development is not a part of the mission of the institution, than this becomes a gray area that needs to be examined more carefully. Academic freedom is essential for learning and research, and there should be no taboo questions or areas of inquiry so that learning can flourish. However, academic freedoms of the individual are constrained by the academic contexts in which they work. Working to support one's institutional mission (or at least not working against it) is considered to be a necessary component of teaching ethically in some codes of conduct, which is where we turn now.

(6) Professional guidelines and codes of conduct

Relevant and helpful resources for determining the limitations and freedoms of expressions of faith in the classroom include ethical codes of conduct. Teachers need to identify the professional codes of conduct that apply to their specific context. There are many available, and the following are provided as a starting point:

- The American Educational Research Association's *Ethical Standards of the American Educational Association* (AERA, 2011);
- The Association of International Educators' *Code of Ethics* (NAFSA, 1989);
- National Educators Association's *Code of Ethics of the Education Profession* (NEA, 1975);
- *A Teacher's Guide to Religion in the Public Schools* (First Amendment Center, 2008).

Although not created for language educators, the following is particularly detailed and insightful and could be used as a resource:

- The American Psychological Association's *Ethical Principles of Psychologists and Code of Conduct* (APA, 2010);
- *Standards of Conduct in the International Civil Service* (International Civil Service Commission, 2013).

Professional ethical codes and standards are a useful source of information that should be part of teacher education programs.

(7) Ethical precautions applied in research (IRB)

Another helpful source of principles in determining ethically appropriate behavior in classrooms includes those applied to research, such as the Belmont Report. The Belmont Report (US Department of Health, 1979) offers three principles that can be applied to determining appropriate pedagogy: respect, beneficence and justice, as described below.

- *Respect* for persons involves two ethical concerns: individuals must be treated as autonomous agents, and persons with diminished autonomy must be protected.

- *Beneficence* has to do with doing good or doing no harm. It strives to maximize benefits and minimize harm to the individual research participant.
- *Justice* refers to fairness in distribution and providing what is deserved. This includes not denying a benefit without good reason or imposing a burden unduly. Treating people equally is also part of justice.

Although these apply to research, the principles are useful for pedagogical practice well.

(8) Sacred and/or seminal texts from one's religious faith tradition or worldview

Sacred and seminal texts can be sources of moral principles that inform our ethical decisions. Since sacred texts are so important to those who follow a specific religious faith, this might be an important source for people of faith, potentially overlapping at least partially with most of the other sources. Sacred texts include the Bible, the Qur'an, the teachings of Buddha and a host of other texts. There are many non-religious seminal texts that should be considered as sources of our ethical and moral decisions as well, including works by poets, philosophers and novelists. For educators, these might include works by Piaget, Dewey and Vygotsky, to name a few.

With this background of the importance of context, the distinctions between morals and ethics, and potential sources that inform our understanding of morals and ethics, we turn now to the dangers and delights of spiritual identity as pedagogy, starting with the delights.

Three Delights of Teacher Spiritual Identity as Pedagogy

Three delights that can result when one allows one's spirituality to inform one's teaching will be described here: gratification of teaching with integrity, joy of meaningful service and satisfaction of critical engagement. The first is introspective and describes the gratification that comes from knowing oneself and being true to oneself. The second has an outward focus – the joy that can come in giving of oneself to others. The last seeks to apply a critical, purposeful and mindful approach in the way one's faith or spirituality is applied to pedagogy.

The gratification of teaching with integrity

An author who provides a rich description of the gratification of teaching with integrity and drawing from one's spiritual self by exploring the 'inner landscape of a teacher's life' is Parker Palmer (2003, 2010). In the 10th edition of his book, *The Courage to Teach*, Palmer states, 'Good teaching cannot be reduced to technique; good teaching comes from the identity and integrity of the teacher' (Palmer, 2010: 10). Oprandy (1999) also discusses the importance of teachers connecting the personal and professional, although not particularly from a spiritual or religious perspective. Oprandy (1999: 144) suggests that teachers ask themselves: how does language teaching fit into my vision of who I am becoming and how I would like the world to be? Sid Brown's (2008) sabbatical reflection on Buddhist teachings focused on this same question. This gratification of teaching who we are is not limited to people of faith, although it does touch on the spiritual.

Some non-religious students on a course that I teach (mentioned at the start of this chapter) have told me that they have enjoyed taking courses at a religious university even though they are not religious. They said the process of being asked to articulate and reflect on their values, worldview and religious beliefs has helped them to connect their teaching to their own spiritual journey and to rekindle their passion for teaching. They noted that the spiritual focus helped them reflect more on why they are teaching rather than just how to teach, and encouraged them to teach more purposefully or, as Palmer says, from integrity of their identity.

The joy of meaningful service

However, knowing oneself, one's giftedness, passions and purpose, is not an end in itself. Understanding gained from introspection finds its full expression and joy in stewardship and service. Joy will be found, according to Palmer (2000), when 'authentic self-hood' leads to a path of 'authentic service' to the world, as he states: 'Our deepest calling is to grow into our own authentic self-hood, whether or not it conforms to some image of who we ought to be. As we do so, we will not only find the joy that every human being seeks – we will also find our path of authentic service in the world' (Palmer, 2000: 16). Frederick Buechner speaks of the joy of service in his definition of vocation, which he says is 'the place where your deep gladness and the world's deep hunger meet' (Buechner, 1993: 119). Volf (1991) describes work in the spirit as cooperation with God. All human work done in accordance with the will of God, Volf argues, is cooperation with God in the preservation and transformation of the world (Volf, 1991: 114). While those with no religious faith can also teach to serve, and those with religious faith might not teach in the service of others, the connection of faith and service is often made, especially among those with an active and critical faith. This leads to the final delight of applying the mind to engage critically.

The satisfaction of critical engagement

Another delight is the satisfaction of critical engagement. I use the term critical here to refer to being aware of our agendas, context, students and the role of power. It involves the application of the criteria for ethical practice as outlined in the previous section and a heightened awareness of our privilege and power as teachers. As Stevick (1976: 159) notes, 'the acts and events of the classroom are always bound up in the relationships of power'. Critical engagement is purposeful and mindful and infused in all we do as teachers – choosing where we work, what we teach, our teaching materials, the way we engage with our colleagues, what we research, how we grade, and a host of other actions. It means asking critical questions and collecting data to reflect on what we are doing and whom it benefits – questions such as: *To what extent does what I am doing, the way I am doing it, why I'm doing it, and who it benefits align with my spiritual identity?* (Wong, 2014a: 18). It is the satisfaction of living out one's beliefs in a way marked by professionalism and sensitivity. It is the opportunity to learn more about our students' religious and spiritual beliefs and allow this to inform our practice. It is the challenge to help students engage critically in thinking about their beliefs, spirituality and faith in order to expose misconceptions and foster the desire to see something from someone else's perspective.

Three Dangers of Teacher Spiritual Identity as Pedagogy

Morgan's (2004) concept of 'identity as pedagogy' speaks to the importance of examining teachers' identity and the influence it has on teaching. The previous section noted three delights of spiritual identity as pedagogy, but now we turn to three concerns. If Foucault (1983: 231) is right that 'everything is dangerous', in what ways is teacher spiritual identity as pedagogy potentially dangerous? There are many examples in history of the ways in which religious fundamentalism and fanaticism can lead to the dismantling of institutions of higher education and the disruption of the quest for truth, and to extreme violence and even genocide. Strong religious views have been the cause of some of the world's worst manmade atrocities, such as the Crusades and the Inquisition. Even recent history has religious-based or -fueled atrocities, such as the armed conflict in Northern Ireland, political instability in South Africa and the Middle East and systematic oppression and forced relocation in many regions of the world. One cannot deny the devastating consequences of religious fanaticism on a global scale and how it has destroyed higher education where once it flourished or stifled the exploration of truth when it violated current (mis)interpretations of sacred texts.

But this should not lead to banning of religious discussions in classrooms. Educating students about religions and creating a better understanding of the 'religious other' and our spiritual connectedness may serve to mitigate religious misunderstandings and minimize religiously fueled conflicts. However, the question remains: how does one allow faith to inform pedagogy without imposing it on students and limiting the free exploration of ideas? Put another way, what are the dangers of spiritual identity as pedagogy, and how can one avoid the dangers while engaging in English language teaching and teacher education? There are many dangers one might consider and this list is not meant to be exhaustive, but it does address three dangers affecting English language teachers who seek to engage in teacher spiritual identity as pedagogy, namely: the threat of the native-speaker quasi-teacher; the menace of the over-zealous oblivious teacher; and the peril of the pariah faith-informed teacher.

The threat of the native-speaker quasi-teacher

Some Christian religious agencies motivated to place people in countries that are not open to religious missionaries recruit and send people who may not have much in the way of teaching experience or qualifications to teach English. Christian mission agencies have been criticized for this, although they are not the only group who may be guilty of the practice. Some Christian mission agencies even go so far as to advertise that no training or experience is needed to teach abroad as long as one is a 'native speaker' (Mahboob, 2009; Wong & Stratton, 2011). This is unethical because students' learning could be hindered due to the inexperience and lack of skills, knowledge and awareness of the so-called teacher. In their book *Teaching Ethically*, which focuses on ethical standards for teaching psychologists, Landrum and McCarthy (2012: 10–11) discuss two APA Standards, 2.01 Boundaries of Competence and 7.03 Accuracy in Teaching, which would be violated by this practice. When a 'quasi-teacher' is sent abroad, student motivation may at first go up due to the novelty factor of a foreign teacher, but this often wanes when it is not supported by sound teaching practices and is ethically suspect.

Another reason that this practice is unethical is because it creates and supports hiring practices that are discriminatory, since this type of hiring is often based on 'nativeness' instead of the quality, experience and qualifications of the teacher. Note that this may not violate the ethical code of the institution that advertises for 'native speakers', but it does violate the policy statement on non-native English speaking teachers (NNESTs) of the largest professional organization in our field, the TESOL International Association. Moreover, it is counterproductive for these mission agencies. Not being able to fulfill their job requirements would undermine the positive impact they hope to make. Thus intentionally sending underqualified 'quasi-teachers' to teach (in this case motivated by religious beliefs, but this could apply to other reasons) is unethical when student learning is compromised and when it supports discriminatory hiring practices. This should not be tolerated and those who are part of such agencies need to strategize ways to move from being accomplices in this discrimination to becoming advocates for change. See Wong and Stratton (2011) for additional discussion and suggestions.

The menace of the overzealous oblivious teacher

Actions of the overzealous teacher are unethical when student learning is diminished because of a misuse of class time which is spent on the teacher's comments or agenda that do not support the learning outcomes. It is problematic because other required content is omitted due to discussions of issues that are not part of the curriculum. This might be related to a plethora of teacher agendas other than faith beliefs, but since teachers' religious views are often strong, it is an area that needs attention. It is unethical when student learning or motivation is diminished due to teachers' actions. In some cases, the teacher may be unaware of the unintended negative impact, which leads to a related danger, the oblivious teacher.

The oblivious teacher is unaware of how the student–teacher power differential may affect students' reluctance to voice dissatisfaction with potential coercion in the classroom. Motivation is a powerful force in language learning, so teachers need to be aware of ways in which they may be demoting their students, whether that is by imposing their religious beliefs on students or subtly disparaging the students' faith. The other extreme is also possible, engaging in a 'null curriculum' and creating a spiritual void by the avoidance, denial or denigration of spiritual aspects and religious practices of everyday life embedded within the cultures of students. A teacher's comments and actions may make students feel that they are not permitted to explore their views on religion or that faith beliefs are unworthy of academic discussion.

Teachers can mitigate this by examining the curriculum and periodically asking for anonymous feedback from students. Teachers also need to seek out information about their students' faith backgrounds and how other stakeholders (such as parents, administrators and colleagues) feel about religious discussions in the classroom. Foye (2014) surveyed 277 teachers in 44 countries about their views on religion in the classroom, and based on the responses concluded that 'there is no need to shy away from religion as a language classroom topic, provided that the subject is handled appropriately' (Foye, 2014: 10–11). The concern regarding being appropriate reinforces the need for teachers to be aware of how power dynamics affect student learning. The Belmont principles of respect, beneficence and justice could be applied here: *respect* for students by getting to know about their faith backgrounds and their desire to speak about religion; *beneficence* by ensuring teachers are not harming students by imposing their faith beliefs or denigrating students' beliefs; and *justice* by not denying students the opportunity to explore faith beliefs and by treating the subject fairly and in a balanced manner.

The peril of the pariah faith-informed teacher

When asked what dangers they perceived when seeking to apply teacher spiritual identity as pedagogy, a group of over 30 Christian English language educators surveyed during a presentation (Wong, 2014b) responded with a list of 15 dangers that included the danger described above of imposing their religious views on students. They noted that teachers with strong religious convictions need to be aware of the danger of 'offending, endangering, overpowering, antagonizing, and damaging' students. However, they also spoke of what I called 'the peril of the pariah (faith-informed) teacher', which they voiced as being 'misunderstood, pigeonholed, essentialized, ostracized, alienated, silenced, fired, and branded as crazy or a proselytizer'. This should be avoided, as it might lead to the de-voicing, silencing and degrading of someone based on their spiritual or religious identity.

Morgan and Clarke (2011: 827–828) note that 'voiced proscriptions against religious identity work in SLE [are] somewhat hypocritical, given the field's preoccupation with ... engaged identities pedagogies'. Johnston (2017: 3) has also voiced this concern and problematizes the 'condescension and scorn' that evangelicals are subject to in our field. He describes an anecdote about academics rolling their eyes and making deprecating comments when a Christian student spoke of his faith. Johnston remarks that this might not have happened if the student were Buddhist or Muslim. He warns that all evangelicals should not be tarred with the same brush, and states, 'no other religious group is treated with such cavalier contempt by supposedly open-minded liberals' (Johnston, 2017: 3).

Some of the 30 Christian teachers surveyed (Wong, 2014b) said that they avoided any discussions or reference to religion in their classrooms out of fear of being misunderstood by students or ostracized by colleagues. Some teachers said that they felt constrained by a curriculum that was void of any religious content. They asked how their faith might inform their classrooms in ways that were sensitive and helpful to students. Research that investigates how faith is used in classrooms and how it impacts teaching and learning, such as Johnston's (2017) study, is a good start in forming a response to this question. Teachers might begin their own inquiries by reflecting on the questions provided in the next section.

Implications

Implications of exploring teacher 'spiritual identity as pedagogy' will vary by individual and context. To start this process of exploration, a set of questions and potential scenarios are provided below. Readers are encouraged to continue to critically engage with these issues and to come to their own understandings of the potential that 'spiritual identity as pedagogy' has in their own classrooms and schools.

Questions to inform teacher spiritual identity as pedagogy

(1) Which, if any, of the three dangers described in this chapter are you facing, and how can you mitigate those dangers?
(2) Which, if any, of the three delights do you experience, and if not, how might you seek to experience them through introspection, service and critical reflection?
(3) When determining a response to an ethical dilemma you face as a teacher, which of the eight sources will you draw from and what priority do you give to each?
(4) What are your 'hot buttons' or agendas, and how can you be aware of ways in which you may be imposing your views on this topic on your students?
(5) How can you learn more about your students' faith backgrounds and worldviews and determine how this may inform your teaching of a particular course?
(6) What professional ethical codes of conduct are you aware of and use as a teacher?
(7) What is the mission statement of the institution where you work, and what are the limitations and freedoms of a teacher's expression of faith and spirituality in the classroom there?
(8) How do you maintain an ethical practice and allow your faith and spirituality to inform your teaching without favoring students who are seeking to learn more about your faith beliefs?
(9) How can you present a broad perspective to include other faith beliefs and a balance of topics among which faith is included but not privileged in a course you are teaching?
(10) How can you expose misconceptions about your faith and other faiths and the diversity of those who hold them within the confines of the courses you teach?
(11) How can you get feedback on students' perceptions of the ways in which faith and spirituality are excluded or included in a particular course?
(12) Describe an ethical dilemma you (might) encounter in teaching related to religion, and describe how you (might) respond.
(13) In answering Question 12, articulate which of the eight sources you used to determine what was the best moral and ethical response for you. What specific personal experiences, cultural traditions, intellectual justifications, religious or spiritual beliefs, institutional mission statements, professional codes or research standards and sacred or secular texts have informed your response?

Sample scenarios

In addition to the scenarios you create in responding to the questions above, also consider the following.

(1) A colleague's after-hours student meetings

(a) You teach in a school that has no explicit faith-based mission in a country where the overwhelming majority of students are of a religion different from yours. You discover that a colleague (of your religion) has started a student group that meets outside school in order for her to explain more about her beliefs. Describe the specifics of your scenario based on these conditions (what faiths, what country, what level of school, etc.). How do you feel about this? What will you do? What are you basing your decisions upon?

(b) If the setting is changed to one in which the overwhelming majority of students are of your religion and the colleague belongs to a religion other than yours, does that make a difference? Does it matter if there is ongoing armed conflict among these religious groups in other parts of the world? Describe the specifics of your scenario based on these conditions (what faiths, what country, what level of school, etc.). What will you do now? What are you basing your decisions upon?

(c) It starts to become noticeable that participants in your colleague's out-of-school group are regularly more successful in her classes. Should you do anything and why? Does your response change for setting (a) and (b) as outlined above?

(2) A colleague's ban on religious discussions

You work in a country in which most students hold strong religious views, mainly for one particular religion. A colleague brings up student reports that the teacher in the advanced reading skills class is dismissive of the students' religion and that they are more or less forbidden to raise faith issues in their discussions or assignments. The teacher concerned, clearly quite hurt by the accusation, replies calmly but firmly: 'Look, this is a pre-university course that is supposed to help them develop into critical thinkers. If all we do is wait to hear what the official line from God is on anything that comes up and the most devout wins, we're not doing very much to help them get on with their studies at a US university, are we?'

They both look at you. What do you say? What informs your response?

Conclusion

This chapter addresses Vandrick's (2009) concern over the lack of a sustained discussion about what is and is not appropriate classroom practice regarding religious faith in the SLE classroom, especially for teachers whose spiritual identity is an important part of how they view themselves and their work. Put another way, what are the limitations and possibilities of teachers' 'spiritual identity as pedagogy'? To answer this question, the context must be considered as well as the potential sources that inform teachers' moral and ethical decisions. Teachers should consider individual (internal) factors that influence decisions on what they believe to be ethical conduct in the classroom, such as personal experiences, cultural traditions, intellectual justifications and religious and spiritual beliefs. Other sources affecting their decisions are more external, such as ethical codes and statements found in institutional mission statements, professional codes of conduct, principles found in ethical standards for research, and the many sacred or secular texts that teachers draw from to inform their practice. Three delights of faith-informed pedagogy are discussed as well as three dangers, so that readers might be more aware of what is at stake by ignoring the spiritual aspect of teaching or, at the other extreme, by allowing it to go unchecked and unexamined. To inform the examination of faith in the classroom, a series of questions and scenarios is provided so readers can continue to think through the implications of teachers' 'spiritual identity as pedagogy' in their particular contexts. It is argued that teachers who seek to apply a 'spiritual identity as pedagogy' approach need to consider how their religious faith can inform their teaching in a way that respects their students and enhances learning. It is hoped that future research in this area might explore the potential of a 'spiritual identity as pedagogy' approach that is contextually appropriate, ethically sound and critically examined.

Special thanks to Julian Edge who provided comments on the chapter and drafts of the scenarios.

Other works that provide dilemmas to discuss include Messerschmitt and Hafernik (2009) and Strike and Soltis (2009). Also see Purgason (2016) for discussions from a Christian perspective.

References

AERA (American Educational Research Association) (2011) *Ethical Standards of the American Educational Association*. See http://www.aera.net/About-AERA/AERA-Rules-Policies/Professional-Ethics (accessed 28 April, 2018).

APA (American Psychological Association) (2010) *Ethical Principles of Psychologists and Code of Conduct* (2002, amended 1 June 2010). Washington, DC: American Psychological Association. See http://www.apa.org/ethics/code/index.aspx (accessed 28 April, 2018).

Braine, G. (1999) *Non-Native Educators in English Language Teaching*. Mahwah, NJ: Lawrence Erlbaum.

Braine, G. (2010) *Nonnative Speaker English Teachers: Research, Pedagogy, and Professional Growth*. New York: Routledge.

Brown, S. (2008) *A Buddhist in the Classroom*. Albany, NY: State University of New York Press.

Buechner, F. (1993) *Wishful Thinking: A Seekers ABC*. San Francisco, CA: Harper San Francisco.

Buzzilli, C.A. and Johnston, B. (2002) *The Moral Dimensions of Teaching: Language, Power, and Culture in Classroom Interaction*. New York: RoutledgeFalmer.

Cahn, S.M. (2011) *Saints and Scamps: Ethics in Academia* (25th Anniversary edn). Langham, MD: Rowman & Littlefield.

Canagarajah, A.S. (2011) Translanguaging in the classroom: Emerging issues for research and pedagogy. *Applied Linguistics Review* 2, 1–28.

Crookes, G. (2009) *Values, Philosophies, and Beliefs in TESOL: Making a Statement*. Cambridge: Cambridge University Press.

First Amendment Center (2008) *A Teacher's Guide to Religion in the Public Schools*. Nashville, TN: Freedom Forum. See http://www.religiousfreedomcenter.org/wp-content/uploads/2014/08/teachersguide.pdf (accessed 28 April, 2018).

Foucault, M. (1983) On the genealogy of ethics: An overview of a work in progress. In H. Dreyfus and P. Rabinow (eds) *Michel Foucault: Beyond Structuralism and Hermeneutics* (2nd edn) (pp. 229–252). Chicago, IL: University of Chicago Press.

Foye, K. (2014) Religion in the ELT classroom: Teachers' perspectives. *The Language Teacher* 38 (2), 5–12.

Hafernick, J.J., Messerschmitt, D.S. and Vandrick, S. (2002) *Ethical Issues for ESL Faculty: Social Justice in Practice*. Mahwah, NJ: Lawrence Erlbaum.

Hornberger, N. (2006) Voice and biliteracy in indigenous language revitalization: Contentious educational practices in Que-chua, Guarani, and Maori contexts. *Journal of Language, Identity, & Education* 5, 277–292.

International Civil Service Commission (2013) *Standards of Conduct in the International Civil Service*. See https://icsc.un.org/resources/pdfs/general/standardsE.pdf (accessed 28 April, 2018).

Johnston, B. (2003) *Values in English Language Teaching*. Mahwah, NJ: Lawrence Erlbaum.

Johnston, B. (2017) *English Teaching and Evangelical Missions: The Case of Lighthouse School*. Bristol: Multilingual Matters.

Kubota, R. and Lin, A. (eds) (2009) *Race, Culture, and Identities in Second Language Education: Exploring Critically Engaged Practice*. New York: Routledge.

Landrum, R.E. and McCarthy, M.A. (eds) (2012) *Teaching Ethically: Challenges and Opportunities*. Washington, DC: American Psychological Association.

Mahboob, A. (2009) Additive perspective on religion or growing hearts with wisdom. In M.S. Wong and A.S. Canagarajah (eds) *Christian and Critical English Language Educators in Dialogue: Pedagogical and Ethical Dilemmas* (pp. 272–280). New York: Routledge.

Mahboob, A. (ed.) (2010) *The NNEST Lens: Nonnative English Speakers in TESOL*. Newcastle upon Tyne: Cambridge Scholars.

Messerschmitt, D.S. and Hafernik, J.J. (2009) *Dilemmas in Teaching English to Speakers of Other Languages: 40 Cases*. Ann Arbor, MI: University of Michigan Press.

Morgan, B. (2004) Teacher identity as pedagogy: Towards a field-internal conceptualisation in bilingual and second language education. *International Journal of Bilingual Education and Bilingualism* 7, 172–188.

Morgan, B. (2009) The pedagogical dilemmas of faith in ELT: A dialogic response. In M.S. Wong and S. Canagarajah (eds) *Christian and Critical English Language Educators in Dialogue: Pedagogical and Ethical Dilemmas* (pp. 193–204). New York: Routledge.

Morgan, B. and Clarke, M. (2011) Identity in second language teaching and learning. In E. Hinkel (ed.) *Handbook of Research in Second Language Teaching and Learning* (Vol. 2) (pp. 817–836). New York: Routledge.

Moussu, L. and Llurda, E. (2008) Non-native English-speaking English language teachers: History and research. *Language Teaching* 41 (3), 315–348.

NAFSA: Association of International Educators (1989) *NAFSA's Code of Ethics*. See www.nafsa.org.

NEA (National Educators Association) (1975) *Code of Ethics of the Education Profession*. See http://www.nea.org/home/30442.htm (accessed 28 April, 2018).

Nelson, C.D. (1999) Sexual identities in ESL: Queer theory and classroom inquiry. *TESOL Quarterly* 33, 371–391.

Oprandy, R. (1999) Making personal connections to teaching. In J. Gebhard and R. Oprandy (eds) *Language Teaching Awareness: A Guide to Exploring Beliefs and Practices* (pp. 122–145). New York: Cambridge University Press.

Palmer, P. (2000) *Let Your Life Speak: Listening to the Voice of Vocation*. San Francisco, CA: Jossey-Bass.

Palmer, P. (2003) Teaching with heart and soul: Reflections on spirituality in teacher education. *Journal of Teacher Education* 54 (5), 376–385.

Palmer, P. (2010) *The Courage to Teach: Exploring an Inner Landscape of a Teacher's Life* (10th edn). San Francisco, CA: Jossey-Bass.

Purgason, K. (2016) *Professional Guidelines for Christian English Teachers: How to Be a Teacher with Convictions while Respecting Those of Your Students*. Pasadena, CA: William Carey Library.

Stevick, E.W. (1976) *Memory, Meaning, and Method: Some Psychological Perspectives on Language Learning*. Boston: Heinle & Heinle.

Strike, K.A. and Soltis, J.F. (2009) *The Ethics of Teaching* (5th edn). New York: Teachers College Press.

US Department of Health (1979) *The Belmont Report*. Washington, DC: US Department of Health, Education, and Welfare, National Commission for the Protection of Human Subjects of Biomedical and Behavioral Research.

Vandrick, S. (2009) A former 'missionary kid' responds. In M.S. Wong and S. Canagarajah (eds) *Christian and Critical English Language Educators in Dialogue: Pedagogical and Ethical Dilemmas* (pp. 141–149). New York: Routledge.

Volf, M. (1991) *Work in the Spirit: Toward a Theology of Work*. Oxford: Oxford University Press.

Wong, M.S. (2009) Deconstructing/reconstructing the missionary English teacher identity. In M.S. Wong and S. Canagarajah (eds) *Christian and Critical English Language Educators in Dialogue: Pedagogical and Ethical Dilemmas* (pp. 91–105). New York: Routledge.

Wong, M.S. (2012) Gender, identity, missions, and empire: Letters from Christian teachers in China in the early 20th and 21st centuries. *Frontiers of Education in China, Special Issue* 7 (3), 309–337.

Wong, M.S. (2013) Called to teach: The impact of faith on professional identity construction of western English teachers in China. In M.S. Wong, C. Kristjánsson and Z. Dörnyei (eds) *Christian Faith and English Language Teaching and Learning: Research on the Interrelationship of Religion and ELT* (pp. 11–30). New York: Routledge.

Wong, M.S. (2014a) The history, nature and future of faith-informed research in English language teaching. *International Journal of Christianity & English Language Teaching* 1, 6–23. Online. See https://static.biola.edu/cook/media/downloads/PDF/ijcelt-volume-1-2014.pdf (accessed 28 April, 2018).

Wong, M.S. (2014b) The dangers and delights of teacher spiritual identity as pedagogy. Paper presented at the Christians in English Language Teaching Conference, Portland, OR.

Wong, M.S. and Canagarajah, S. (eds) (2009) *Christian and Critical English Language Educators in Dialogue: Pedagogical and Ethical Dilemmas*. New York: Routledge.

Wong, M.S. and Stratton, D.J. (2011) From accomplices to advocates: Recognizing and reducing discrimination among 'non-native' speakers in mission organizations. *Evangelical Missions Quarterly* 47 (4), 440–447.

Wong, M.S., Kristjánsson, C. and Dörnyei, Z. (eds) (2013) *Christian Faith and English Language Teaching and Learning: Research on the Interrelationship of Religion and ELT*. New York: Routledge.

3 Buddhist Principles and the Development of Leadership Skills in English Language Program Administration and Teaching

MaryAnn Christison

When most people think of Buddhism and Buddhists, a number of visual images likely come to mind: orange-robed monks slowly making their way to early morning temple prayers; thin, scantily clad, wandering ascetics indulging in austerities and denying themselves most of the comforts accessible to modern humans; or people seated in the traditional lotus position in front of a Buddhist statue. Few people think of the growing number of individuals, like myself, who are not represented by these visual images and who live typical, ordinary lives. We are known as lay Buddhists, and we are not part of the *Sangha*. In other words, we are not monks, nuns or similar clergy who take vows to renounce their worldly possessions. Nevertheless, we are serious about our commitments and try to live lives that are consistent with Buddhist teachings. In communities where there is a presence of the *Sangha*, lay Buddhists provide support to the *Sangha*, and throughout history lay Buddhists have given offerings, fed the *Sangha*, and built temples and kept them running. If it were not for the lay Buddhists, many *Sangha* communities would not thrive as they do and have done throughout history.

Most lay Buddhists are attracted to Buddhism because of a shared belief that the mind is the creative center of human experience and that it has an infinite capacity for change and growth. This concept is central to the notion of intelligent leadership (Christison & Murray, 2009). In this view of leadership, intelligence is defined quite differently from traditional views, which consider intelligence as a single, static construct that remains unchanged throughout one's lifetime. In intelligent leadership, intelligence is viewed from the perspective of multiple constructs, and it is dynamic (Chen *et al.*, 2009; Gardner, 2011a, 2011b). In his book entitled *Leadership IQ*, Murphy (1996: 2) states that '... leadership can be defined and measured as a form of intelligence'. In other words, the behaviors of effective leaders can be studied, and leadership skills can be developed over time. In support of the notion of intelligent leadership, it is my position that Buddhism offers a set of guidelines that can be useful in the development of leadership skills in educational contexts (Meshram, 2013).

In this chapter I examine some of my experiences as an English language teaching professional from the perspective of a lay Buddhist to show how the basic principles of Buddhism can serve as a useful guide when one is working across the international boundaries of language and culture, focusing on developing skills as program administrators and leaders (Goodman, 2009). I will first provide you with some basic history about Buddhism and how it began. Then I will present each of the basic principles of Buddhism known as the Eightfold Path and discuss them against the backdrop of my own experiences in English language teaching and leadership with a focus on how the Eightfold Path has assisted me in navigating the challenges I have faced. I will also offer suggestions for the application and discussion of some of these ideas as they relate to the practice of English language administration and leadership.

An Introduction to Buddhism

Buddhism is not a religion in the traditional sense of the word. The Buddha is not considered a messiah or savior; there is no church to attend and no baptism or ritual that constitutes membership. One can become a lay Buddhist simply by saying that one is Buddhist. In order to understand Buddhism and, therefore, the relevance of its teachings to the development of leadership practices in the English language teaching profession, it is helpful to know something of its history and its basic teachings.

Buddhism originated in India in the 6th century BCE and slowly spread throughout Asia. Today it is estimated that around 500 million individuals from all over the world (about 6–7% of the Earth's population) are following some aspects of Buddhist philosophy (see http://www.buddhanet.net/e-learning/history/bud_statwrld.htm). It began with a man known as Siddhartha Gautama who came to be known as the Buddha. He was the son of an aristocrat and the long-awaited heir to his father's kingdom, so he grew up in a world of great affluence. He renounced his privileged circumstances, and this act gave force to his later teachings that individuals were worthy of honor only through their behaviors and not because of their titles or worldly possessions. The Buddha's ideas are similar to intelligent leadership (Murphy, 1996), which states that effective leaders are not born but made, and that one is considered to be an effective leader not by the position one holds but by the actions and behaviors that are consistent with effective leadership.

There are many traditions, stories and myths that have grown up around the Buddha and his teachings (Gowans, 2003). It is beyond the scope of this chapter to review even a small portion of them; however, there are general training rules or guidelines that Buddhists undertake voluntarily to live what Buddhists call a moral life. In Theravada Buddhism (the type of Buddhism with which I am most familiar) the guidelines are known as the Eightfold Path – right understanding, right thought, right action, right livelihood, right effort, right mindfulness, right speech and right concentration.

The Eightfold Path constitutes a basic doctrine known as the Middle Way. The observance of the Eightfold Path supplies the preliminary groundwork for the cultivation of a purposeful life and for the development of one's mind, but it also contributes to the peaceful co-existence among members of a community and, consequently, helps promote social growth and mutual trust (Harvey, 2000). Promoting social growth and mutual trust is a common goal for English language teaching programs; consequently, it is not a stretch to see that understanding the basic Buddhist doctrine may be useful for English language program administrators and leaders as they seek to develop leadership skills.

Each of the eight steps in the Eightfold Path must all be given attention. Although the steps are generally unfolded in the way in which I present them in this chapter, they are not meant to be completely linear in nature. The steps can and should be repeated and recycled until each step is mastered. I wish I could say that I have mastered even one of these steps, but that is not the case even though I have been practicing the Middle Way for most of my adult life.

Right Understanding

Right understanding (*samma ditthi*) is sometimes a difficult concept for the Western mind to grasp. It stems from the Buddha's realization that life is suffering. This doctrine may seem to be a very pessimistic view of life for many people because as humans we resist this analysis and set out in pursuit of happiness in our lives as if it were a constant. In the Buddha's view, it is 'this very belief in the attainment of lasting happiness, in conventional human terms, that is the true source of suffering' (Ross, 1981: 75). Conditions in the external world are constantly changing. If we base our happiness on external factors such as getting the job we want, marrying the person we love or getting the pay raise we think we deserve, we become unhappy every time we are not able to achieve these things. Fame, material security, success or power cannot bring the peace and satisfaction we seek because they are external markers of happiness and, therefore, changeable and impermanent.

Buddhist philosophy focuses on internal happiness and finding contentment in the here and now (Harvey, 2000). Most of us know people who seem to have everything in life, such as money or even fame, and yet have not found happiness. If leaders and administrators in the English language teaching profession can focus on the truth that happiness is an internal state, then whether we are able to control events in the external world is not likely to be a factor affecting our happiness.

When I first became an English language program administrator many years ago, I was establishing a new intensive English program (IEP), designing the curriculum, and implementing it in an institution of higher education (IHE) in the United States, an IHE that had never previously had an IEP or large numbers of international students learning academic English as a second language (L2). Like the days of most IEP administrators, my days were filled with many challenges and emotional ups and downs as I tried to negotiate the politics of the institution and figure out how to create a curriculum for an academic unit that no-one seemed to understand and get it approved by a group of individuals who had little or no background in L2 pedagogy. English language program administration is often difficult, and leaders will always run up against roadblocks related to space, money, the curriculum, staffing and institutional policies. I have spoken with many administrators who agree that nothing in their academic preparation had prepared them for the emotional upheavals and turmoil that they experienced as new administrators.

As I tried to negotiate my way through these challenges, the Buddhist principle of right understanding ultimately became my saving grace. I remember the precise moment when I realized that disappointments and challenges were going to be constant in my work as an administrator. Prior to that moment, I had been thinking that once I solved the current problems, then everything would be 'normal' and I would be happy. However, putting off being happy or content until all of the problems were solved was resulting in an almost permanent state of emotional upheaval for me because there are always challenges and problems in English language program administration. When I solved one problem, there was always another one there to take its place. Once I realized this fact about the nature of problems in my role as an English language program administrator, then I could begin to develop right understanding.

I have no idea if my process will work for others; however, for English language program administrators and leaders who are interested in pursuing right understanding, I offer my experiences as a place to begin the process. At the beginning of each workday, I tried to access positive internal feelings by devoting just five or 10 minutes to thinking about what made me happy, what I was looking forward to or what I was grateful for outside of my work. I also created a mantra, a statement that reminded me that my internal state was separate from external events, and I repeated it when necessary throughout the day. I also developed a non-personal orientation to problem solving in which I expected problems to occur and stated that no problems were unsolvable (Murphy, 1996). When problems arose, I focused on finding solutions and involved others in the process. Eventually I noticed that my internal state began to change even when I faced disappointments and difficulties. I also noticed that my work environment, in terms of my interactions with others, became more positive and supportive. Because of my own experiences I believe that leaders and administrators who develop right understanding can not only be more effective in solving problems and experience less stress and more personal happiness as individuals, but they can also have an overall positive impact on their programs.

Right Thought

Right understanding deals with the content and direction of what we think, whereas right thought (*samma sankappa*) is concerned with understanding the relationship between thoughts and actions and determining what drives our thinking (Meshram, 2013). The Buddha described two types of thoughts – wandering and directed. Our minds are generally filled with random or wandering thoughts; however, we have the power to direct or cultivate our thoughts for the achievement of certain goals. There is a cause/effect relationship between thoughts and actions, so it is easy to see how positive and optimistic thoughts are more likely to result in positive and optimistic actions.

Leaders in any workplace environment are confronted by problems, and leaders in the field of English language teaching are no exception to this rule. According to Murphy (1996), average leaders spend 30% of their time solving problems and 45% of their time on maintenance activities involving paperwork. However, effective leaders embrace problem-solving activities and spend up to 60% of their time solving problems that will move their work forward and only 10% of their time on maintenance work. Creating an optimal balance between maintenance activities and planning or problem-solving activities is an issue for most program administrators and leaders. Very often program administrators' days are wrapped up in the minutiae of maintenance rather than on planning and solving long-term problems (Christison & Stoller, 2012).

The best problem solvers use a straightforward, linear and analytical process to keep their work focused. Using an analytical process for problem solving brings together the principle of right understanding with right thought, because problem solvers are seen as scientists who search for data to find workable solutions, thereby allowing them to focus on finding solutions to problems and maintaining positive and optimistic attitudes. Students, teachers, staff and other stakeholders look to leaders for constancy, stability and optimism. When leaders have positive and optimistic attitudes even in the face of difficulties and challenges, such as when enrollments decline and teachers are at risk of losing their jobs, they are able to demonstrate right thought and have a powerful influence on colleagues and peers. Thoughts influence actions, so the development of right thoughts can bring about actions that have the potential to result in positive change in the work environment.

In Buddhism, right thought also refers to uncovering what drives private thoughts and learning to be honest with ourselves. For example, if we participate in an activity or a task or develop a relationship because we hope to get a promotion or secure additional money, we simply need to be honest with ourselves and admit that these are our motives. Such honesty is a challenge for leaders because the motives we have may be different from the motives that others may expect us to have. A leader who is not honest about his or her motives risks becoming trapped in the political complexities of an institution and its organizational systems, thereby allowing other people to drive the daily agendas and ultimately control their lives.

Early on in my career, I remember being asked to chair committees and task forces for my institution. Although I did not want to participate in these activities, I would say 'yes' because I hoped that if I did these things I would be able to get more money for the program's budget or that I could compel loyalty from colleagues in other units. I seldom enjoyed participating in these activities and my participation seldom resulted in accomplishing the objectives I originally sought. Eventually I came to realize the value of right thought as it applied to uncovering my own motives. Ultimately, I would say things such as: 'Well, I have to be honest with you; I don't really want to chair this committee, and if I agree to do it, I may not be doing it for the right reasons. Of course, I will always do my best, but my heart is not in it.' Sometimes I had to take on the task anyway; however, in those instances, I knew that I had at least been honest with myself about my motives. In developing right thought, English language program administrators and leaders may sometimes find tensions developing between the need for personal honesty in developing right thought and meeting the expectations of others.

Right Speech

When I think of right speech (*samma vaca*), I am reminded of a wooden sign that my paternal grandmother used to display on the wall at the top of her basement stairs. It said, 'Be sure your brain is in motion before opening your mouth'. Our family always laughed at this little sign, and I always thought about its message, which is basically the same as right speech. Right speech is perhaps the most challenging step in the Eightfold Path for leaders in English language education because our jobs require face-to-face communication with students, parents, teachers and other stakeholders on a daily basis, and these communicative encounters often take place across languages and cultures, thereby creating numerous challenges for the interlocutors involved.

Learning to apply the principle of right speech in the work environment is a valuable tool for administrators and leaders. In the Buddhist tradition, right speech is explained in terms of avoiding four types of harmful speech: lies, divisive speech, harsh speech and idle chatter. To apply the concept of right speech, administrators and leaders must focus on giving themselves thinking time before speaking. Thinking time gives us a chance to focus on the purpose or motivation for speaking and determine whether we really need to speak or not.

To determine the purpose of speech, leaders should determine if they can answer 'yes' to the following question: Does what I have to say serve a purpose? If it is not possible to answer 'yes' to this question and articulate the purpose, then leaders should opt to say nothing until the intention is clear. Giving information, providing clarification, promoting trust and harmony or offering comfort are important purposes related to right speech. Finding the words to promote right speech is often difficult when one is feeling marginalized or upset. Although it is sometimes frustrating to say nothing, there is wisdom in following this process.

Students, teachers, staff and other stakeholders associated with an English language program look to leaders to offer renewal and hope and help transcend differences. Most people are aware that saying the right thing at the right time is a critical skill for leaders. On the other hand, knowing when not to talk is also an important skill. By knowing when to speak and not speak, leaders can be healers (Christison & Murray, 2009; Murphy, 1996). English language teaching programs are often recovering from crises – budget cuts, decreases in enrollments, changes in policies – and administrators and leaders often need to function as healers. A healer's job is first and foremost diagnostic; it is a job that involves determining how to interact with the individuals. Leaders who are healers focus on right speech because it is through right speech that leaders can promote trust and harmony in the workplace.

Right Action

The fourth step in the Eightfold Path is right action (*samma kammanta*), with its focus on how to behave in the modern, physical world. In essence, right action in the Buddhist tradition means to refrain from killing another human being, lying, stealing, sexual misconduct and overindulgence. While all of these concepts are certainly important and contribute to right action, it means much more than the sum total of these refrains for English language program and administration. In most Western religious traditions, principles are organized around opposites, for example sin versus virtue, thou shalt versus thou shalt not. However, Buddhism has no such absolutes. Right action begins with statements, such as *it is better to* or *it is better not to*, so that the choice for action is contextualized and must be determined by the individual. In this way, right action is consistent with emerging views in critical applied linguistics (Pennycook, 2001), in which applied linguists approach their work in terms of ethical, epistemological and political considerations. No action we take is ever simply black or white, right or wrong, effective or ineffective. Our praxis must be considered against the backdrop of the context(s) in which we work.

In the last decade I have become increasingly aware of the contextual nature of the work we do as applied linguists, as I negotiate my interests in language pedagogy in English language teaching and my interests in language revitalization and the fate of endangered language communities around the world. I recognize that the work I do in promoting a majority language such as English may contribute either directly or indirectly to the decline of linguistic diversity (Grenoble & Whaley, 2006), which impacts the work I do in language revitalization. On the other hand, the work that I do in language maintenance and revitalization could be seen by a number of English language educators as a political statement against an increased interest in globalization or a political statement about the position of English as world language. As Edge (2006) points out, 'to work to improve the quality of experience available to the inhabitants of a situation can be seen, from another perspective, as working to support those in power in that situation'. My work in teaching English to students of other languages (TESOL) and in the revitalization of endangered languages is contextual in that it involves a complex set of factors. Understanding and counterbalancing the forces that cause the language shift requires that I treat each context as unique. When I conduct teacher education workshops for teachers of minority languages, I draw on my decades of experience in working with teachers of majority languages. While I realize that not everything I do in one domain is directly applicable to another, there are definitely cross-over points and areas in which we come together. If English language administrators and leaders are to pursue right action in their work, there will be few black and white answers. In order to provide effective leadership, it is important to determine the best course of action by looking at the problems and the decisions that need to be made in the contexts, both local and global, in which they occur (Gates, 2005).

Right Livelihood

The development of right livelihood (*samma ajiva*), the fifth step in the Middle Way, is a bit tricky in modern, contemporary life (Ross, 1981). To practice right livelihood means that English language administrators and leaders have to find a way to earn a living and support themselves without doing harm to others. The influential British economist, E.F. Schumacher (1975), points out that Buddhist economics differs radically from the economics of modern materialism because, in Buddhism, daily work is seen as a means for the purification of the human character (Ross, 1981), and administrators and leaders who are committed to developing right action in their work lives will find that it is a complex and growth-producing experience.

The global economy of the 21st century complicates ideas of right livelihood because, as English language program administrators and leaders, we depend on one another to support ourselves. Globalization means that the citizens of the world are more closely linked than they ever have been. Even if the job we directly pursue and enjoy does not require harmful or unethical actions from us, it is possible that the multinational company or institution for which we work or which we do business with may knowingly or unknowingly do harm or be associated with unethical actions. For example, Kumaravadivelu (2006) highlights the dangerous liaison that exists between the forces of globalization and TESOL wherein 'TESOL professionals end up serving the profit motives of global corporations and the political motives of imperial powers' (Kumaravadivelu, 2006: 23). Most jobs in English language program administration provide endless opportunities to practice right livelihood; however, the problems that arise for Buddhist lay practitioners are subtle and complex.

In addition, there is the politics of language itself and issues of how race and class play into the discourses on English language teaching (Kubota, 2006). As an example, Lo Bianco (2002) points out how bilingualism in the United States is an interesting paradox. Bilingualism among immigrants and the poor is seen as a social evil to be done away with, whereas bilingualism among the English-speaking elite is seen as an accomplishment. There are also pressing problems of ecology and the environment in today's world which are considerations for right livelihood. Because Buddhism stresses the interrelatedness of life, concerns of non-violence and non-destructive attitudes are critical to this concept, and administrators and leaders who wish to apply right livelihood to their working lives must be vigilant in determining how right livelihood can be actualized in our globalized and interconnected world.

Right Effort

Right effort (*samma vayama*) can be described in simple terms as the ability to use our inner strength or willpower to alter the 'habitual patterns of our thought processes and thus effect changes in our character' (Ross, 1981: 85). If you have ever tried to change something you habitually do, such as trying to get up an hour earlier, stop smoking cigarettes or give up desserts, you know how difficult making such changes can be. The process of change requires constant vigilance and patience, as it takes a considerable time for new behaviors to become part of our everyday routines. The process of right effort is really a cycle of commitment, focus, ongoing observation and recommitment. This cycle or iterative process is the same one that most of us have used to change physical behaviors, so it is likely familiar. What may be unfamiliar is its application to changing our thought processes.

Some years ago, one of my colleagues asked me why I was so negative about a particular person at work. This person was not a part of our work unit but was someone we needed to work with on a regular basis. Although I had experienced many difficulties with this person in terms of stressful interpersonal communication, attempts to obstruct the growth and development of program, and the quality of the person's work over the years, I also realized that my negative thoughts and unmonitored comments about this person were detrimental to a positive work environment in the English language teaching program that I was hoping to build.

I knew that I needed to change my thought processes, but I also knew that the negative feelings I had were quite strong and were not likely to change overnight. In the beginning, I could not make the commitment necessary for right effort. Consequently, I decided to begin with right speech, a task to which I believed I could commit. I decided to see where it would take me in terms of making the changes that I knew were necessary. At first, I focused on the purposes of my speech and on whether my comments would establish trust and bring peace and harmony to the interactions in our workplace. I concluded that nothing I had to say about this person would further the process of right speech. Consequently, when this person's name came up, which was often, I usually said nothing because my comments would have been outside the parameters of right speech. Over time, my staff and the teaching faculty began to view me as neutral relative to this individual, and once my personal views were removed from the process of solving problems, we made progress and were able to develop a process for working with this person that allowed us to get important work done. Through the experience of silence concerning this individual, I came to see how destructive my thought processes had been for me personally and for the program. Once I came to this realization, I was able to commit to the process of developing right effort.

The process of developing right effort can be described in steps. First, we must commit to the process. Such a commitment means that we must truly want to make a change and must make every effort to get rid of or change the disagreeable or harmful states of mind that have already arisen, as was the case with the negative thoughts I had about someone in my own workplace. Secondly, we must focus on the process. Focusing means that we must be aware of the disagreeable or harmful states of mind as they arise and monitor these. The third step in the process is observation. When negative thoughts arise, we must be willing to observe our thought processes without taking action. I ultimately found that keeping a written journal was helpful for me during the observation stage as writing down my thoughts gave me opportunities to further examine them. My journals also included observations of others' actions and comments. I did not purposely try to rid myself of my negative thoughts, but recorded them, studied them and tried to understand them. Then I would recommit to the process again. I wish I could say that the process resulted in the obliteration of my negative thoughts, but this would be an untrue statement. What the process did was allow me to understand my thought processes. It also made me aware of how detrimental negative thoughts can be to individuals and to programs, how important it is to have a process for working with negative thoughts, and why right effort is so important for English language administrators and leaders who have the capacity, simply by virtue of the positions they hold, to influence the thoughts and actions of others.

Right Mindfulness

In order to explain right mindfulness (*samma sati*), I draw on Admiral E.H. Shattock's experiences in a Burmese monastery in Rangoon (Shattock, 1960). In his book, *An Experiment in Mindfulness*, Shattock explains that he was given two basic exercises to do at the monastery. One was to walk back and forth for a short distance and concentrate on the separate actions involved in each step he took, and the other was to concentrate on his breathing, on the rise and fall of his abdomen. At first, the exercises seemed as if they would be simple, but they turned out to be very difficult. In short order, Shattock discovered that his mind was not disciplined. In the beginning, he could concentrate for only a few moments. He was constantly fighting with intrusive and random thoughts which made it very difficult to accomplish these two basic tasks.

Although Shattock studied for a relatively short period of time, he made progress and eventually became mindful of his breathing and movements for longer periods of time. He realized that the rise and fall of the abdomen in the process of breathing was representative of the transient nature of the human body in which nothing is permanent. He learned to notice his breath and to watch it come and go, while at the same time noticing the intrusive thoughts without fighting them or passing judgment on them. This meditative process of watching and noticing one's breath or movements without attachment is designed to ease tension so that a person can become present in the here and now.

My own experiences with right mindfulness have been very similar to Shattock's and many others. When I first started to meditate, I very quickly came to the realization that I have a very undisciplined mind. Over time, I also learned that the practice of meditation helped me focus, slowed me down and eased the tensions I experienced on a daily basis. When difficulties arise in the workplace, I find that five, 10 or 15 minutes of meditative practice is extremely helpful. I close and lock my office door, close my eyes, notice my breath, become aware of my bodily movements, listen to sounds in the environment and watch my thoughts come and go. A short, meditative break restores me and helps me listen to and focus on others and maintain steadiness and patience in my work rather than on my own thoughts and issues.

Right Concentration

Right concentration (*samma samadhi*) is the most difficult stage to explain in terms of its immediate application to the work of English language teaching professionals. There is no adequate translation for this final stage in the Eightfold Path. In essence, this stage is about developing wisdom by moving from the observation of life, to participation in life and, finally, to absorption into life. In a sense, right concentration is similar to 'an ocean entering a drop' of water. In the Theravada tradition, this stage is comprised of various exercises that fall into the following three main areas: (1) contemplation on one's faith in personal effort and in the belief that heightened consciousness can be attained; (2) seeking support for one's endeavors; and (3) expressing gratitude for others and having a strong desire to help others.

In Murphy's (1996) model for intelligent leadership, personal effort is the number one factor contributing to success as a leader. Successful leadership is not about whether the boss likes us or whether we are in the right place at the right time, but about our own personal effort and initiative. Leadership intelligence can be developed through hard work and effort, and this view is consistent with right concentration. Seeking support for our endeavors and finding and expressing gratitude are essential to the work that we do as English language program administrators and leaders. Seeking support for our endeavors is an important step in recognizing our interconnectedness and in not separating ourselves from others in a unit or institution. Expressing gratitude is an important step in feeling compassion. Although globalization means that our world has become metaphorically smaller, it also means that our communication has become more complicated, resulting in political tensions, misunderstandings and, left unchecked, violence. Ross (1981) shares a beautiful injunction which is intended to create a state of being focused on benevolence, compassion and loving-kindness for one's fellow humans. Its message stands in sharp contrast to the tensions and misunderstandings prevalent in the world today and is at the heart of a lay Buddhist's practice.

> May all beings be happy and at their ease. May they be joyous and live in safety! All beings, whether weak or strong – omitting none – in high, middle, or low realms of existence, small or great, visible or invisible, near or far away, born or to be born – may all beings be happy and at their ease. Let none deceive another, or despise any being in any state; let none by anger or ill-will wish harm to another! Even as a mother watches over and protects her child, her only child, so with boundless mind should one cherish all living beings, radiating friendliness over the entire world,

above, below, and all around without limits; so let him cultivate a boundless goodwill towards the entire world, uncramped, free from ill-will or enmity. (Ross, 1981: 91)

Conclusion

Understanding the simple but penetrating principles of Buddhism is a lifelong pursuit. In this short chapter, I have provided an introduction to the tenets of the Eightfold Path or the Middle Way – right understanding, right thought, right action, right livelihood, right effort, right mindfulness, right speech and right concentration – along with my personal interpretation of the doctrine as it applies to a lay Buddhist and a practicing English language teaching professional in the 21st century. My purpose in doing this has been to help administrators and leaders in English language education develop skills for working effectively across borders of languages and cultures (Wisadavet, 2003). I also believe that application of the Buddhist principles in the Eightfold Path can provide us with opportunities to learn about ourselves and others and that learning more about ourselves and the individuals with whom we communicate and interact in our work environments contributes to developing a rewarding and satisfying professional life.

References

Chen, J.-Q., Moran, S. and Gardner, H. (2009) (eds) *Multiple Intelligences around the World*. San Francisco, CA: Jossey-Bass.

Christison, M.A. and Murray, D.E. (2009) A model for leadership in English language teaching: An introduction to leadership IQ. In M.A. Christison and D.E. Murray (eds) *Leadership in English Language Education: Theoretical Foundations and Practical Skills for Changing Times*. New York: Routledge/Taylor & Francis.

Christison, M.A. and Stoller, F.L. (2012) Time management principles. In M.A. Christison and F.L. Stoller (eds) *A Handbook for Language Program Administrators* (2nd edn) (pp. 263–282). Miami Beach, FL: Alta Book Center.

Edge, J. (2006) Non-judgemental discourse: Role and relevance. In J. Edge (ed.) *(Re)locating TESOL in an Age of Empire* (pp. 104–118). London: Palgrave Macmillan.

Gardner, H. (2011a) *Multiple Intelligences: New Horizons in Theory and Practice* (3rd edn). New York: Basic Books.

Gardner, H. (2011b) *Multiple Intelligences: Frames of Mind*. New York: Basic Books.

Gates, G. (2005) Awakening to school community: Buddhist philosophy of educational reform. *Journal of Educational Thought* 39 (2), 149–173.

Goodman, C. (2009) *Consequences of Compassion: An Interpretation and Defense of Buddhist Ethics*. Oxford: Oxford University Press.

Gowans, C. (2003) *Philosophy of the Buddha*. London: Routledge.

Grenoble, L.A. and Whaley, L.J. (2006) *Saving Languages: An Introduction to Revitalization*. Cambridge: Cambridge University Press.

Harvey, P. (2000) *An Introduction to Buddhist Ethics*. Cambridge: Cambridge University Press.

Kubota, R. (2006) Teaching second languages for national security purposes: A case of post-9/11 USA. In J. Edge (ed.) *(Re)locating TESOL in an Age of Empire* (pp. 119–138). London: Palgrave Macmillan.

Kumaravadivelu, B. (2006) Dangerous liaison: Globalization, empire, and TESOL. In J. Edge (ed.) *(Re)locating TESOL in an Age of Empire* (pp. 1–26). London: Palgrave Macmillan.

Lo Bianco, J. (2002) Uncle Sam and Mister Unz. *Australian Language Matters* 10, 8–10.

Meshram, M. (2013) The significance of Buddhist ethics in modern education. *International Journal of Research in Humanities, Arts and Literature* 1 (4), 17–24.

Murphy, E.M. (1996) *Leadership IQ*. New York: John Wiley.

Pennycook, A. (2001) *Critical Applied Linguistics: A Critical Approach*. New York: Lawrence Erlbaum.

Ross, N.W. (1981) *Buddhism: A Way of Life and Thought*. New York: Vintage Books.

Schumacher, E.F. (1975) *Small is Beautiful*. New York: Harper & Row.

Shattock, E.H. (1960) *An Experiment in Mindfulness: An English Admiral's Experiences in a Buddhist Monastery*. Boston, MA: Dutton.

Wisadavet, W. (2003) The Buddhist philosophy of education: Approaches and problems. *Chulalongkorn Journal of Buddhist Studies* 2 (1), 159–188. See http://www.chinabuddhismencyclopedia.com/en/images/3/31/The_Buddhist_Philosophy_of_Education.pdf (accessed 24 April, 2018).

4 Attempting Interfaith Dialogue in TESOL: A Duoethnography

Joel Heng Hartse and Saeed Nazari

Introduction: Impetus and Purpose

In recent years, interest in scholarly dialogue about various aspects of religion and spirituality in English language teaching (ELT) has increased. The publication of books (Wong & Canagarajah, 2009; Wong *et al.*, 2013) and articles (e.g. Edge, 2003; Pennycook & Coutand-Marin, 2003; Pennycook & Makoni, 2005; Varghese & Johnston 2006) on religion and teaching English to speakers of other languages (TESOL) has created a welcome space for an academic discussion of sometimes contentious issues among ELT scholars from different backgrounds. This chapter, inspired by recent efforts at scholarly dialogue on religion and TESOL, takes a distinctly interpersonal, autobiographical approach: we are both ELT professionals and with differing religious perspectives and backgrounds (namely, Christianity and Islam) who have an interest in interfaith dialogue in our profession.

While the impetus for our interest in interfaith dialogue in our profession is, in part, the conflicts and contentious issues involving Christianity and Islam which have been cited in applied linguistics literature (see, for example, Hadley, 2004; Karmani, 2005, 2006; Pennycook & Coutand-Marin, 2003), our approach was purposefully open ended. It was difficult to know what, if anything, the actual outcome of such a dialogue would be before we began meeting, talking and writing together. We note, however, that attempts at dialogue between Christians and Muslims – or at 'interfaith' dialogue in general – are lacking in the applied linguistics literature; the volume from which we drew inspiration for dialogue (Wong & Canagarajah, 2009) includes dialogues between applied linguists who self-identified as (evangelical) Christian, agnostic, spiritual, non-religious, atheist and other (see the 'spiritual identification statements' of the contributors to that volume for a more complex and nuanced picture).

The original stated goal of our project was to discover the common values of our different faiths through a discussion of our profession of ELT and our respective religious backgrounds, beliefs and practices. We could not assume that either of us had the information about each other's backgrounds, or what the other's position would be on various religious, political or professional issues. Our original intention was to produce a document which affirmed common Christian and Muslim values that can be put into practice in English language teaching and scholarship.

While we did eventually produce such a document, it became clear that the text we had written was less than suitable as a contribution to the scholarly conversation on religion in TESOL. It was at once too personal to be relevant to a wide audience and too abstract to serve as a practical model of interfaith dialogue. Thus, we shifted our focus from producing a conceptual paper on common values shared by Christian and Muslim TESOL professionals to what has instead emerged below: a collaborative, autoethnographic, qualitative analysis of our own 'interfaith dialogue in TESOL', an excavation of a two-year process of collaboration, dialogue and co-writing.

In what follows, we use the method/genre (the research and writing processes being inextricable) of duoethnography (Norris *et al.*, 2012; Sawyer & Norris, 2013) to explore the possibilities and challenges of interfaith dialogue in TESOL. We adopted this approach for two reasons: first, to emphasize the importance and usefulness of qualitative, autobiographically oriented research for studying the deeply personal areas of spirituality and identity in education; and, secondly, to offer a more faithful representation of the ambiguities, failures, unexpected outcomes and overall 'messiness' of the project of interfaith dialogue between TESOL professionals.

In this chapter we begin by situating our project in the larger conversation about 'dialogue' on religious issues in TESOL, an issue which was foregrounded in Wong and Canagarajah's (2009) dialogically organized edited volume, *Christian and Critical English Language Educators in Dialogue*. We discuss various approaches to dialogue by that volume's contributors, arguing for the necessity of a more interpersonal approach to scholarly dialogue. We then describe the unique affordances of duoethnography for studying (and indeed participating in) interfaith dialogue.

The 'meat' of the chapter is the duoethnography itself, which would traditionally be called the 'results' section of a research article; here we (re)present, contextualize and analyze personal narratives and excerpts of data collected from our two-year interaction, including emails, meeting notes, drafts of collaborative writing, and memories and reflections on the process.

Interfaith Dialogue in TESOL: Methodological Issues

One of the challenges of interfaith dialogue in TESOL is determining a conceptual and/or methodological framework for dialogue. Much of the work on 'dialogue' in this area has been at the conceptual level – that is, scholars writing for an audience of scholars – rather than interpersonal. This section reviews approaches to 'dialogue' on religious issues described by English language teachers, and then describes the features of duoethnography, explaining our decision to proceed with this approach rather than simply producing a conceptual text.

Johnston (2009), in his chapter on challenges to evangelicals and non-evangelicals in ELT, provides two distinct modifiers for the word 'dialogue' when defining its nature and uses. In educational contexts, he uses the term *exploratory dialogue* to address spoken or written exchanges of perspectives, stories, questions and voices to form mutual ideas and views. He further proposes *conciliatory dialogue* as a way to include the differing positions of Christian English teacher (CET) and non-CET communities or political parties, since the opposing sides are presumably considered too involved in their own perspectives to be open to modifying their viewpoints. Such dialogue is essentially concerned with not altering the beliefs of the other position, but rather understanding the opposite standpoints and surmounting biases and preconceptions of either position (Johnston, 2009: 36).

Pennycook (2009) describes a more pessimistic perspective on dialogue with religious believers in ELT; to him, 'to have to engage with ancient organized religions in their new incarnations, with claims to the existence of an almighty being still, seems a desperate regression' (Pennycook, 2009: 60). Pennycook (2009: 60) points out that, for many, the prominence of religion is 'not welcome'. We recognize Pennycook's insights into the sometimes uneasy and tense interactions between committed religious and decidedly non-religious individuals. However, we also note that religion is not likely to disappear; Berger (1999) and others have argued that 'secularization theory' – the notion that 'modernization necessarily leads to a decline of religion, both in society and in the minds of individuals' – is 'essentially mistaken' (Berger, 1999: 2).

We also, however, recognize that religious beliefs and identities are complex and multifaceted, and assume that productive, open-ended discussions between people with religious differences is possible through what Canagarajah (2009) introduces as *transformative dialogue*, a collective achievement that provides the ground for mutual progress of both parties in their personal transformation. In a holistic manner, the dialogue ultimately accommodates the possibility of change to the participants' views, relationships and values. We regard this type of dialogue as a common ground for an exchange of perspectives, ideas and values, and find that the qualitative research methodology known as duoethnography (described below) is well suited for exploring the possibilities of transformative dialogue, as this method is 'ultimately … about transformation' (Norris *et al.*, 2012: 200).

Duoethnography

Duoethnography is a methodologically rigorous approach to interpersonal scholarly dialogue, which operates by 'critically juxtaposing the stories of two or more disparate individuals who experience a similar phenomenon' (Norris, 2008: 233). Rooted in the narrative tradition in autobiographical research, duoethnography provides the tools and framework needed to approach a complex issue like religious identity via a dialogic process in which differences, disagreements and our own unique subjective engagements with research, theory, beliefs and each other are embraced as a vital part of the research itself.

Duoethnography is a form of dual autoethnography in which 'two or more researchers work in tandem to dialogically critique and question the meanings they give to issues and constructs. Examining personal artifacts, stories, memories, compositions, texts, and critical incidents, duoethnographers excavate the temporal, social, cultural and geographical cartography of their lives, making explicit their assumptions and perspectives' (Sawyer & Norris, 2009). The inspiration for this method is Pinar's concept of *currere* (cited in Norris *et al.*, 2012), which views 'a person's life as curriculum' (Norris *et al.*, 2012: 12) and involves 'an act of self-interrogation in which one reclaims one's self from one's self as one unpacks and repacks the meanings that one holds' (Norris *et al.*, 2012: 13). Crucially, duoethnography involves more than one individual undergoing this process at the same time, 'in tandem with the Other' (Norris *et al.*, 2012: 13). Differences between co-researchers is assumed and even necessary for duoethnographies; examples from the growing literature in this tradition include collaborations between researchers who are, for example, gay and straight (Sawyer & Norris, 2004), black and white (McClellan & Sader, 2012) and immigrant and non-immigrant (Nabavi & Lund, 2012). The juxtaposition of these differences often results in scholarly conversations which are deeply personal.

Norris (2008: 35) identifies four basic tenets of duoethnography. First, the methodology 'must remain open', because its aim is 'to promote and articulate research conversations in dialogue'. Secondly, each researcher's voice is made explicit; the final product is not agreement or synthesis, but 'the conversations present both thesis and antithesis'. Thirdly, duoethnography does not aim at 'uncovering meanings' but rather 'creating and transforming them', and changes of perspective are expected and encouraged throughout the conversation as 'the researchers/writers are open to (re)storying their own lives'. Finally, differences are viewed as a strength: 'duoethnography is not looking for universals but rather examines how different individuals give both similar and different meanings to a shared phenomenon.'

During the course of our work on the original, 'conceptual' version of this paper, we aimed to create a simple synthesis which described harmonious aspects of Muslim and Christian theology and practice and how these impact our lives as English teachers. During the course of our writing and discussions, however, it became clear that we had different understandings of concepts like 'Muslim', 'Christian' and 'religion', and the ways in which these impact us both personally and professionally. We began to look for theoretical models that could accommodate a more subjective understanding, including sociological concepts of religious habitus (Mellor & Shilling, 2010), communication perspectives on interfaith dialogue (Brown, 2013), and autobiography and *currere* (Pinar, 2011). Ultimately, duoethnography emerged as the most effective method for us both to engage in and to model the type of interpersonal scholarly dialogue we believe is missing and necessary when it comes to understanding the role of faith in TESOL. Thus, we write this chapter not simply as representatives of various religions, or even solely as TESOL practitioners or scholars, but ultimately as 'different individuals trying to make meaning of their life histories and then reconceptualizing those meanings' (Norris *et al.*, 2012: 178).

Methods: Writing our 'Interfaith Dialogue in TESOL'

There is very little separation between 'data collection' and 'writing' in duoethnography; because the method involves individual life histories, autobiographical writing is, in a sense, both the data and the analysis for such a project. However, we did create a 'data set' to aid our analysis: an 80-page document comprising every email we sent to each other (and, occasionally, others, like the editors of this volume) from June 2012 to October 2014. Supplementary data included our original drafts of our first paper, which included autobiographical narratives and descriptions of religious values, and our individual notes from the seven face-to-face meetings we had over the course of the two years.

As this is a duoethnography, the dialogue through which we engage in 'data analysis' is necessarily open ended, and is guided by this basic question: How did/do we approach the project of undertaking 'interfaith dialogue in TESOL', based on our own beliefs and life histories, and what were the differences, disagreements and failures, as well as the commonalities, agreements and successes, as defined by the participants (us)? Below, we present the duoethnographic dialogue in which we each attempt to come to some better understanding of these questions.

'Interfaith Dialogue in TESOL: A Duoethnography'

Joel: I am almost embarrassed now at the goal I had when we started this project, Saeed. We first met in the summer of 2012 because I had mentioned to your wife, who is a classmate in my PhD program, that I was interested in religion and TESOL. I had written a review of the *Christian* *and Critical Language Educators in Dialogue* book, and the publisher had sent me two copies of the book by mistake, so I brought one with me to a meeting of my TESOL writing group to see if anyone wanted it. That meeting started a kind of casual conversation about religion among members of the group. In my own life I had been thinking about my Christian faith and how little I knew about Islam and other faiths in general, and my interest in the perceived 'clash' between Christianity and Islam in TESOL led me to be interested in pursuing a project on dialogue between Christian and Muslim ELT professionals. At that time I don't recall what I had in mind, but I remember when your wife first introduced us to each other at the coffee shop on campus, you enthusiastically suggested that we co-write or co-edit a book on the subject! I remember being somewhat shocked (we had only just met and now we are writing a book?), but excited about the prospect. Nothing like this had been done and I saw it as vitally necessary. It was not until much later that I began to see my approach to this project – which I saw as more or less a 'Christian and Muslim' version of the *Christian and Critical* book – as somewhat misguided or naïve. Later, we ended up signing a contract to do this chapter and decided to see what would come of it before actually doing a book. But I think after what we've been talking about for the last two years, that book would not be possible for us to write!

Saeed: I will never forget our first meeting on a rainy day in that coffee shop with a spectacular view. Heading home after teaching English intensive classes on that Friday, on the bus on my way to our meeting, I took a second look at the volume you had lent me, *Christian and Critical Language Educators in Dialogue*. I liked the style of the dialogues between Christian and critical scholars; however, I thought something was missing. Coming from a country where the dominant religion is Islam, I was wondering how I could facilitate a chance of dialogue between Muslim and Christian scholars. Since I considered an inter-religious dialogue as an exchange of thoughts between two religious groups, in our first meeting I mainly focused on a larger scale, failing to notice an interpersonal dialogue between us. Overlooking our personal differences led into the first draft on 'Common values of a Christian and Muslim TESOL professional'. My learning from our first attempt, however, encouraged me to revisit my ideology, leading into a more critical perspective. Now, I have many questions:

Before initiating a dialogue between two religious TESOL practitioners, a pivotal question is 'is an interfaith dialogue possible'? This might initially seem a naïve question. Provided that we simply consider that the dialogue is between two religious TESOL professionals who self-identified as Christian and Muslim, is there a clear definition for 'Christianity' and 'Islam'? Thinking about the multiple divisions of each religion, if there is not a definite answer for the proposed question, how would we label ourselves as Christian and Muslim? Do all Christian or Muslim

TESOL professionals share the same ideological perspectives, which are transferable or communicable to new circumstances, contexts, people and professionals? Is it possible that a Christian or Muslim individual, who happened to be a TESOL practitioner, is uniquely different from other believers in that religion? If yes, would other professionals in the field benefit from the findings of an interfaith dialogue? If what the authors are going to achieve is *not* generalizable by any means, what is the objective of this dialogue? Is this project going to provide insight mainly for the authors? If so, why should they publish their very personal dialogue? And many more unanswered questions are crossing my mind as I am drafting my thoughts. Despite all these concerns and uncertainties, I hope that sharing our lived experiences in different (religious) ideologies formed in certain contexts will ultimately bring some insight to us and our readers.

Joel: These are very important questions, and the idea of labelling ourselves as 'Christian' or 'Muslim' is a much more complicated one than I realized before we began meeting. In our original draft, I wrote a narrative section about my upbringing as an evangelical Christian in the United States. In it, I quoted an essay I had written a few years previously about a conversation I had with a Catholic classmate in high school:

> 'So, what are you?' he asked.
> I didn't understand the question.
> 'I mean, like, I'm Catholic. You're not Catholic, so what are you?'
> 'Nothing,' I said. 'Just Christian. Just regular.' (Heng Hartse, 2010: 38)
> My sense of 'regular' was being an evangelical Christian. ... I often feel that before any other significant category, my having been brought up in an evangelical environment has shaped my understanding of myself – more so than being American, or 'White,' or male, or middle-class, I think of myself as 'A Christian.' (I put this in quotes because evangelicals tend to refer to our tradition as simply 'Christian,' with no modifiers.)

While I didn't realize it at first, I now feel that the way I conceived of 'Christian–Muslim dialogue in TESOL', as I first labelled the shared Dropbox where we collected drafts and documents, was unfair to you in the way I pigeonholed you as 'A Muslim' in the same way that I was accustomed to thinking of myself as 'A Christian'. Towards the end of one of our meetings, I'm sure you remember that I said, in mock frustration, something like 'for this project to work, I need you to be a Muslim!' This was after we had several discussions in which I felt you were emphasizing concepts like the oneness of humanity, the similarities of religions, and so on, whereas I wanted to talk about the particularities and the differences between Christianity and Islam, and the tensions that exist in the world of ELT because of religious ideologies. I really enjoyed reading what you wrote in the first draft about your religious background, your experience of Arabic as a language of faith, and so on, but you also wrote about many things that were unrelated to religion. Am I right in assuming that even at that point you were trying to, in a sense, get out of the box I was – and maybe others were – trying to put you in as 'A Muslim ESL teacher'?

Saeed: I am really grateful that you raised a truly important issue. Ideology, to my understanding, can take the shape of the context it is applied to. In a mutual communication, not only might a specific religion condition the people in a certain context, but the people also have an equal chance to structure the received religion, either experienced voluntarily or imposed by force. Therefore, Muslim people in different regions of the world might represent varying beliefs which might not necessarily be approving of each other's. And this is not limited to a specific religion, as you might be well aware of disagreements in different divisions of Christianity as well. To go further, my recent reading in curriculum and ideology (e.g. Pinar, 2011) confirms to me that, as individuals, our perceptions and lived experiences of a certain religion can be distinctively different. Therefore, at a more personal level, there is a secondary mutual communication between a specific religion and each single individual exposed to that religion. In this exchange, not only would the individual learn from the religion, but also the religious practices might be transformed by the individual's lived experiences, and consequently transform its original content, meaning or message. Therefore, each individual's religious identity might go beyond the conventional labels. However, it is common that people might be looking for a stereotypical label among religious terminologies to grasp a general understanding of an individual's perceived identity. The terminologies might be insufficient and religious labels have the capacity to bring up misunderstandings. That is why, I assume, our initial inter-religious dialogue on the common values of a Christian and Muslim TESOL educator turned into a duoethnographic interfaith dialogue on lived experiences, giving it a personal tone.

At this level, to know about the religious identity of an ESL educator, one needs to take a journey into the individual's life history within a specific religion. Moreover, in assigning a certain religious label to an English language educator, like myself, we are also prone to ascribe undesired sociopolitical connotations in an ideologically sensitive context like North America. When I simply compare your currencies as being a Christian, white American (Aujla-Bhullar & Grain, 2012) with my (self/other)-identified Muslim, Middle Eastern identity in North America, I can easily understand how we can undergo two quite different lived experiences in a shared context, and why I feel reluctant to assume a mere religious label.

Joel: I see more clearly now why you resist being labeled with an oversimplified 'Muslim' identity. And I have thought about why I *want* to label myself with a Christian identity and think about my own professional life 'Christianly'. As we have talked about during the last few months, moving our project from the original 'shared values' one to this more dialogical one, I have come to terms with my desire to identify myself *more* with the label of 'Christian', not less. Early on in one of our brainstorms on religious values, I mentioned that in my experience American evangelicals tend to view ourselves as a 'minority' or even 'persecuted' vis-à-vis mainstream American culture. And while a lot of this is exaggerated, given the enormous amount of political and symbolic capital Christianity has in the United States, it has also shaped the way I think about bringing my religious identity to my scholarship and teaching. When I attended a Catholic high school and a Methodist university, I liked the idea that I was somehow resisting certain dominant narratives in American society. I do believe that Christian institutions and Christian individuals have different guiding principles from 'secular' ones. Because I experience my Christian faith as the anchor of my identity in a world I often view as hostile to a Christian vision of human flourishing, I do weird things like pray for my students before class (sometimes), and I do find the source of many of my values as a teacher in my faith. Possibly, being an American evangelical is the reason why I somehow feel a need to *proclaim* these things, but I also want to be honest with myself and admit that this is important to me. Writing in our original draft about my 'religious values' was a deeply meaningful exercise for me, because I had to articulate how I desire the cardinal Christian virtues of faith, hope and love to actually function as guiding principles for my work, not just as smug platitudes. Did writing the 'religious values' section work for you in our previous draft? You brought in many 'non-religious' sources, as I did, to describe your values as an educator. Would you be comfortable now in describing how/whether your spiritual values/beliefs influence what you do as an English language teacher and/or scholar, or is that the wrong question for you at this point?

Saeed: Thank you so much for raising this question and giving me a good chance to elaborate on it. I would like to build again on my lived experience to picture another perspective of my religious identity to answer your question. In Iran it is typical that people adopt their religious values through reading the literature of poets such as Sa'di, Hafiz and Mawlawi (Rumi), just to name a few. Although all three Persian scholars are Muslim, believing in God, the holy Qur'an and the Prophet Muhammad (pbuh) as indicated in the literature, their approach to Islam is distinctly different. Sa'di holds a more classical approach to Islam, focusing on social and moral thoughts. Hafiz mainly concentrates on faith and exposing hypocrisy. Mawlawi is considered a Sufi mystic theologian. Many people in Iran, depending on their lived experiences, are familiar with one or more Persian poets and learn about Islam through their frameworks. I am personally interested in and engaged with Mawlawi's theology and Sufism, which to my understanding presents a wider perspective of religion. In many places in his poetry, Mawlawi believes that he does not fit into a specific ideology and is beyond the frameworks ordinary people of his time attributed to him. When I as an ESL educator learn about Islam through Mawlawi's indefinite framework in the light of my lived experience, the outcome might be something different from his originally conveyed message. Therefore, as you have noticed, my perception about Islam is dynamically changing, growing and transforming. How is it possible to assign a stereotypical label to this dynamic transformation?

Joel: I'm wary enough of labels now that I wouldn't be able to even try! I want to go back to something you just briefly mentioned. You referred to yourself as an ESL educator in your last paragraph, even though most of what you talked about was more personal than professional. Perhaps this is another reason why our original attempt to discern common religious values for TESOL practitioners 'failed' – our goal of learning about each other's different religious backgrounds has become so personal that we have rarely had time to discuss our identities as English language educators and how our spirituality impacts this. Indeed, I sometimes feel I should shy away from talking about my faith in my professional life, even though it is important to me. Canagarajah's (2009) chapter had a statement that resonated with me: he expresses discomfort at having to 'loudly invoke the labels I would rather quietly live by' (Canagarajah, 2009: 15). I have the sense that speaking up about religious values in 'mainstream' settings is frowned upon, as Pennycook (2009) suggests. Perhaps it is only possible for me to be comfortable in talking about my faith and profession when I am in a 'safe house' with other evangelicals (Canagarajah, 2007). I remember at a TESOL conference a few years ago I was on a bus with a Christian colleague who was searching for a tenure-track position; she said: 'So, I've just been putting that out in into the universe – oh, wait, I don't have to change the discourse here to make it palatable to agnostics: I've been praying about it.' I thought that was so funny, but such a true example of the way most of us feel the need to speak guardedly about things that mean so much to us, like faith or politics or other intensely personal beliefs. Maybe it is because you and I know each other personally but not professionally (we have never worked together) that we have had less success in 'applying' religious or spiritual values to TESOL in our discussion.

Saeed: That might be a possibility. I think another reason why we have not been able to apply our religious values to TESOL in a dialogic exchange is that my values have been fairly heavily affected by the curriculum (Pinar, 2009) in my previous and current contexts. In my previous context, religious teachings are considered a serious issue, and the majority of people are Muslim. I was born into a family in Tehran favoring this religion. Although I initially believed that people with this religion have a privilege over 'other' Abrahamic religions such as Christianity and Judaism, and was thankful for the 'merit', I found out later that this belief might have been formed by the social forces favoring it. This feeling grew more robust when I noticed that other religious people (Abrahamic or non-Abrahamic) shared a similar viewpoint, promoting their experienced religions. And for me and many more people, from a Bourdieuian perspective, being religious simply means being born in a context and acquiring the thought systems imposed by the field and experienced by the agents like Saeed and Joel. And we all might admit that states literally use religion as a tool in their power games (Bourdieu, 1991). We have also noticed that many religious individuals within one single religion, ideology or division might be opposing each other at a personal level due to their lived experience, especially when their interests are in conflict.

Knowing these simple facts, our interfaith dialogue helped me to learn about another religion in the light of your personal perspective. However, it was not surprising for me to find out that my exposure to a certain ideology equipped me with a judgmental system of what is good and what is bad. And at this point of my life, I am looking into how to get rid of judgment and gain a more objective experience of the world and the people in it. This process of religious exploration gets more complicated when the power dynamics in my North American context would prefer to label me as a Muslim. My understanding of the power games in my new context is that for the rules of the game to be set precisely, I need to assume a Middle Eastern Muslim identity which seems to me a pre-molded label for an immigrant from that region. And you know what this labeling carries with it in the political field of North America. That is perhaps another reason why I strive to avoid my attached label and focus on 'we-ness' to make up for it.

Joel: Remember when you told me you liked John Lennon's song, 'Imagine', and I said I can't stand it? For some reason, I resist what I see as simplified notions of 'unity' because I feel like the smoothing over of differences can be dangerous. But maybe the whole reason I want to engage with the idea of religious 'difference' is that it is safe for me to do so from my position as someone with the 'right' kind of cultural capital in North American society. Kubota (2016) has pointed out that it is popular now in applied linguistics to talk about multilingualism and pluralizing languages, embracing hybridity and difference and so on – but this is done by top scholars at elite institutions who can 'afford' to do it. While academia is not exactly hospitable to evangelicals (and certainly in Canada the public discourse about, for example, Christian higher education can be quite hostile), I am sure I do not have to face the same kinds of possible discrimination that you might when I want to talk about my 'religious differences' from secular teachers/scholars.

I remember very clearly a turning point in our work together on this project, and I think in our friendship in general. We were sitting together on the campus of a Christian graduate school (it was a convenient location for us both to meet), and I looked around and realized that we were utterly 'on my turf', as it were. I could not have been more 'at home': we were surrounded by people with my same religious background, most of whom go to my kind of church; we were right next to a bookstore full of books that I like to read and magazines that I have written for; there were Bible verses and crosses all around us. This was 'normal' for me, but it was not until that moment that I started to consider that if I wanted us to have an 'interfaith dialogue', we were not at all on a level playing field.

Saeed: Exactly. And I assume in our North American field, power games are strategically planned and maintained in this way. At this point, I would like to raise a related question regarding the influence of religion, faith or spirituality on our practice as TESOL professionals, unanswered above. The question is how my religious or spiritual values and practices would influence my practices as a TESOL professional in the classroom. This question can hold two distinct answers – theoretical and practical. In theory, in ESL schools where I have taught as a non-native teacher, I have the freedom to keep my own religious faith as long as I do not communicate it to my students. In practice, though, I have always attempted to hide my religious or spiritual values in my Canadian context and feel really anxious if a student tries to know about my religious identity. In contrast, I recall when I was teaching as a tenured lecturer in Iran, in a university with over 6000 students and classes packed with up to 60 learners, I invariably started my teaching with an Arabic or Persian phrase written on the top right-hand corner of the whiteboard, which translates into 'In the name of God, the compassionate, the merciful'. It actually provided a pleasant spiritual feeling for myself and the other students as well. Do you think in my current context I dare to put such a phrase on the board? Therefore, practical representations of my religious identity are kept confidential in my verbal and nonverbal communications. To give you a clearer view of how shaky the ESL school market in the Canadian context is, I should say many schools still prefer to hire NNESTs with Anglicized names. They think it is more marketable and Canadianized. How would you feel when your students call your 'Middle Eastern' name in such a field?

Joel: This question of 'hiding' is interesting. It saddens me that anyone would have to hide an important part of their identity, but of course it happens all the time and not only with religion – sexuality, gender, class and race are all things people may be compelled to hide or downplay in classrooms or teaching contexts. When I taught in both the United States and China, I was aware of an assumed secular norm – 'separation of church and state' in the United States and 'official atheism' in China. I was guarded about mentioning that I was a Christian – not because it would be stigmatized, but because I thought it was somehow 'inappropriate' or 'unprofessional'. As an evangelical, I come from a community that views 'witnessing', or spreading the message of Christianity (also known as proselytizing), as vitally important (this is one of the 'pillars' of evangelicalism; see Bebbington, 1989), but personally I have been uncomfortable with how this tends to be carried out by evangelicals, and I have rarely, if ever, participated in evangelism. When I got involved in TESOL I found that many evangelicals view it as a 'mission field', and when I told other evangelicals I was going to teach in China, for example, some people assumed I was a missionary, which I decidedly am not. On the other hand, now that I am a more experienced teacher, I usually feel comfortable talking about my religion if a student or colleague asks about it, without fear that I will be seen as 'unprofessional'. (Again, I may have more freedom to do this because of social and political circumstances being in 'my favor', so to speak.)

I remember that a student in China once asked me, point blank, in front of the whole class, what I believed the meaning of life was. I stammered out something about the importance of loving people and my faith. This led to a longer discussion with a different student after class in which I just barely mentioned being a Christian; this student later told me she had been baptized a Christian. This was meaningful to me, but I have no idea if she remained a Christian. I remember thinking about this as I watched her Facebook profile gradually change from having a lot of Christian references in it to very few, and in fact this was one of the first times that I started to think about religious identity as potentially being more fluid than I was accustomed to. I am certainly more comfortable with ambiguity in religion than I used to be, even as I continue to embrace Christian practices and beliefs.

Saeed: Here is another fine difference; you are openly expressing your beliefs, and I am somehow striving to. There is still another meaningful reason why I am uncomfortable with openly expressing my religious identity, and it probably lies in my early educational experience, which has implemented a self-censorship mechanism in me. Heavily loaded with ideology, the curriculum I have undergone in public school has probably left some traces on my subjectivity. This experience is common among those who were exposed to a certain ideology in their educational experience, I believe. As we might agree, religious faith deals with absolutes in contrast to relatives. People who are exposed to religious fields might acquire the absolute values widely practiced in their specific context. Absolutism might leave insufficient space for the subjectivity of individuals within a certain field, especially when supplemented by power. It can potentially turn into an ideologically autocratic system in which ideology supports power and power upholds ideology. Minorities, like children educated in an ideologically autocratic curriculum, typically experience a schooling in which their subjectivity might be suppressed at the price of the power games in the field. When confronting questions such as religion, ideology or faith, quite unconsciously, I might strive to avoid those specific terminologies bringing up the experience. The struggle exists between my subjectivity which looks for an opportunity to prosper and grow, and my subconscious mind being exposed to a certain ideology. This consciousness has provided a good chance to be well aware of the power of the terms assigned in my North American context. Perhaps the reason I focus on we-ness in an interfaith dialogue in such a context as opposed to otherness is because, quite automatically, my subjectivity is seeking a refuge in we-ness, preventing it from being 'othered' any further.

Joel: So how do we end this phase of our dialogue? In our original document I came up with several suggestions for interfaith dialogue, and I think I still would promote them, even after going through our two-year struggle to come up with 'common values'. In it, the conclusion encouraged the following:

- more empirical, qualitative religion-related research in TESOL;
- an attitude of openness to discussion of religion and faith in TESOL;
- Christian and Muslim English language teachers (and students) learning more about each other's backgrounds and religions;
- acknowledging differences and embracing common values in discussions of religion and TESOL.

I would still endorse these, but would add some additional caveats. First, I would even more adamantly insist on the absolute importance of qualitative research in order to find out how people view their own relationship to faith, how they define it and how it affects their experience with language teaching/learning. I still endorse the second and third points, but would underscore the extremely subjective nature of both 'discussion' and 'Christian and Muslim'. The intersubjective nature of interfaith dialogue cannot be underestimated, and we cannot hope to learn about 'Christians' or 'Muslims' so much as getting to know our colleagues and students on a personal level. For the last point, I would again emphasize how important differences are, and encourage all of us not to gloss over differences in the hope that we will find more commonalities – hope is certainly a good thing, but we need to be realistic about difference.

Finally, I would encourage more acknowledgment of power differences and inequalities among people with various religious backgrounds in different settings. Just as you face many difficulties as someone who is perceived in a certain way in North America, certainly there are issues for teachers and students of minority faiths in contexts like China, Iran, Indonesia and various European countries, to name a scant few. There is more work to be done in the areas of faith and language teaching/learning, and I for one really hope to see more work that engages with Islam, Buddhism, Hinduism and other major faiths, not only Christianity – something that I believe this volume is doing. Evangelical scholars have done a good job of making faith an area of research in the mainstream of applied linguistics, but also, very important (and difficult) work can be done when people with different backgrounds and beliefs work together. This is something I think we have started here – even if, in duoethnography, we don't really come to any 'conclusions' or simple explanations as to how to 'do' interfaith dialogue in our profession. In the end I'm deeply gratified that we have become friends, shared difficult and meaningful conversations about faith, scholarship and life, and so on. We can't answer any of these questions, but we've 'lived the questions' together for several years.

Saeed: This dialogue will never settle on a certain conclusion. Since duoethnography is, to my understanding, an exploration of self in a dual exchange, and self is literally bottomless, we will never be able to get to an end. The outcome of our interfaith dialogue, however, is the surprising fact that our subjectivity can interact with faith to build a new personality, identity or orientation in us. Living in North America has provided a unique experience for me to learn about various ideologies and beliefs. When my religious *habitus* (Bourdieu, 1991) is confronted with new ideologies, inertia would naturally prefer to stay with and maintain my existing faith. Confronting this static inertia, an evolving self, who is growing and becoming every moment, would like to keep itself open and welcoming to new thoughts, beliefs and perspectives. My question is: 'Is it possible to maintain your previous beliefs and welcome new ones?' The answer is straightforward to me; it is our subjective decision that can make all the difference.

If our disposition or inclination is towards change and transformation, we might prefer to welcome new ideas, beliefs and thoughts. However, this stage might seem intimidating or frightening for many people. Perhaps an essential ingredient of our being is the beliefs we possess. Although they are acquired through exposure to certain teachings, and with different teachings we could probably presume different beliefs, this process has formed through our life history and has inculcated a religious identity in our being. Sometimes accepting new ideas, thoughts or beliefs feels like denying our being, since we might be unable to separate our beliefs from our 'selves' due to the critical time they were molded in us in our childhood. Therefore, we might prefer to let the self be as it is – secure and protected. And if we are among those people who prefer to keep their beliefs untouched, are we potentially thinking of the similarities in religions or the differences? Are we in favor of oneness in humanity or uniqueness in essence? Are we thinking about ourselves or other selves? How would an intersubjective interfaith dialogue influence us, then? How can it contribute to our interfaith transformative learning? Can we embrace a duoethnographic dialogue in which mutual learning, growing and becoming are endorsed?

These are some of the unanswered questions I prefer to end my dialogue with and enjoy thinking about. One unforgettable experience, however, which I definitely was able to achieve with you in our dialogue was the supportive care that you provided generously from the onset of our dialogue, and especially through the sharp curves I experienced in my personal life during the period. And I am simply grateful for that.

References

Aujla-Bhullar, S. and Grain, K. (2012) Mirror imaging diversity experience: A juxtaposition of identities in cross-cultural initiatives. In J. Norris, R. Sawyer and D. Lund (eds) *Duoethnography: Dialogic Methods For Social, Health, and Educational Research* (pp. 199–222). Walnut Creek, CA: Left Coast Publications.

Bebbington, D.W. (1989) *Evangelicalism in Modern Britain: A History from the 1730s to the 1980s*. London: Unwin Hyman.

Berger, P. (1999) The desecularization of the world: A global overview. In P. Berger (ed.) *The Desecularization of the World: Resurgent Religion and World Politics*. Washington, DC: Washington Ethics and Public Policy Center.

Bourdieu, P. (1991) *Language and Symbolic Power*. Cambridge, MA: Harvard University Press.

Brown, D.S. (2013) *Interfaith Dialogue in Practice: Christian, Muslim, Jew*. Kansas City, MO: Rockhurst University Press.

Canagarajah, A.S. (2007) There is something furtive about the behavior of evangelicals in TESOL. *CETC Newsletter* 11 (3).

Canagarajah, A.S. (2009) Can we talk? Finding a platform for dialogue among values-based professionals in post-positivist education. In M.S. Wong and S. Canagarajah (eds) *Christian and Critical English Language Educators in Dialogue: Pedagogical and Ethical Dilemmas* (pp. 75–86). New York: Routledge.

Edge, J. (2003) Imperial troopers and servants of the Lord. *TESOL Quarterly* 37, 701–709.

Hadley, G. (2004) ELT and the new world order: Nation building or neocolonial reconstruction? *Issues in Political Discourse Analysis* 1 (1), 23–48.

Heng Hartse, J. (2010) *Sects, Love, and Rock and Roll*. Eugene, OR: Cascade Books.

Johnston, B. (2009) Is dialogue possible? Challenge to evangelicals and nonevangelicals in English language teaching. In M.S. Wong and S. Canagarajah (eds) *Christian Educators and Critical Practitioners in Dialogue: Ethical Dilemmas in English Language Teaching* (pp. 35–45). New York: Routledge.

Karmani, S. (2005) TESOL in a time of terror: Toward an Islamic perspective on applied linguistics. *TESOL Quarterly* 39 (4), 738–748.

Karmani, S. (2006) Good Muslims speak English. *Critical Discourse Studies* 3, 103–105.

Kubota, R. (2016) The multi/plural turn, postcolonial theory, and neoliberal multiculturalism: Complicities and implications for applied linguistics. *Applied Linguistics* 37 (4), 474–494.

McClellan, P. and Sader, J. (2012) Power and privilege. In J. Norris, R. Sawyer and D. Lund (eds) *Duoethnography: Dialogic Methods for Social, Health, and Educational Research* (pp. 137–156). Walnut Creek, CA: Left Coast Publications.

Mellor, P.A. and Shilling, C. (2010) Body pedagogics and the religious habitus: A new direction for the sociological study of religion. *Religion* 40 (1), 27–38.

Nabavi, M. and Lund, D. (2012) Tensions and contradictions of living in a multicultural nation in an era of bounded identities. In J. Norris, R. Sawyer and D. Lund (eds) *Duoethnography: Dialogic Methods for Social, Health, and Educational Research* (pp. 177–198). Walnut Creek, CA: Left Coast Publications.

Norris, J. (2008) Duoethnography. In L.M. Given (ed.) *The Sage Encyclopedia of Qualitative Research Methods* (Vol. 1) (pp. 233–236). Los Angeles, CA: Sage.

Norris, J., Sawyer, R.D. and Lund, D. (eds) (2012) *Duoethnography: Dialogic Methods for Social, Health, and Educational Research*. Walnut Creek, CA: Left Coast Publications.

Pennycook, A. (2009) Is dialogue possible? Anti-intellectualism, relativism, politics and linguistic ideologies. In M.S. Wong and S. Canagarajah (eds) *Christian Educators and Critical Practitioners in Dialogue: Ethical Dilemmas in English Language Teaching* (pp. 60–65). New York: Routledge.

Pennycook, A. and Coutand-Marin, S. (2003) Teaching English as a missionary language (TEML). *Discourse: Studies in the Cultural Politics of Education* 24, 337–353.

Pennycook, A. and Makoni, S. (2005) The modern mission: The language effects of Christianity. *Journal of Language, Identity and Education* 4 (2), 137–155.

Pinar, W.F. (2009) *The Worldliness of a Cosmopolitan Education: Passionate Lives in Public Service*. New York: Routledge.

Pinar, W.F. (2011) *The Character of Curriculum Studies. Bildung, Currere, and The Recurring Question of the Subject*. New York: Palgrave Macmillan.

Sawyer, R.D. and Norris, J. (2004) Null and hidden curricula of sexual orientation: A dialogue on the curreres of the absent presence and the present absence. In L. Coia, M. Birch, N.J. Brooks, E. Heilman, S. Mayer, A. Mountain and P. Pritchard (eds) *Democratic Responses in an Era of Standardization* (pp. 139–159). Troy, NY: Educators International.

Sawyer, R.D. and Norris, J. (2009) Duoethnography: Articulations/(re)creations of meaning in the making. In W.S. Gershon (ed.) *The Collaborative Turn: Working Together in Qualitative Research* (pp. 127–140). Rotterdam, The Netherlands: Sense Publishers.

Sawyer, R.D. and Norris, J. (2013) *Duoethnography: Understanding Qualitative Research*. New York: Oxford University Press.

Varghese, M. and Johnston, B. (2007) Evangelical Christians and English language teaching. *TESOL Quarterly* 41 (1), 5–31.

Wong, M.S. and Canagarajah, S. (eds) (2009) *Christian and Critical English Language Educators in Dialogue: Pedagogical and Ethical Dilemmas*. New York: Routledge.

Wong, M., Kristjánsson, C. and Dörnyei, Z. (eds) (2013) *Christian Faith and English Language Teaching and Learning: Research on the Interrelationship of Religion and ELT*. New York: Routledge.

5 Response to Part 1. Possibilities for Nonattachment: Investigating the Affective Dimension of Imposition

Ryuko Kubota

Introduction

The preceding three chapters by Wong, Christison, and Heng Hartse and Nazari address multiple issues about the intersection between teacher identity and spirituality from Christian, Buddhist and Islamic perspectives. Although each chapter presents a unique approach and content, I identify the following overarching question to explore: How can we come to terms with the problem of imposing one's perspective onto others? This question is related to another issue: How can we deal with our emotional attachment to a certain belief or view, which may conflict with the beliefs and views of others? These questions raise the broader issue of how to attain a deeper level of engagement with difference, as opposed to mere respect for difference, in considering diverse perspectives, opinions and beliefs. This deeper engagement with difference encompasses a willingness to both interrogate difference, which addresses the intellectual domain, and an openness to empathizing with different positions, which focuses on the affective domain. While both domains require students and teachers to practice situated ethics and hyper-self-reflexivity, recognizing the affective domain directs our attention to the need to exercise nonattachment, a practice that promotes increased open-mindedness and awareness of the peril of imposition. These explorations are relevant not only to religious beliefs and spirituality – the main focus of this book – but also to social and professional activities in general, including teaching and research.

In this chapter, I will first discuss the link between religious identity and emotional attachments (hereafter attachments), followed by a liberal pluralist approach to teaching about controversial issues, which emphasizes the presentation of multiple perspectives in a balanced and neutral way. I will then contrast this approach with a poststructuralist intellectual approach to examining knowledge production. However, neither of these two approaches can escape a teacher's imposition of their personal views when little attention is paid to the affective dimension. This discussion will lead into an exploration of exercising nonattachment and situated ethics for increased openness and a more profound engagement with difference.

Religious Identity and Attachment

The relationship between spirituality and language teaching can be discussed at two levels: the social/ideological level and the individual level. On the broader social and ideological level, Christianity, in particular, has been a target of ideological scrutiny for its role in the spread of English language teaching worldwide. Several scholars have critiqued covert or overt efforts for religious conversion associated with this activity (e.g. Edge, 2003; Pennycook & Coutand-Marin, 2003). Conversely, on an individual level, a teacher's religious faith or spirituality constitutes a sense of their identity with affective investment. Empirical research has revealed that Christian teachers of English, for instance, have a range of subjectivities as evangelical professionals, and that it is untenable to draw simplistic associations between evangelical Christian teachers of English and the proselytization mission or the American Empire's neoconservative agenda (Varghese & Johnston, 2007; Wong, 2009).

This empirical research indicates that, similar to other identity markers, a religious or spiritual identity can sometimes become a target of discrimination in contexts where a majority group holds either a secular view or another religious faith. Just as women and people of color are often associated with negative attributes, evangelical Christians are sometimes unanimously constructed as proselytizers, reinforcing essentialism and alienation. This danger is pointed out in the preceding chapters.

Although all identities are socially constructed rather than innate, religious/spiritual identities may be developed with greater individual agency. Although some individuals are obviously born into religious families or societies that expect certain beliefs to be ingrained in their habitus, others consciously choose and pursue their religious/spiritual identity, as seen in the case of Christison. This means that following a religious faith or spiritual path involves one's conscious investment, which leads to a sense of attachment to it.

A sense of attachment is involved in other everyday activities, including professional, scholarly and political engagements. We tend to be attached to a particular academic perspective or a political view that we strongly support. In theorizing emotions as cultural politics, Ahmed (2014) argues that emotions circulate and move across individuals but they also become attached to individuals as sticky objects, forming a sense of cohesion among a group of individuals and directing them to cling to certain objects – not only tangible but also intangible objects, such as words, concepts and thoughts (see also Benesch, 2012). A sense of attachment can compel us to impose our belief onto others, which may cause others emotional pain, and it also can prompt us to vehemently defend our beliefs when they are questioned by others; this will most likely hurt others as well. Viewed in this way, the problem of imposition as well as that of conflicts among diverse beliefs, as raised by Wong, Heng Hartse and Nazari, can be situated within the broader challenge of handling diverse opinions and managing our sense of attachment in the classroom and beyond. In what follows, I will draw on scholarly discussions on teaching about controversial issues (e.g. social, historical, political, economic, scientific and religious topics; Kubota, 2014) and discuss how imposition is mitigated in a liberal pluralist approach which respects difference and yet is limited in several ways.

Respect for Difference: A Relativist and Neutral Stance of Liberal Pluralism

Being attached to a certain belief or opinion often makes it difficult for us to engage in an open dialogue with people who have different beliefs or opinions. It also creates the danger of imposing what we believe in onto others. Therefore, in a classroom discussion especially on a controversial issue, a teacher may choose to present multiple perspectives by striking a balance and strategically taking a neutral position so that students feel encouraged to express their own views without fear. This approach is supposed to promote respect for difference and reflects liberal pluralism. It also echoes the more general educational goal of developing critical thinking. Presenting multiple perspectives also helps avoid the indoctrination of students into a single point of view. Although presenting multiple perspectives in a balanced and neutral way to encourage dialogues may work in some circumstances, this approach has certain limitations.

First, it runs the risk of falling into absolute relativism, discouraging participants from making individual judgments of any sort and becoming informed and responsible citizens who can form their own opinions in a rational manner. Secondly, absolute relativism may allow extremely biased or unethical ideas to be expressed without being challenged. When this happens, a teacher may take a position and try to lead students in a direction considered to be more appropriate. Nonetheless, how can we determine that a certain view is more ethical than others, especially in a context in which different cultural and religious values are in competition with one another?

Just as a relativist approach can be problematic, teacher neutrality also poses some challenges in practice. First, teacher neutrality may not actually be conducive to learning, since it diminishes the role of the teacher as an experienced professional citizen, preventing students from engaging in informed discussions in the classroom. Secondly, and importantly, progressive teachers or critical pedagogues in particular will find it difficult to remain neutral on an issue that they feel strongly about. These teachers often feel that progressive perspectives on social, political, historical, economic and environmental issues are marginalized in the curriculum by dominant conservative perspectives and therefore want to foreground alternative worldviews in their teaching. No doubt these teachers believe that their teaching is founded on ethical and moral decisions (cf. Wong's chapter). Nonetheless, the presentation and discussion of these issues, no matter how ethical they may appear to be, can be interpreted as indoctrination (Ellsworth, 1989; Kubota, 2014; Pessoa & Urzêda Freitas, 2012). Even if the teacher explicitly tells the students that he or she has no intention of imposing a particular view, the unequal relation of power between teacher and students may compel the students to adopt the teacher's perspective. Thus, no perspectives – conservative, progressive, critical or religious – can escape the possibility of imposition, regardless of their ideological orientations.

The liberal pluralist approach to exposing students to diverse perspectives in a balanced and neutral way is meant to promote respect for difference. It requires teachers to temporarily detach themselves from their own values and opinions. However, the issues delineated above indicate that complete detachment is untenable and often unattainable. Furthermore, this approach may not necessarily guide students to a deeper understanding of the issues discussed, but instead it may reinforce the beliefs that students already have (Cotton, 2006). Thus, this approach to respecting difference does not always solve the problem of attachment; nor does it lead to truly engaged learning. One alternative is to take a poststructuralist approach to unpacking knowledge construction.

Interrogating Difference: Intellectual Approach to Examining Knowledge Construction

A liberal pluralist approach treats different perspectives with equal weight. A poststructuralist approach to examining knowledge construction also assumes that every knowledge brought to a given discussion is legitimate and worth discussing. However, this legitimacy is recognized within a particular context; in other words, each knowledge is understood as contextual and only partial and incomplete rather than absolute or universal (Andreotti, 2011). Rather than simply treating different perspectives as objective facts, the approach focusing on knowledge aims to unpack the meanings attached to the differences (Nelson, 2009). It focuses on the mechanism of meaning production by examining how divergent views, including one's own, have been constructed socially, historically and politically; what social, political and ideological meanings are embedded within particular forms of knowledge; and what implications they have. It raises such questions as: 'How can a certain statement be interpreted differently in different contexts? What assumptions are behind the statements? What could shape a certain understanding of a reality? Who decides what is real and who benefits from the judgment? What are the limitations and contradictions of a perspective? Whose interests are represented in the statement?' (Kubota, 2014: 204; see also Andreotti, 2011). Contrary to absolute relativism, this poststructuralist approach to knowledge construction adopts contextual relativism, in which the existing knowledge is viewed as heterogeneous and dynamic, as well as socially, culturally, historically and politically situated (Andreotti, 2011).

The contextuality of meaning is especially important in thinking about moral and ethical engagements, as Wong argues. For instance, the ethical review guidelines of institutional review boards (IRBs) for research studies involving children are based on the Western understanding of human rights and the legal protection of research participants. However, research on children in the Global South poses an ethical dilemma in that consent letters presented to parents are often culturally incomprehensible and, moreover, archiving research data in these countries may allow access and surveillance by the government, making the participants vulnerable (Asselin & Doiron, in press; Kapoor, 2004). Furthermore, cultural difference is entangled with political, economic and sometimes religious interests. Reflecting on her research involving children in Ethiopia, Marlene Asselin speculates about complex reasons behind some mothers' resistance to signing consent for their children. Not only do these mothers fear that the government would obtain their information, but they view their children as personal possessions rather than individuals with human rights, and they are also afraid that their children may be subtly converted to Western values through participating in programs supported by particular religious organizations (personal communication). In these situations, ethics are clearly contextual and contentious. Furthermore, the question of 'who benefits?' is raised when researchers from the Global North conduct participatory action research in the Global South (Kapoor, 2004). When applying these difficult questions to issues of religion and spirituality, it becomes clear that our knowledge and beliefs are shaped socially, culturally, historically and politically. The sample scenarios presented towards the end of Wong's chapter demonstrate how different contexts will affect the multiple ways in which a given incident is interpreted. Christison's comment on the Buddhist philosophy of avoiding dichotomous absolutes and instead valuing contextualized action as 'right action' also demonstrates the significance of situated ethics.

However, to imagine a different meaning or different reality takes a great amount of effort and investment not only intellectually but also emotionally. This is particularly the case when confronted with a perspective that contradicts the one that we feel attached to. Heng Hartse's dislike for the song 'Imagine' as opposed to Nazari's favorable stance is one example; my own dilemma of dealing with students' denial of the Nanking Massacre of 1937 expressed in the classroom is another (Kubota, 2014). It seems to me that interrogating knowledge construction is certainly useful in recognizing the contextuality and provisionality of knowledge, but it is also necessary to address the emotional dimension in order to reach a more profound level of awareness and understanding.

Compared to the liberal pluralist approach of respecting difference, a knowledge construction approach addresses difference at a deeper level. However, as a rational and intellectual exercise, it does not address the emotional significance in dealing with difference.

Engaging in Difference: Focusing on the Affective Domain

Neither the liberal pluralist focus on respect for difference nor the poststructuralist approach to intellectually interrogating difference scrutinizes our emotional adherence to particular views or beliefs. In academic discussions, we typically resort to a rational approach to understanding and analyzing issues and assumptions. Yet our sense of attachment significantly affects our ability to genuinely engage with differences – especially with different positions that are opposite to what we believe in. Obviously, we endorse a certain perspective because we think it is ethical and moral. As such, our commitment to the principles and values underlying our views should be respected. However, this clinging can become an obstacle for considering the alternative perspectives to which others are committed.

In the intellectual domain, contextual understanding of a certain perspective contributes to understanding knowledge production. Conversely, in the affective domain, contextuality rests in the affective capacity to imagine what it is like to espouse other views and beliefs. Such engagement with difference may take a greater amount of effort – perhaps a kind of 'right effort' as discussed by Christison. To be able to intensely imagine not only another point of view but also how others who subscribe to that view feel requires detaching ourselves temporarily from the perspective that we cling to. In a personal anecdote narrated by Christison, a more positive work environment was established through her effort to refrain from making any comments about a colleague towards whom she had held negative feelings. In this case, her detachment from negative feelings led to a positive outcome.

Exercising nonattachment is not easy. In Kubota (2014), I reflected on my inability to competently deal with the conflicting opinions expressed among teacher candidates on the Nanking Massacre in a class I was teaching in Japan. I was unable to encourage my students to examine the origin and the meaning of the historical revisionist view, precisely because it was not imaginable for me to think from this denial perspective, which I had rejected on scholarly and ethical terms. For critical educators, the view expressed by these students, which parallels a denial of the Holocaust, is certainly outrageous and needs to be dismissed (Nieto, 1995). However, it is likely that my emotional resentment towards this denial view paralleled the emotional disturbance possibly felt by the students who expressed the denial view – they were exposed to my non-revisionist stance, which was reflected in my choice of the topic and exposure of the students to guest lectures on campus highlighting a non-revisionist perspective. My insistence that they consider my non-revisionist stance may have disturbed them. My strong attachment to the perspective I regarded as ethical was perhaps interpreted as an imposition in that context.

Nonattachment enables us to make an effort to step outside of our own convictions and enter into others' worldview. It is consistent with the notion of 'non-coercive rearrangement of desire' (Spivak, 2004: 532; see also Andreotti, 2011; Motha & Lin, 2013), in which 'One should open possibilities without attempting to coerce and one should not judge learners' provisional choices of existence' (Andreotti, 2011: 181), even if one's view might appear more ethical and moral. It requires 'a suspension of the conviction that I am necessarily better, I am necessarily indispensable, I am necessarily the one to right wrongs' (Spivak, 2004: 532). This critical openness is part of hyper-self-reflexivity (Kapoor, 2004) – intense vigilance in reflecting on one's own role in complex power relations.

Spiritually speaking, nonattachment is consistent with a Buddhist principle. Buddhism is ingrained in the culture in which I grew up, and it influenced me significantly at one point in my life. Although I do not currently consider myself a devout follower of Buddhism, I find the concepts of nonattachment and emptiness helpful in thinking about the affective domain and the problem of imposition in teaching. Matsubara (1993) invites us to imagine our mind as a whiteboard. Numerous words are written down, representing our past experiences, knowledge and thoughts, leaving no space for new ideas to be added. But once we have erased everything and regain a blank whiteboard, we can start anew to re-examine all that was written before – we can pick up what still seems valid, abandon what does not and start writing anew. In this process, even what we used to regard as ethical or moral is erased altogether, because it may not be so from a broader perspective.

Although I find nonattachment to be a useful approach to achieving greater engagement with difference, it is difficult to practice. I find myself continuing to cling to my beliefs in my daily professional activities, which has probably had the effect of alienating some people around me. In addition, the concept of nonattachment is a particular spiritual practice that may be incompatible with other orientations. My intention here has been to shed light on the affective dimension in understanding difference and the peril of imposition, as well as to explore possibilities for engaging difference in more profound and situated ways.

Conclusion

The three previous chapters demonstrate how religious faiths and spirituality occupy a significant part of our professional lives. They also allude to emotions such as feeling hurt, alienated, ambivalent, negative and so on, which are likely to be caused by others' attachment to and consequently imposition of an opposing perspective. While some scholars' criticism that the activities engaged in by evangelical Christian teachers have a hidden agenda of conversion is a legitimate argument in its own right, such a criticism can also cause Christian teachers emotional pain. Thus, when the notion of imposition is viewed broadly, it is likely exercised by anyone who participates in a debate on a contentious issue and it stems from our sense of attachment to a particular view. This indicates that, even if a teacher intellectually explores a certain topic by presenting multiple perspectives in a balanced and neutral way or interrogates knowledge production from a poststructuralist perspective, sidestepping the effects of emotional attachment may prevent them from achieving a deeper understanding of difference.

It seems to me that profound engagement with difference requires genuine openness among the participants in the discussion. The duoethnography performed by Heng Hartse and Nazari demonstrates the importance of remaining open in a dialogue across differences, in which differences are viewed as strength for enriching dialogue and not merely as positions to be defended. Considering contextual and situated ethics, as discussed by Wong, enables teachers and students to broaden their perspectives. Overcoming negative feelings, as narrated by Christison, leads to more open interpersonal relationships. Such openness requires letting go of one's sense of attachment to particular beliefs, feelings and perspectives.

Controversies and conflicts will never cease to exist. I acknowledge that my inclination to such notions as openness, nonattachment and hyper-self-reflexivity come across as naïve or unrealistic. Nevertheless, it may serve as a humble small step towards a more profound engagement with difference.

References

Ahmed, S. (2014) *The Cultural Politics of Emotion* (2nd edn). New York: Routledge.

Andreotti, V. (2011) *Actionable Postcolonial Theory in Education*. New York: Palgrave Macmillan.
Asselin, M. and Doiron, R. (in press) Reflections on and recommendations for ethical research with children in international contexts. *Canadian Children*.
Benesch, S. (2012) *Considering Emotions in Critical English Language Teaching: Theories and Praxis*. New York: Routledge.
Cotton, D.R.E. (2006) Teaching controversial environmental issues: Neutrality and balance in the reality of the classroom. *Educational Research* 48, 223–241.
Edge, J. (2003) Imperial troopers and servants of the Lord: A vision of TESOL in the 21st century. *TESOL Quarterly* 37, 701–709.
Ellsworth, E. (1989) Why doesn't this feel empowering? Working through the repressive myths of critical pedagogy. *Harvard Educational Review* 59, 297–324.
Kapoor, I. (2004) Hyper-self-reflexive development? Spivak on representing the Third World 'Other'. *Third World Quarterly* 25, 624–647.
Kubota, R. (2014) 'We must look at both sides' – but a denial of genocide too?: Difficult moments on controversial issues in the classroom. *Critical Inquiry in Language Studies* 11, 225–251.
Matsubara, T. (1993) *Shin yaku hannya shingyô* [*The Heart Sutra: A New Translation*]. Tokyo: Sanshûsha.
Motha, S. and Lin, A. (2013) 'Non-coercive rearrangements': Theorizing desire in TESOL. *TESOL Quarterly* 48, 331–359.
Nelson, C.D. (2009) *Sexual Identities in English Language Education*. New York: Routledge.
Nieto, S. (1995) From brown heroes and holidays to assimilationist agendas: Reconsidering the critiques of multicultural education. In C.E. Sleeter and P.L. McLaren (eds) *Multicultural Education, Critical Pedagogy, and the Politics of Difference* (pp. 191–220). Albany, NY: State University of New York Press.
Pennycook, A. and Coutand-Marin, S. (2003) Teaching English as a missionary language (TEML). *Discourse: Studies in the Cultural Politics of Education* 24, 337–353.
Pessoa, R.R. and Urzêda Freitas, M.T. (2012) Challenges in critical language teaching. *TESOL Quarterly* 46, 753–776.
Spivak, G.C. (2004) Righting wrongs. *South Atlantic Quarterly* 103 (2/3), 523–581.
Varghese, M. and Johnston, B. (2007) Evangelical Christians and English language teaching. *TESOL Quarterly* 41 (1), 5–31.
Wong, M.S. (2009) Deconstructing/reconstructing the missionary English teacher identity. In M.S. Wong and S. Canagarajah (eds) *Christian and Critical English Language Educators in Dialogue: Pedagogical and Ethical Dilemmas* (pp. 91–105). New York: Routledge.

Part 2

Religious Faith and Pedagogical Practice

6 A Buddhist in the Classroom Revisited

Sid Brown

This chapter explores some daily Buddhist practices and stories and the moment-by-moment transformations of teacher, student and classroom that arise from them, informed by a definition of religion based on how religion functions. It revisits insights discussed in Brown (2001). Examination of some of these changes in light of 'private' religious practice gives us the eyes with which to see some of the complexities of religion in our globalized world today.

What are we teaching when we walk into the classroom with our religious commitments – in my case, to Buddhism? What are we handing down, besides the more overt curriculum, as we do so? A partial answer is clear: a teacher has no choice but to have values (humans do) and in some ways express them to students (if only because teachers and students communicate with each other over time), so a teacher's values are present and public, more or less, and part of the legacy. Being teachers, we are obliged to be self-conscious about our values and how overtly we call attention to them. And we must be committed to examining them, knowing what they are, and recommitting ourselves to them or abandoning them. Further, teachers, as I see us, should discern the problems of the world to the best of our ability and help students develop the skills, perspectives and values necessary to discern and solve world problems.

As a scholar of religious studies, I care and am knowledgeable about the ways in which religion has caused both good and harm at individual, societal and global levels – how people have used religious reasoning, categories, symbols and rituals to cultivate love, compassion, clarity, understanding and societal harmony, and how people have used the same to cultivate greed, hatred and delusion, harming and killing others. For many years I was trained, too, to refrain from bringing my own religion into the classroom in any way. In this view, my own religious commitments were irrelevant, and I was to teach *about* religion, understanding the classroom as a secular space for the intellectual investigation of religious phenomena. Things religious could and should be investigated in the same way in which other aspects of society could and should be investigated, removed from personal religious commitments.

Over the years, however, I have noticed some problems with this approach, problems best made clear by viewing religion using a functional definition. Different definitions of religion reveal and conceal different things, of course. Functional definitions emphasize how religion operates; religion in this understanding consists of rituals, symbols, stories, institutions and ethics that create worldviews. Viewing religion functionally calls to mind the fact that a classroom society, defined at least in part by the instructor, consists of rituals, symbols and stories, and is part of an educational institution (which is part of larger institutions, too), which holds and expresses certain ethics. In short, a functional definition reveals the tentativeness of the supposed secularity of a Western classroom; it reveals how classroom rituals and stories and the institutions of which a classroom is part function to create worldviews.

Here I examine some of the rituals and stories that create the worldview of the classroom I hold, a worldview I make more or less transparent to students through my syllabus and through what I say to them and what we do together. Time in the hermeneutic circle reveals some of the transformations of at least this Buddhist in the classroom.

Before I walk into the classroom to teach, I pause at the door and take a full breath, bringing awareness to the fact that I am beginning my classroom time with these students. At some time during the class, I pause again to remind myself that I am in the middle of a class. At the end of the class, I take another breath and a pause and remind myself that the class is coming to an end. I learned this recognition of beginnings, middles and endings from a Tibetan Buddhist teacher.[1] This practice makes me aware of what I am doing – a critical element of Buddhist practice rooted in the enlightenment experience of the Buddha, when he was 'awakened' (the meaning of the honorific 'Buddha') to 'how things actually are'. (In a Buddhist understanding, one sees things as they 'actually are' when one sees them as dependent on causes and conditions, in a net of causality.) One can use other kinds of reminders to be mindful in the moment – one can use doorways, the ring of one's phone, the sound of a received email or text. One simply tries to remember that these particular stimuli are there to help one become aware of what is happening right now, right here, and the more one remembers that, the more often one is aware in the moment, not so much informed by circular and habitual kinds of thinking. Such an awareness is helpful, as scientists are discovering, in relieving anxiety, stress and depression, but it is also useful, from a Buddhist view, to help one see things clearly, respond to things with love and compassion, and to be more honest.

This practice certainly helps me be a better Buddhist, but how does it affect my pedagogy? For one thing, it allows me to be more aware of myself and others at a time when simple awareness of this sort seems least possible – when I am in a room with 20 or so young people, guiding them in what I hope will be a learning experience. Even this brief practice invites a moment of the kind of metacognitive reflection that helps me 'simplify and clarify complex subjects' and complex class dynamics (Bain, 2004: 16). The ritual reinforces my respect for my students and what we are doing – it reminds me to see the classroom as sacred space, to see class time as sacred time, deserving of a particular kind of attention. It has also led me to look more deeply into what kind of 'learning experience' I am actually giving my students. In short, my religious practice (this one so private and yet performed in public) reminds me of one aspect of what can make teaching at least good and sometimes excellent: it reminds me of the importance of the time I share with my students. It reminds me that I am not just teaching about religion, although of course that is why I have been hired and what I have been trained to do. In the larger view I am afforded by moments of calm and complex understanding in the midst of my class, I see that I am teaching my students one way that an adult has found to be in this world now – valuing calm, recognizing many different causes that bring a single event about, often attempting to articulate that complexity to the best of my ability. Needless to say, this is a humble goal for teaching: to stand in the middle of the web of problems humanity faces in this 21st century, and represent one adult view. But this ritual (and others like it) repeatedly lands me in a fruitful countercultural position, eschewing the rush that defines mainstream American society today and standing not for more and faster information but for deeper wells of wisdom cultivated more slowly, and the more aware I become of taking this stand repeatedly, the more significant the stand becomes, even in its humility.

My worldview is also informed by stories from Buddhist texts such as one of my favorites, the *Ambalatthikarahulavada Sutta*, 'Advice to Rahula at Ambalatthika'. This sutta (discourse, dialogue) was purportedly given by the Buddha to his son Rahula when he was seven years old. At the beginning, the sutta notes that the Buddha was living at Rajagaha in the Bamboo Grove, the Squirrels' Sanctuary, while Rahula was living somewhere else, and one evening the Buddha arises from meditation and goes to see Rahula.

The problem that the Buddha approaches Rahula about is that evidently Rahula has been caught lying. With the use of a cup, the Buddha demonstrates to his son how bad it is to lie, how lying means you would not stop at anything, that you have given up utterly on having any kind of admirable character, of being respected by your peers ... you would do *anything* now. For example, he indicates the small amount of water in the cup and says, 'Even so little, Rahula, is the recluseship of those who are not ashamed to tell a deliberate lie'; he disposes of that water and compares throwing it away to how someone who lies throws away his discipleship (Bodhi, 2005: 523).

After exploring the problems of lying using the metaphors related to the cup, the Buddha moves beyond the description of how bad lying is and the need to refrain from doing it to recommendations of an active practice in which Rahula can engage. The Buddha asks his son, 'when you wish to do an action with the body, you should reflect upon that same bodily action thus: "Would this action that I wish to do with the body lead to my own affliction, or to the affliction of others, or to the affliction of both?"' (Bodhi, 2005: 524). In this context, something that leads to affliction, to more suffering, is something that leads to greed, anger or delusion. If the answer to the question is yes, he should refrain from doing that action. But if the action is a wholesome one (motivated by virtues such as generosity and love) with pleasant consequences (leading to lovingkindness, generosity, clarity and understanding), he should do that action. All well and good. But then the Buddha tells his seven-year-old that *while doing an action*, he should reflect in the same way and interrupt his action should he determine it to be an unwholesome one with unpleasant consequences. And *then*, the Buddha tells him that *after* he does an action he should view the action informed by the same questions, and if he finds that the action has led to the affliction of himself or others, he should 'confess such a bodily action, reveal it, and lay it open to the Teacher or to your wise companions' and 'undertake restraint for the future'. If he finds that the action was wholesome and with pleasant consequences, the Buddha assures him he 'can abide happy and glad, training day and night in wholesome states' (Bodhi, 2005: 525). And as though all that were not enough, the Buddha then goes on to advise a similar approach to actions of speech and actions of mind. (That is a lot for anyone, never mind a seven-year-old!)

I like this beginning to the sutta for one reason, because I relate to the context. Just as the Buddha seems to arise from meditation with clarity in relation to a pressing problem, so do I. By disciplining my mind, by setting aside inclinations to think, rethink, obsess and ruminate, and inviting my mind to do something else – attend gently to my breathing, systematically cultivate lovingkindness – solutions to problems simply arise as though what the solutions needed was actually a lack of a certain kind of attention to trying to find them. It is easy for me to imagine the Buddha having heard of a problem with his young son, and having meditated, and because of that meditation, the best way to approach the problem arose. So he just ends meditation and sets out to see Rahula in the same way that I get up from my meditation cushion and move directly to my desk to confront, skillfully I hope, a particular problem that has been nagging me.

I enjoy the cup metaphor part of the sutta too, not only because I appreciate the Buddha's pedagogical use of everyday objects, but because I take the precept not to lie regularly and aspire to keep it and have found that trying to refrain from lying gives me a foundation to stand on, allows me to see my flaws more clearly and quickly and allows me to treat people better.

What I most appreciate about this sutta, however, is the Buddha's high demands for reflections before, during and after an action. (When I read this sutta with students once, a young woman exclaimed with surprise that she did not think she had *ever* reflected on *any* of her actions in this manner. The possibility of this kind of reflection amazed her as much as the magnitude of the task.) As a human and a Buddhist, the sutta demands that I take every action seriously, which means also that as a teacher I must take every action seriously.

My beginnings-middles-and-ends practice parallels the practices recommended in this sutta. It reminds me of the significance of every act of the body, speech or mind, and it reminds me of the possibility of awareness and choice in response to every such act *before* the act, *during* the act and *after* the act. The practice functions both as rudder and keel. It steers me to more honest and careful behavior while stabilizing my heart and mind on principles related to refraining from harm and encouraging the best in others. How this sutta affects me as a Buddhist overlaps well with my pedagogical commitments: I am committed to doing what I can in my position as a teacher to bring greater peace to the world, to cause less harm, to seek to respond to the greater needs of the world as I teach about religion. Teaching religious literacy is important, but unless I assist my students in cultivating and communicating respect and curiosity and seeking fairness as they speak across religious divides and take stands in a religiously pluralistic world, I am just clocking in as a teacher.

Needless to say, my aspirations exceed my abilities, as aspirations do. Recently, during a class discussion, I watched as a student reached into his pocket and took something out just enough to see it. Enraged by his checking a phone text message in class, I raised my arms straight out in front of me with my hands clasped together, forming a gun. I was a police officer, confronting a fleeing criminal in a dead end alley. ('Put your hands up!') I shot my gun, making an explosive noise with my mouth, raising my hands up as though experiencing the kickback of the gun.

I shot my student directly in the chest.

The students in the class seemed to take the action with amused ease – another professorial antic in the classroom, nothing to be bothered by. We moved onto the next thing as a class fast enough that the conversation was not stilled; no stretching moment of awkwardness was allowed to yawn. I was aware, however, that even the mock shooting of a student was not a good thing for me to do. The action was motivated by anger and was evidence that my mind had made that student into an enemy, someone profoundly separated from me, different from me (a delusion in Buddhism as it obscures our love and compassion and denies our interrelatedness). My gun 'play' isolated the student and it made real an idea that he was somehow more alienated from what was going on in the classroom than the rest of us were, despite the fact that there are moments, hours and days when I, too, welcome a distraction from our conversation – something true for everyone in the room.

After class, in a private conversation, the student told me that he had not been checking for a text at all but was rather looking at the time on his cell phone. For my part, in the wake of the incident I became more aware of other ways in which I created a chasm between that particular student and myself and why and how this chasm led me to be overly judgmental, unfair and unkind to the student. There was more subtlety in these negative responses than in my outright (mock) shooting of him in class, but that subtlety did not make it right or better. It took the shooting to make me see my own behavior clearly enough to address it.

Why did I dislike the student? I cannot be sure, as I suspect there are a lot of reasons beyond my ability to know. Mostly, though, I think I disliked him because of our different expectations for the class: he wanted a different approach to learning what we were studying, and I could not and did not use that approach. I was frustrated that he wanted something I could not give, frustrated that we had to be together every day, me offering what I had and he finding that offering wanting. I suspect he felt the same way – that he had something to offer, but evidently not in this classroom at this time.

In time, as my feelings with respect to this student became clearer, I put his name on my home altar to be included in my sending of lovingkindness every morning. I increased my practices of the four brahmaviharas (the divine abodes: lovingkindness, compassion, appreciative joy and equanimity) in hopes of changing my heart and perhaps making this particular student feel as welcome in my classroom and in my presence as anyone else.

Despite my commitment to treating this student well, there was no great victory here. While he and I had a number of good conversations and I wished him well as he took the LSATs and aimed for law school, he clearly dismissed me at the end of the semester with an attitude of good riddance. On the few occasions we had the opportunity to see each other before he graduated, he more often averted his eyes than met mine. I was sad for that, but I understood it, too. While I had struggled with a dislike for him and done what I could, we were both glad when the strain was over. On further reflection it became clear to me that the sudden anger I had felt on seeing him doing something with his phone had roots both afflicted and not. That is an interesting thing about anger – it is one of the afflictions, one of the motivations out of which Buddhists try not to act, but it is also one that, especially when it is so strong, can signal something true and important – injustices, for example. The unafflicted roots included my care, a profound concern for the happiness and resilience of a generation that faces such great challenges to cultivating attention. I see the results of these problems in students struggling with anxiety and depression, and I see it all the time as students reach for something outside themselves for distraction instead of taking the time to reach inside themselves for maturation and growth.

My students reach outside themselves for solutions all too often. Some of them buy things to be cool. Some go to parties and numb their neocortexes so they can go to bed with one another. Some students take anti-anxiety drugs and antidepressants or take medicine for their attention deficit disorder. No wonder. They are acculturated largely in a society in which we seek external objects in order to find happiness, well-supported in this effort by the advertising industry, 'probably the greatest effort in mental manipulation that humanity has ever experienced – all of it to no other end than defining and creating consumerist needs' (Loy, 1997: 287). These students have become habituated to asking themselves, 'What do I need now [to be happy]?' The idea that they may need nothing outside themselves at any moment does not naturally occur to most of them. The medical-industrial complex also supports this repeated and immediate turn to external things to address problems. And their distractions are legion: they are attuned to the gentle humming of their phones set on vibrate and become excited at the sound; their computers hold entire universes. As a Buddhist, I am particularly troubled by a society that encourages distraction because Buddhism prizes attention as one important aspect of a path to wisdom.

I have given examples here of how I work on becoming a person who reduces harm in the world as I teach. Is it enough, however, for a professor to work on his or her own spirituality? Is that enough spirituality for any classroom? I used to think so, yes. Educated to teach *about* religions, I felt uncomfortable inviting students to engage in activities that did not seem to be about memorization, analysis, evaluation and synthesis – obviously cognitive skills. And there was the problem of assessing the kinds of activities that invite students to reach inside, to recognize and develop their interior lives. I had rubrics for grading all kinds of things, and especially fine rubrics for grading writing, but I had no rubrics for spiritual development and practice and the thought of such rubrics repelled me. In fact, my own experience of having been graded on a meditation journal once still confused me. (Why a 'B'? What made that journal be judged as a 'B'?)

Yet I kept finding myself including in my classes exercises that were oriented to the students' own inner lives, their own spirituality. I hid this orientation from myself and felt quite awkward about it. I certainly never used the word 'spiritual', and how I ended up grading these assignments was either (1) easily (so other assignments were graded more severely), or (2) by simply giving the students credit if they did the assignment (credit/no credit). (The former caused some confusion for me as well, as I heard comments from weaker students that they were 'good' at this one kind of assignment, when in fact every single person in the class had got an 'A' on that one.) I was also very concerned that most of the kinds of exercises I included in classes were secularized versions of Buddhist practices. I supported contemplative practices in other traditions such as centering prayer, and I brought people into my classes to teach those kinds of practice, but I could not represent the great diversity of religious practices. Yet the ones I brought clearly nourished the students in some way. I agree with Judith

Simmer-Brown when she writes, 'it is important to distinguish between religious or spiritual practice and educational pedagogy in the methods we are bringing into our classrooms. We must skillfully develop precise and appropriate approaches that remove any prerequisite of religious belief from our pedagogies, and design them to serve the larger educational journeys of our students' (Simmer-Brown, 2013: 34). But the separation of religious belief from pedagogical practices does not totally address the complexity of the situation when one views it through a lens informed by a functional definition of religion.

My students text in class but also try not to. They try to give up their anti-anxiety drugs and antidepressants.[2] They take stress reduction classes and learn to meditate, to do yoga and to be respectful of their bodies and minds. They give up Ritalin and Adderall and take walks in the woods. They volunteer for the emergency medical services team and in the local schools. Although largely acculturated in a consumerist society, they feel in their bodies and minds the constant sense of lack created when they ask themselves only 'What do I need/want now?' They listen to each other and try to do things differently.

More and more I incorporate 'experiments' into classes to give students support as they explore reaching inside. One experiment in an environmentally related class was to refrain from buying anything for a week. For a lark, I allowed this week to be the one that included Valentine's day that semester. The timing challenged one young man in particular – he loved his girlfriend and wanted to do something very special for her. So he bent the rules a bit: before the no-buying week began, he bought a gift certificate for a restaurant he knew she liked and gave it to her with a wink, saying that if she found she wanted to use that certificate on a certain day, he thought that was fine and in fact had made a reservation at the restaurant for that evening. He also bought her another gift before the week began to give to her that night. As Valentine's day drew near, however, he still felt these expressions of love were inadequate, yet he could not buy her anything else because of the experiment. So he took over an hour to write a letter to her describing what he most loved about her and gave it to her at dinner that night. Needless to say, it was the letter that meant the most to his girlfriend – his grateful reflections about her, formalized and crystallized in a form that allowed her to revisit and treasure them.

The obligations of a teacher include helping students to memorize, analyze, synthesize; they include compelling students to frame and encourage critiques of our culture and world and its values, and they include sharing wisdom and inspiring gratitude, love and care. Our students need more than to know how to think as they try to respond to the larger problems of society and the world as best as they can despite the obstacles in their way. In some ways this work is hopeless, yet what could be more hopeless than to give up? Everyone working for a better world has to engage in the work while simultaneously abandoning all hope of fruition.

But what of the intricacies of creating in a classroom the neutral, safe space in which religious commitments are irrelevant? Again, I used to think that was possible at the same time as I started each semester telling students that they were bound to be offended in a class on religion. I expected students to leave their religious (and anti-religious and non-religious) commitments and questions at the door, until I found that if they did so they could not walk into the room; the experiences and practices that have formed them and their (non- or anti-)religious commitments are how they (and we) are in the world; these commitments and questions form their eyes and move their legs. So far my work in this area as a teacher is tentative. In my Asian Religions class I now assign 'Where I stand' essays that are not graded – either the students write them and get credit for them or do not write them and do not get credit. I protect their anonymity and simply give them points for turning something in. These assignments ask them to respond personally to questions posed by what we do in class; they ask them for their personal responses to definitions of religion, to religious diversity, to their possible responsibilities at the end of the semester, now that they know more about Asian religions than many around them.[3] The students love these casual writing assignments as they help them integrate what they are learning in the class into their lives and recognize that they do, indeed, have personal reflections on the class material. I love reading the assignments because the writing is raw, sincere and honest; I can feel their struggle as they seek to grow and learn and respond. More and more I invite students to share with each other these personal reflections – just to share them, to learn how others are thinking and feeling about what we are doing. At this point I agree with Kwame Anthony Appiah when he says that 'intercultural "conversation does not have to lead to consensus about anything, especially not values; it's enough that it helps people get used to one another"' (as cited in Jacobsen & Jacobsen, 2012: 91).

The challenges of forming a classroom in which students can own up to religious formations, commitments, experiences and questions (or the lack of them or to stand against them) in such a way that all students have voices and the dialogues are lively and important are huge, and sometimes I am frankly afraid of these challenges. But religious diversity needs to be recognized and discussed, and in our increasingly global world I need to give my students practice in engaging in these ways. The rawness and sincerity that make the 'Where I stand' papers so compelling is also what makes this work exciting.

I will continue to pause at the door to my classroom, during class and at the end of it, and I will continue the kinds of reflection the Buddha encouraged of his seven-year-old son. I will do this for the sake of my interest in cultivating love and attention, and I will do this also so that students are more likely to cultivate love and attention. They will learn about religions in my classroom and the challenges of studying religion, but they will also learn a little bit more about how at least one adult is approaching the complexities of living in an exceedingly challenged world. As the Buddha says at the end of that sutta, 'Whatever [contemplatives in the past, present or future] purify their bodily actions, verbal actions, and mental actions, all do so by repeatedly reflecting thus' (Bodhi, 2005: 526).

Notes

(1) This teacher was Judith Simmer-Brown, Professor of Religious Studies, Naropa University. I remain grateful for the Contemplative Pedagogy Workshop I attended at Naropa University, Denver, CO, 2–7 August 2007, of which Professor Simmer-Brown was a leader.

(2) Although there are students who are rightly prescribed anti-anxiety drugs and anti-depressants, there are many more students who are prescribed these drugs too quickly and we do not know the consequences of this over-prescription on both the young and our society.

(3) By the end of my Asian Religions class, my students are part of the 6% who have been to a Hindu temple or part of the 10% who have been to a Buddhist temple, which makes them a little less insulated than most people in the United States (Hickey, 2012).

References

Bain, K. (2004) *What the Best College Teachers Do*. Cambridge, MA: Harvard University Press.

Bodhi (ed.) (2005) *The Middle Length Discourses of the Buddha: A Translation of the Majjhima Nikaya* (3rd edn) (trans. Nanamoli). Boston, MA: Wisdom Publications.

Brown, S. (2001) *A Buddhist in the Classroom*. New York: SUNY Press.

Hickey, W.S. (2012) Religious prejudice in the United States: Why we don't get along and what helps. *Dharma World* 39. See http://www.rk-world.org/dharmaworld/dw_2012octdecreligiousprejudice.aspx (accessed 3 May, 2018).

Jacobsen, D. and Jacobsen, R. (2012) *No Longer Invisible: Religion in University Education*. Oxford: Oxford University Press.

Loy, D. (1997) The religion of the market. *Journal of the American Academy of Religion* 65 (2), 275–290.

Simmer-Brown, J. (2013) 'Listening dangerously': Dialogue training as contemplative pedagogy. *Buddhist-Christian Studies* 33, 33–40.

7 The Relevance of Hinduism to English Language Teaching and Learning

Bal Krishna Sharma

During a class activity on the English grammar *prefer x to y*, while I was teaching at a high school in Kathmandu, Nepal in 2007, I noticed that one group of students had gone completely silent. Following the instructions in the textbook entitled *Meanings into Words*, which was published in the UK and prescribed by the Nepali board of higher secondary education, I had asked my students to work in small groups and practice the above grammatical pattern by taking turns and picking one out of the pair of objects assigned to them. When I asked the seemingly confused group of students what had happened, they told me they did not understand the meaning of the pair of words they had been assigned: *ham* and *steak*. I promptly provided them with the literal meanings of the words and moved on to listen to other groups. After a while, I noticed that those students had still not initiated a conversation: they were just smiling and looking at each other. It then occurred to me that neither steak nor ham was part of the food culture in Nepal's predominantly Hindu society – so it was little wonder that the students didn't know what to do with the pair of words that they were working on.

When the incident above occurred in my class, I realized how important it was to consider students' and teachers' cultural, religious and spiritual traditions and values in language teaching and learning, especially when they are not so explicit and striking as the above. The values may not only be a part of the content of teaching and learning, but they could form the very foundation of what it means to teach and learn. My teacher education courses in Nepal taught me that all 'modern' innovations in education and pedagogy have their origins in the West. I was trained to think that learner centeredness, teacher and student autonomy, discussion and argument-based classroom participation, and transformative pedagogy, among other current trends, were more modern and hence superior to the indigenous educational ideas and practices of the Indian subcontinent. Viewed from the perspective of the mainstream and respected theories that I studied at university, local pedagogical traditions such as the Vedic *Gurukuls* promoted *only* rote learning and authoritarian teacher roles, jeopardizing students' creativity and reasoning skills. And because local teachers like me were educated in the more 'global' and 'advanced' ideas and practices about education, we embraced and internalized the idea that the local and surviving forms of educational practices and methods were nothing but obsolete and backward in terms of content and pedagogy. Indeed, they were considered unworthy of studying or practicing any more due to the spiritual and religious values that undergirded any vestiges of those educational practices. In spite of our awareness about how contexts, conventions and values shape the notions of quality and worth, there was little in the direction of making us think otherwise.

The classroom incident and reflection on my own education above suggest that there is a need to understand and contextualize the value of local cultural, spiritual and philosophical traditions in language teaching. In the first case, the textbook authors must have been largely unaware of the local spiritual traditions of contexts such as Nepal and of other contexts in which the books would be used. Due to the inclusion of supposedly 'universal' content, the task lacked context sensitivity among certain groups of students in Nepal. Because I was familiar with the local Hindu spiritual tradition, I replaced these words with the appropriate food items; if I did not know about such traditions, I would not understand why the students were not engaged in the activity. This suggests that, regardless of a (lack of) affiliation to a particular religious tradition, textbook writers, test writers and language teachers should have some degree of awareness of the local spiritual traditions if those traditions are an important part of the students' lives. Some knowledge and awareness of such traditions can greatly help them in producing locally appropriate curricular materials, tests, pedagogies and teaching philosophies. Instead of looking up to Western-originated philosophical and pedagogical traditions for their professional development, English teachers in the periphery can reflect on their own philosophical and spiritual background if such background is an important part of their teaching life. Most teacher education courses and the discourse in applied linguistics and teaching English to students of other languages (TESOL) contain assumptions, such as non-Western traditions being inferior to Western ones (Kumaravadivelu, 2003).[1] Considering my own teaching, until very recently I did not have the awareness and training to reflect on and critically assess whether some of the local Hindu spiritual thoughts and practices were very similar to the 'modern' innovations in language teaching that I studied as a teacher in the making. The fact of the matter is that certain modern and Western values and practices of education, such as student-centered teaching/learning, were in existence in one form or another in the Vedic education schools centuries ago in the Indian subcontinent. Also, some Hindu educational philosophies and ideas relate to current work in critical pedagogy in the field of applied linguistics.

In this chapter I provide a historical survey of Hindu views and practices of learning, teaching and student–teacher relationships, and argue that some of what have been regarded as standard practices and innovations in language pedagogy in the Western world today, especially in Anglo-American educational contexts, were similar to some ideas in the traditional Hindu educational ethos and practices found in the Vedic traditions in the Indian subcontinent. In the second part of the chapter, I discuss how English language teachers can benefit from Hindu spiritual-philosophical bases in order to pay attention to the social responsibility dimension of language teaching. Understanding Hinduism can help English teachers address some critical issues, such as respect for students as individuals and members of a particular culture/community, peace and social harmony, human relationship with nature and an awareness of environmental crisis, among others.

Introduction to Hinduism

Hinduism is a West-given label during British colonization in India, designed to explain the dominant religious traditions of a majority of the people who inhabit the Indian subcontinent. Hinduism is so diverse that there is hardly any one binding principle that captures its essence. This tradition spans nearly 5000 years of diverse traditions, beliefs and practices, which makes the task of providing a generalization or an overview of education extremely challenging. Unlike many other religious, philosophical or cultural traditions of the world, Hinduism does not have a clear founder, a central text or for that matter a clear historical beginning (Sheshagiri, 2011). Hinduism is also known as a *sanatan dharma*. *Sanatan* means 'eternal', and *dharma*, which is often translated as 'religion', actually encompasses such notions as 'duty', 'righteousness' and 'natural law', thus suggesting a much broader understanding than that generally accorded the term 'religion' in the West (Reagan, 2005). Although scholars and historians acknowledge the diversity of Hindu traditions, the core version of Hinduism is the Vedic tradition. Within this tradition there is a body of sacred writings, including different kinds of literature. Ancient Hindu literature is divided into two elements: *shruti* and *smriti*. *Shruti*, meaning 'listening' or 'hearing', consists of sacred texts and scripts like the *Vedas* and the *Upanishads* which are traditionally understood as divine revelation. They are principally oral texts and can best be transmitted as such. *Smritis*, which means 'that are remembered', are sacred writings which originated from human authors and comprise codes of conduct for human life (Monk, 1968). Examples include the *Mahabharata*, the *Ramayana*, the *Manusmriti*, the *Bhagvat Gita*, etc.

I join scholars in interpreting Hinduism as a tradition that is more than a set of religious rituals and practices. It is a spiritual tradition in the Indian subcontinent, encompassing philosophies of religion, science, education, life and human development, which are treated as inseparable from one another (Thaker, 2007). For that reason, I will be using the terms 'philosophical' and 'spiritual' interchangeably here and they refer to the same Vedic tradition unless stated otherwise. Western philosophers have documented that Hindu philosophy and the Indian subcontinent were home to a significant portion of the world's mathematics, astronomy, philosophy, linguistics, ethics and psychology. Hinduism is also a source of origin of yoga. There were great educational centers of excellence and higher education in the subcontinent such as Takshashila, Vikramashila and Nalanda. Hindu philosophers also had an influence on the development of European and Asian languages and linguistics. Panini's grammar from 500 BC (with over 4000 precise rules) became the source of inspiration and model for the entirely new fields of philology and linguistics in the West. In East Asia and Southeast Asia, the Indian subcontinent exerted a great influence on literature. Indic ideas have profoundly shaped modern philosophy, psychology and Western spirituality and its emerging worldview (Malhotra, 2014). Therefore, there is historical, educational and intellectual significance in going back to the ideas and practices of Hinduism (Sharma, 2013).

As hinted in the previous paragraphs, the ideas and practices of Hinduism in this chapter are mainly drawn from its scriptures, such as the *Vedas*, the *Upanishadas*, the *Bhavat Gita* and the *Mahabharata*, among others. Similar to Canagarajah's (2009) suggestion for reading religious scriptures, my interpretation of such scriptures is flexible and open: Hindu scriptures are socially constructed; truth derived from scriptures is constantly reinterpreted; and scriptures are not closed sources, but subject to change as time and location change. And, when I discuss Hindu educational practices, this mainly means teaching and learning traditions as practiced in *Gurukuls* and other centers of learning in the Vedic educational tradition, but not the modern religious practices of Hindus in contemporary South Asia or in other parts of the world.

I wish to mention some caveats here before I go further. Hinduism was diverse but its educational practices were sociohistorically limited. Although a majority of the people in the region followed the Hindu religion, only a few of them had the educational opportunities it offered. Only *Brahmins* and a few *Chhetriyas*, mostly males, had access to education (Sheshagiri, 2011). Secondly, Hinduism is supposed to have given birth to the hierarchical caste system[2] and created a strongly patriarchal and gendered society in South Asia. As a result, it only privileged the lives of people from the upper stratum. This implies that when I refer back to the ancient educational institutions and practices of Hinduism, I am discussing the practices of just a handful of social and spiritual male elites of that time. These educational ideas, nevertheless, can be useful to modern societies that are more inclusive and democratic. I will show this in the later sections. In addition, it would be of great interest and significance to unearth what was there in the Hindu scriptures that was kept confined to a few *Brahmins* and *Chhetriyas*. Imparting and receiving education in the Sanskrit language helped the elites control the knowledge from its vernacularization for centuries. Following the same argument, I also acknowledge that there existed immense indigenous knowledge and literary traditions passed along the generations orally in local cultures and their vernacular languages which were not based on Hinduism. It does not mean that I am not aware of or ignoring other forms of cultural and educational practices, but this lies beyond the scope of this chapter.

Here, I also try to make my positionality and affiliation to Hinduism clear to my audience so that readers can understand why I want to privilege one tradition, not others. Since I grew up in a Hindu family in Nepal, the cultural practices in my family and society (e.g. rituals of birth, marriage, death, festivals and food, etc.) and my understanding of the relationship between humans and the cosmos have shaped my childhood and have greatly influenced who I am today. I regard Hinduism not only as existing/going beyond a set of religious rituals, but as a comprehensive philosophy of spirituality, of life and of education. Hindu ideas and practices of yoga, Ayurveda (a traditional, alternative medicinal practice in the South Asian region) and non-violence have inspired my life. I am also open to the possibility of reinterpretation and adaptation of Hindu institutions in accordance with the changing nature of our societies. I provide a space for the eclecticism of multiple philosophies and faith backgrounds when needed. My motivation to explore Hinduism is the result of my proximity to it as well as my interest in a quest for space for an alternative spiritual-philosophical tradition in TESOL.

According to the traditional Hindu social system, I am a Brahmin male – a member of the so-called uppermost stratum in the caste hierarchy in Nepal. This identity privileges as well as limits my role as a Nepalese scholar writing on topics of spirituality and education. It privileges in the sense that I am an insider member of the Hindu community and have lived a 'Hindu life' so far. It also limits me in the sense that I do not 'represent' the voice and perspective of the entire Hindu community, particularly of those who have been socially and historically disadvantaged due to discriminatory Hindu spiritual, cultural and educational traditions as they are practiced now.

Hindu Educational Practices

In this section I review Hindu educational principles and practices in terms of three basic elements of pedagogy: (1) learning, (2) methods of teaching and (3) student–teacher relationships. Since non-Western philosophical and educational traditions are still under-documented, poorly understood and vastly stereotyped in most parts of the Western academic world (Shin & Crookes, 2005), a review such as the present one helps to question some myths and stereotypes language educators in both Western and non-Western contexts may have. Researchers continue to claim that there exists a stereotypical dichotomy of the East (particularly Asia) versus West, essentializing their pedagogical practices on historical and cultural grounds: the East being more teacher centered, static and authoritarian while the West is more student centered, dynamic and egalitarian (Kubota, 1999; Kumaravadivelu, 2003; Shin & Crookes, 2005). Consequently, there is a danger that language professionals' lack of knowledge of historical and philosophical traditions – theirs and others – may reinforce a distorted essentialist position and lead them not to question the cultural appropriateness of supposedly West-originated curricular innovations, implying that cultural inappropriateness would lead to a lack of success in non-Western contexts. In the following section I identify the key aspects of traditional Hindu education and discuss them, whenever possible, in relation to some similar educational thoughts and practices in TESOL today.

Learning

According to Hindu educational principles and practices, a knower possesses two kinds of knowledge: *para vidya* and *apara vidya*. Through *para vidya*, the supreme goal of life, i.e. self-realization, is attained. *Apara vidya* encompasses the phenomenal world, that is, anything that can be objectified by our senses or mind. It is based on the belief that humans need secular knowledge in order to navigate through the material world successfully before they realize the value of higher knowledge and it prepares them to achieve it (Devi & Pillai, 2012). Perhaps the following quote by Thaker (2007) best summarizes the Hindu view of learning:

> In Hindu theory there are two types of learning, each with its own goal and its own method. The first has the aim of gaining knowledge from the world, so it is outer-directed. Its source is environment, and its methodology is two-fold – formal study of sacred writings and the informal interaction with the world known as experience. The second type of learning has self-understanding as its aim. Its source is the person's own spirit, and its methodology is introspection as achieved through meditation. (Thaker, 2007: 61)

Hinduism believes that true empowerment emerges through an understanding of the sources of knowledge, not just its components, which in turn leads to unity with the universe. Thus, the Hindu view of learning does not limit itself to the learning of facts and figures, but emphasizes developing wisdom by forming a connection between mind, body and spirit (Thaker, 2007). This is different from the dominant Western view of learning which seeks cause-and-effect relationships with the worldly phenomena and believes in learning components as part of a whole. When we survey learning from a more formal and pedagogical perspective, it requires us to uncover methods of learning about the outer world by studying scriptures under the supervision of gurus. Memorization constituted one of the major techniques of learning in the Vedic educational tradition. This form of learning by memorization seemingly has parallels with behaviorist principles of repetition, practice, memorization and habit formation (Sheshagiri, 2011). However, I argue that we need to go beyond such accounts for at least two reasons. First, this practice has to be interpreted within the sociohistorical context of the region. Given the oral tradition of literacy and knowledge making, memorization and rote learning could enhance the archiving of knowledge in the form of songs, chants or poems which would be available for future generations.

Hough *et al.* (2009) add that together with rhymes and rhythms, other strategies like repetition, body movements and gestures can help contextualize the information in the form of a narrative. No wonder these elements were partly reflected in the educational practices of that time. Secondly, it is to be noted that learning by heart without understanding the meaning of Vedic hymns, and without reflection, was condemned (Ghosh, 2007). As an example, Narain (1993: 18) cites from the *Nirukta*, 'he is only the bearer of burden, the blockhead who having studied the Veda does not understand its meaning'. The education was considered to be a process of inward meditation and thinking, focusing on opening up the mind and enhancing the understanding of the universe and the self. This kind of learning is not based on rote learning, but much deeper comprehension involving reflection, questioning and exercising judgments (Sheshagiri, 2011). There were a lot of opportunities for learners to gain knowledge by observing, inferring, performing and practicing. The traditions of ancient learning systems displayed much diversity, blurring the boundaries between process and product (Canagarajah, 1999). Narain (1993) laments that under the modern system, the three processes of teaching, learning and evaluation seem to be treated as working almost independently in the context of South Asia, and hardly any integration or synchronization exists among them. In ancient times, all three processes were integrated well.

Education in the Vedic and Upanishadic times was not confined to the development of the self alone, but would also encourage the students to work for social change upon graduation from *Gurukuls*. Students were groomed in an ambience to inculcate the social and moral obligations of a good citizen to serve the society (Devi & Pillai, 2012). Narain (1993) provides evidence from the *Yajurveda* that every student owed three *gurudakshina*, or debts, which must be repaid – one being *Rishi* (guru) debt, owing to learning and acquiring knowledge. Spreading and distributing that knowledge to the people, to the society (Ashok & Thimmappa, 2006) was the only way to pay this back. When students obtained learning and knowledge, they would wander from place to place fearlessly and preach to the masses with honor and respect. They were responsible for the society, not for themselves (Mishra, 1998). Such debt has also been regarded as a *dharma* of a human being, meaning the privileges, duties and obligations of a person towards their society (Bai, 1996).

In sum, the Hindu view of learning encompasses diverse ways of gaining knowledge, including the study of scriptures, experience by interacting with the external environment, and introspection or self-revelation. In addition to memorization, reflection, questioning and exercising of judgment are useful learning techniques. Learning goes beyond individual growth, including the goal of bringing about social change.

Methods of teaching

The *Gurukul* system of education in the ancient Indian subcontinent provides us with insights into methods of teaching during that time and helps us make comparisons with popular pedagogical models today. Students would live with their guru as members of a single family. The system of teaching was communal although there were ample occasions when the teacher explained something to the individual pupils (Mishra, 1998). The educational instruction, to begin with, from early Vedic or Upanishad times, took place in a familial environment where the seeker of knowledge had to take up residence in the home of the teacher. The word 'Upanishad' itself suggests that it is learning received by sitting with the master. The students had to serve their guru with determination, discipline, sincerity and intelligence for years to acquire the knowledge in the different subjects the guru had attained through his study, experience and self-realization.

In addition to the teacher-fronted, product-oriented guru-shishya system, teaching was substantially based on a practice-based apprenticeship system (Sheshagiri, 2011). Students engaged in a process of collective learning in a shared domain of human endeavor. As the pupils interacted regularly, more experienced members helped the new members acquire the community norms and the Vedic educational ethos through their mutual engagement in learning activities. The learning system was notably non-formal, blurring the differences between philosophical and technical knowledge, facts and skills, and knowledge and life. This process was more inductive and process oriented, and teaching methods were diverse, depending on learner, context and subject matter (Canagarajah, 1999). Such practices resonate with the principles of such models of teaching and learning as Lave and Wenger's (1991) communities of practice and the situated learning theory. The relatively recent legitimate peripheral participation framework within the situated learning theory is a popular model to explain professional practice, teaching and learning in many fields today but, as can be seen, ancient Hindu educational practices enjoyed a diversity that encompasses a view of learning consistent with this theoretical position.

In addition to the communal learning in *Gurukuls*, there was another, non-formal mode of learning promoted by freelance teachers called *charakas*, the wandering scholars, who spread education in far and wide regions of the subcontinent. They were the mobile education providers enabling education to reach the unreachable, opportunities similar to those that today's distance mode of education offers. Devi and Pillai (2012) note that the *charakas* provided education at the doorsteps of the needy which in the modern period open universities are trying to emulate through distance modes of education. In *Gurukuls*, teachers exercised total autonomy over curriculum and organization (Sheshagiri, 2011). Pupils also enjoyed some degree of autonomy in choosing institutions or teachers; for example, they could move from one *Gurukul* to another for better knowledge. Sometimes even the teacher could advise the students to go to another teacher to satisfy their queries. Also, the *Gurukul* system did not rule out the possibility of self-study and learning. Ghosh (2007), for example, notes that during the *Brahmacharya Ashram*, people could still achieve the knowledge of the Absolute or Brahma by self-study.

Methods of debate, discussion, speculation and argument were salient features of education in the *Gurukul* system of education. Discussions and debates would take the form of intellectual challenges between the guru and the students or among the students themselves (Dharampal, 1983). Typical of present-day symposia, many learned persons from far-off places used to assemble and participate in the debates and discussions that regularly took place at the Vedic educational centers. Such use of discussion as a method of teaching later led to the development of a logic called *Vakovakyam* or *Tarkashastra*, or the science of disputation. Such a tradition of arguments can be substantially exemplified by dialogues between Krishna and Arjuna in the Bhagavat Gita – a small section of the epic the *Mahabharata*. Mahalakshmi and Geetha (2009) summarize the patterns of Tarkashastra, which typically follows the argumentation pattern of five-stage inference: statement, reason, example, application and conclusion.

> Statement is an argument where things to be proved are stated; reason is the supporting evidence which strengthens the proof; example is a similar case that has occurred prior to the statement; the idea of example can be derived and applied to the statement which shall be concluded towards the end of discussion. … There is also a role of defect exploration in this process, which consists of initially analyzing a given input argument and later highlighting the argument's defects or holes in terms of concept and relation elements of argument. These defects, otherwise called reason fallacies, are connected with inferential reasoning. Overcoming these fallacies or defects is called 'removing the holes' from the submitted argument. An argument is futile when the reverse of what it seeks to prove is established for certain by another proof. (Mahalakshmi & Geetha, 2009: 319)

During defect exploration there is a role of refutation, which means arguing against the proponent with valid inferences. Mahalakshmi and Geetha (2009) note that if the information contained in the proponent's argument is agreeable, the members display an 'agree' message or else a 'disagree' message. The discussion continues until a disputing member offers a voluntary exit from the discussion by an 'exit' message, which means that the volunteer has no interest or ability in further discussion about the current subject. Alternatively, any volunteer wishing to exit an arguing team in the middle of argumentation may offer a 'quit' message to quit the discussion. Ghosh (2007) observes that this method of argument shares some similarities with the art of Socratic dialogs in ancient Greek tradition. Such discussion-oriented teaching is based on the idea of promoting democratic values and fostering student-centered learning. Henning (2008: 2), for example, argues that discussion-based teaching leads to 'gains in general subject mastery, reading comprehension, conceptual understanding, problem-solving ability, moral development, attitude change and development, and communication skills'. This is a major pedagogic technique in many academic institutions today, although teachers both in the center and at the periphery may be hardly aware that such a pedagogical tool existed in Hindu educational practices in the Indian subcontinent centuries ago.

To sum up, in addition to a transmission model, Hindu educational tradition allowed teachers curricular and teaching autonomy and students some degree of autonomy, and it exhibited diversity in teaching methods including learner-centered techniques like debate and discussion. Teaching was both communal and individual and focus was on the product as well as the process of learning.

Student–teacher relationship

In the ancient Hindu system of education, education was highly individualized. There would be only a few selected students enrolled, and teachers knew individual students very closely. Teachers loved students as if they were their own children, and were fully aware of what had been learned by each student, including areas of weakness. In fact, the Vedic students are regarded as twice-born: first from their mother and secondly from their guru at the start of their Vedic education (Thaker, 2007). A teacher had to possess the highest moral and spiritual qualifications and to be well-versed in the sacred lore and dwelling in the *Brahman* or the *Brahmanishtha* (Ghosh, 2007). A similar situation was true in higher educational institutions. This may seem to suggest a stereotypical 'traditional', 'hierarchical' teacher–student relationship and a supposedly 'authoritarian' role of the teacher in Vedic educational practices. Of course, in any period, educational practitioners in South Asia, as in any other location, might misuse a teacher's power for non-pedagogical purposes. However, the topic of student–teacher relationships has to be understood and interpreted with reference to the sociohistorical context of pedagogical practices of that time, in contrast to their use in pedagogies of modern times. Traditional Hindu educational tradition gave more responsibility to teachers beyond classroom teaching. Reverence was given to the teachers for their position in the social and moral hierarchy. Teachers, while clearly occupying such a high social status, were expected to mutually participate with students in the classroom, in the playground and in activities related to the management of the school (Bai, 1996). Of course, it cannot be said that the teacher and the students enjoyed an equal relationship. However, it should be noted that the teaching and relationship was not solely controlled by the teacher, and the students could initiate questions and topics for discussion and debate (see also Canagarajah, 1999).

Good teachers or gurus were considered to be role models in their virtues and morality, to live exemplary lives and to change human society towards wellbeing. They were enlightened people who led ascetic lives. The literal translation of the Sanskrit word 'guru' as 'teacher' carries with it deep reverence for the teacher. Reverence is different from respect: 'Reverence calls for respect only when respect is really the right attitude' (Woodruff, 2001: 6). In contexts where problems of classroom management and student discipline frequently cause 'professional vulnerability' (Gao, 2006) among teachers, requiring them sometimes to protect themselves from personal dangers in their professional lives, reverence can be a strong tool for creating conducive teaching environments. If students lack a certain level of obedience to authority in the classroom, there is a risk that teaching and learning will become counterproductive. Kumaravadivelu also shares a similar experience: 'Indian schools and colleges have always faced, and still face, what is called a *perennial discipline problem*' (Kumaravadivelu, 2003: 711, emphasis in the original). When teachers and students meet in the classroom with the right attitudes, this promotes what has been recognized as the 'intellectual safety' of the teacher. Ancient Hindu educational practices did not ignore the agency and voice of the students.

As mentioned in the *Dharmasutra*, a teacher should not restrain the students for his own advantage in such a way that hinders their studies (Bai, 1996). Teachers were not given the power to refuse instruction to students unless they found a defect in them. In addition, teachers did not appear to have encouraged blind obedience from the pupils. The *Dharmasutra* clearly mentions that students can confidentially draw the attention of the teacher to any transgression of religious injunctions that he may commit, deliberately or inadvertently. Students can forcibly restrain the teacher from wrongdoing either by themselves or with the help of their parents. The teacher not imparting knowledge did not indeed deserve the designation of teacher. Kumaravadivelu also draws from Matilal and Chakrabarti (1994) and comments on the oft-quoted declaration of Buddha, 'Do not trust my words; rely upon your own light' as a traditional Indian attitude towards authority. Emeneau (1955) also accolades the Hindu traditional cultural characteristics of 'intellectual thoroughness, and urge toward ratiocination, intellection, and learned classification' (Emeneau, 1955: 145). All this suggests that although teachers enjoyed a certain degree of authority and reverence, they did not compromise the learning potential and agency of the students.

Hinduism and the Social Responsibility Dimension of TESOL

Hinduism conceives of the entire course of human life as consisting of four *Ashramas* or successive stages. The stage of studentship is called *Brahmacharya Ashrama* and it was spent in the Vedic schools. The *Upanayana* ceremony, meaning taking charge of a student, was considered the foundational state of starting the *Brahmacharya* stage in the Vedic education. The second stage as *Grihastha* or householders began when people entered family life. The third state of *Vanaprasthan* started when they left home for the forest to become hermits. And in the final stage of *Sanyasashram*, they become homeless wanderers with all earthly ties broken. The chief aim of education was to achieve emancipation or liberation by detaching oneself from worldly matters and activities. Emancipation was achieved through *sravana, manana* and *nididhyasana*. *Sravana* means listening to the words or texts from the teacher or guru, *manana* means deliberation or reflection on the topic, and *nididhyasana* means meditation through which truth is to be realized (Ghosh, 2007). The ultimate goal of education according to Hindu educational philosophy and practices is the attainment of the *Brahman* or the highest knowledge, the Absolute. I elaborate on this notion in the following section.

The concept of *Brahman* or the Absolute can provide pedagogical insights for socially responsible language teachers who want to incorporate spiritual beliefs and awareness into their teaching philosophies. *Brahman* urges teachers to understand human life as inseparable from and even embedded in the ecological environment. According to this thought, individuals, society, the universe and the cosmos are all interrelated and integrated (Ashok & Thimmappa, 2006). The *Upanishads* suggests that human beings are not autonomous entities operating independently or in isolation, but a part of *Brahman* interconnected and interrelated to all other beings. The *Atman* or self is not higher or different from the *Brahman*. Hinduism regards nature or *prakriti* as a form of the Goddess *Devi*, and believes that any modifications or changes in the state of nature create imbalance in the life of its creatures and vegetation.[3]

Another related dimension of *Brahman* is the notion of holistic peace. Hindu philosophy is characterized by transformative dictums such as *Ahinsha paramo dharma* (अहिंसा परमो धर्म = non-violence is the ultimate religion), *Vasudaiva kutumbaram* (वसुधैव कुटुम्बकम = the whole world is our family), *Lokah Samastah Sukhino Bhavantu* (लोक: समस्तः शुखींनो भवन्तु = May all the beings in all the worlds become happy) and a prayer like *Om shantih, shantih, shantih!* (ॐ शान्तिः शान्तिः शान्तिः॥ = Peace, peace and peace be everywhere!). Such discourses on peace have become embedded into the Hindu conception of human life and this holds rich potential to unfurl edifying pedagogies to explore spirituality as potent sites for peace building[4] (Upadhyaya, 2010). The *Vedas* and the *Upanishads* provide one of the earliest references to a global family. When all the inhabitants of the cosmos are treated as members of a family, this makes it irrelevant to have conflicts among different nations and people over geographical and political boundaries and identities. The holistic notion of peace, therefore, is directly relevant to some of the major conflicts that matter to people today.

Revisiting spiritual sources such as the ones I have mentioned above will be advantageous to language professionals today as they have the potential to provide alternative perspectives that can inform language teachers' teaching philosophies as well as curricular practices on critical issues that matter to us now. Spiritual ideas have the potential to provide us with a philosophical basis for what it means to be a language teacher. This comes, for example, with language teachers' commitment to teach beyond 'language', providing a space for a pedagogy of possibility in fostering responsibility towards ecology and peaceful human society at large. Focusing on the centrality of the Hindu philosophical concept of *Brahman*, I argue for a relationship of spirituality with the social responsibility aspect of TESOL. The Hindu notion of *Brahman* is guided by a spiritually grounded moral position of reverence and care towards all creation and ecology – human, animals and plants. Such a focus on critical topics also responds to a recent call by Canagarajah (2009) that these topics are serious concerns for practitioners approaching language pedagogy from both critical and spiritual perspectives, since both take a critical stance on dehumanizing, utilitarian and pragmatic orientations towards learning and teaching. This meeting point is an example of the relevance of Hinduism to contemporary pedagogy in the field, particularly from a critical perspective (e.g. Freire, 1972).

TESOL practitioners have long been interested in issues of peace and the environment. For example, Pennycook (1989) in his seminal article reminds us that teachers are transformative intellectuals who must see themselves as 'professionals who are able and willing to ... connect pedagogical theory and practice to wider social issues, and who work together to share ideas, exercise power of the conditions of our labor, and embody in our teaching a vision of a better and more humane life' (Pennycook, 1989: 613). Brown (1994) echoes a similar voice in interpreting professionalism in TESOL:

> You are not merely a language teacher ... You are an agent for change in a world in a desperate need for change: change from competition to cooperation, from powerlessness to empowerment, from conflict to resolution, from prejudice to understanding ... Our professional commitment drives us to help the inhabitants of this planet co-communicate with each other, to negotiate the meaning of peace, of goodwill, and of survival on this tender, fragile globe. (Brown, 1994: 442)

Crookes (2010) also notes that peace and 'green' are two important strands in critical pedagogy and have a long history in curriculum theory, but there is less literature than one might expect in applied linguistics. He encourages language professionals to explore possibilities, suggesting 'the green/environmental line is occurring so widely that to use curriculum material that advocates peaceful citizen action to decrease global warming is not going to get you into trouble' (Crookes, 2010: 340).

The philosophical notion of *Brahman* in Hinduism can, thus, offer a philosophical basis for language teachers and encourage them and their students to rethink their relationship with the world and connect local issues to global environmental and social concerns. It invites them to question the taken-for-granted human activities towards nature and other species and to work for the common good rather than only for their individual interests. When teachers and students view their language classrooms and communities through a spiritual lens, they are encouraged to ask such questions as: What do my spiritual beliefs say about:

- the human relationship with ecology and other animals?
- the quality of our local environment and what can be done to improve it?
- the extent to which our school and society promote eco-justice and peace? In what ways?
- how the resources spent on weapons and wars could be used for alleviating world hunger and poverty?
- the consequence of today's human activities on future generations?
- the materials used in this class – newspaper articles, videos, photographs, etc.?
- how the activities in the classroom can promote the learning of peace vocabularies and communication strategies?

Beyond the prescribed curriculum, language teachers also implement their own beliefs and ideologies while teaching their classes. Such an agency on the part of language teachers helps them incorporate spiritual concerns towards ecology and peace into their instruction. Such teachers can choose to add spiritually motivated activities and materials into the existing curriculum, e.g. discussions about newspaper articles, videos or pictures that in some way reflect these critical concerns. I personally have drawn on the Hindu notion of holistic peace to discuss matters of both domestic and global conflicts and wars, and have emphasized the importance of peace, respect and harmony. I have referenced Hindu scriptures in order to discuss the dynamic, interdependent and interacting nature of human relationships to the world in teaching literature-based English classes to the high school students in Nepal, and encouraged the learners to critically analyze human actions towards the environment. For example, in teaching a lesson on 'environment and human population', I have asked my students: Why is there an inadequate amount of monsoons in Nepal? I have discussed why the world should preserve its forests. I have also drawn students' attention to the Hindu ethos of revering nature and discussed human relationships with the rest of the animals and plants on earth. Meanwhile, I have drawn on the discourses of global warming and climate change and connected them to the Hindu notion of *Brahman* in order to emphasize human relationships with nature. Such discussions have raised students' critical awareness of the fact that Nepali people have to save the forests, not because they want money from the World Bank, but because they want to show their deep appreciation for and intertwined relationship with the environment.

Conclusion

Anchored in a gradual introduction and development of modern linguistic theories and language teaching methods in Europe and North America from the late 19th century onwards, the English language teaching field has resulted in non-attention to, if not outright dismissal of other systems, cosmologies and understandings of learning and pedagogy. With the resurrection of interest in spirituality in academia (e.g. Wong & Canagarajah, 2009), proposals have emerged suggesting that spiritual traditions have the potential to offer pedagogies of alternative possibilities. As a preliminary attempt along these lines, I have provided a review of Hindu educational practices focusing on learning, teaching and student–teacher relationships. I have presented arguments and historical evidence to show that some supposedly Western educational standards and practices occupied important space in ancient Hindu educational traditions. Within the seemingly dominant practices of teacher-frontedness, learning by heart and the transmission model of education in the Hindu ethos of learning and teaching, there indeed were agendas and practices of more student-centered, practice-based approaches and methods that fostered learning, teaching and autonomy. In many places in the chapter, I have identified places of similarities and differences between ancient Hindu education and modern Western educational traditions, and possible places of misunderstandings and myths of Hindu education. As an example of how an idea from Hinduism can be employed in English pedagogy, I drew on the concept of *Brahman* and discussed how Hinduism can provide a philosophical basis for understanding human relationships with other humans and with the rest of the world. Spiritually minded language teachers can address such critical concerns as ecological crisis and conflicts in their curricular materials and teaching practices.

While going through this chapter, it might be assumed that educational practices in the Indian subcontinent today reflect a Hindu philosophy of life. While this may be partly true, modern education in the region has been a blend of recent educational developments during and after British colonization, ongoing sociopolitical changes in the region as well as 'innovations' in the West. I am not trying to suggest that whatever was there in Hindu educational ideals and practices was good and desirable and that every aspect of our lost heritage should be revived. Nor am I implying that the Hindu pedagogical practices should be reclaimed in their entirety and that we should adopt an exclusionary position. Such a fundamentalist position is neither possible nor acceptable. My point is that a philosophical and historical overview like the one outlined here may urge local teachers in the subcontinent to critically re-examine modern transformative approaches to English language teaching. As a result, these are less likely to be seen as 'innovations' and 'foreign' to their native contexts. Global material developers, textbook writers, test developers and language teachers can also develop their awareness of the local traditions and practices in South Asia. Teachers, particularly those from Euro-American backgrounds teaching in South Asia, can benefit from the ideas reviewed and presented here by informing themselves about the region's dominant spiritual-educational beliefs and practices. Today's international TESOL profession should acknowledge and include diverse pedagogical and philosophical traditions so that English teachers are better prepared to accept alternative pedagogies, through both revival and innovation.

Acknowledgement

I thank John Wiley and Sons for allowing me to reproduce some content from my previous article published in *Language and Linguistics Compass* (Sharma, 2013). I would also like to acknowledge the constructive feedback from B. Kumaravadivelu, Graham Crookes, Sthaneshwar Timalsina, Suresh Canagarajah and Shyam Sharma received during the different phases of the development of this chapter. All remaining weaknesses, however, are mine.

Notes

(1) I am aware that the notions 'Western' and 'non-Western' are more complicated than they appear to be. Although this practice seems to reproduce an essentialist tradition, I am using them for a strategic benefit as suggested by the postcolonial theorist Gayatri Chakravorty Spivak (1988).

(2) There are counter-arguments as well. Some would argue that caste in ancient times was not understood in a hereditary sense, but on one's learning aptitude and occupational preferences.

(3) The *Mahabharata* refers to trees as life-bearing objects that can experience all the different emotions (pleasure, sorrow, awe, etc.) that humans do. According to Hindu physical theory, the human body is made from *pancha mahabhoota*, or five great elements – *prithvi* (earth), *jal* (water), *tej* (fire), *vayu* (air) and *akash* (aether) – and upon death the human body dissolves into these five elements of nature, thus balancing the cycle of nature. The *Yajurveda*, therefore, has emphasized the *puja* of all these five elements for life and for peace.

(4) There are several examples of guiding principles of peace in Hindu scriptures. For example, the *Yejurveda* notes 'One who sees all the creatures as if they were his own selves and himself in others – his mind rests in peace' (cited in Upadhyaya, 2010). A

celebrated piece from *Atharvaveda* also invokes that 'Peace to earth and airy spaces! Peace to the heaven, peace to the heaven, peace to the plant and peace to the tree' (cited in Upadhyaya, 2010). Upadhyaya (2010) comments that such collective Hindu thought offers a 'holistic' vision of peace in which the human community, ecology and planetary concerns are tied in a mutually enriching manner.

References

Ashok, H.S. and Thimmappa, M.S. (2006) A Hindu worldview of adult learning in the workplace. *Advances in Developing Human Resources* 8 (3), 329–336.

Bai, E.R. (1996) The pattern of education in Dharmasutra texts. In V.V. Bedekar (ed.) *Education in Ancient India: Shri S.B. Velankar Facilitation Volume* (pp. 56–69). Thane, India: Itihas Patrika Prakashan.

Brown, H.D. (1994) *Teaching by Principles: An Interactive Approach to Language Pedagogy*. White Plains, NY: Pearson Longman.

Canagarajah, A.S. (1999) *Resisting Linguistic Imperialism in English Teaching*. Oxford: Oxford University Press.

Canagarajah, S. (2009) Introduction: New possibilities for the spiritual and the critical in pedagogy. In M.S. Wong and S. Canagarajah (eds) *Christian and Critical English Language Educators in Dialogue: Pedagogical and Ethical Dilemmas* (pp. 1–18). New York and Abingdon: Routledge.

Devi, S.S. and Pillai, K.N.M. (2012) Genesis and evolution of education in ancient India. *PRAGATI Quarterly Research Journal*, 14–34.

Dharampal, A. (1983) *The Beautiful Tree: Indigenous Indian Education in the Eighteenth Century*. New Delhi: Biblia Impex Private Limited.

Emeneau, M.B. (1955) India and linguistics. *Journal of the American Oriental Society*, 75, 143–153.

Freire, P. (1972) *Pedagogy of the Oppressed*. New York: Herder & Herder.

Gao, X. (2006) Teachers' professional vulnerability and cultural tradition: A Chinese paradox. *Teaching and Teacher Education* 24, 154–165.

Ghosh, S.C. (2007) *History of Education in India*. New Delhi: Rawat Publications.

Henning, J.E. (2008) *The Art of Discussion-based Teaching: Opening Up Conversation in the Classroom*. New York: Taylor & Francis.

Hough, D.A., Thapa Magar, R.B. and Yonjan-Tamang, A. (2009) Privileging indigenous knowledge: Empowering multilingual education in Nepal. In T. Skutnabb-Kangas, R. Phillipson, A.K. Mohanty and P. Minati (eds) *Social Justice through Multilingual Education* (pp. 159–176). Bristol: Multilingual Matters.

Kubota, R. (1999) Comments on Ryuko Kubota's 'Japanese culture constructed by discourses: Implications for applied linguistics research and ELT': The author responds. *TESOL Quarterly* 33, 745–749.

Kumaravadivelu, B. (2003) Problematizing cultural stereotypes in TESOL. *TESOL Quarterly* 37, 709–719.

Lave, J. and Wegner, E. (1991) *Situated Learning: Legitimate Peripheral Participation*. Cambridge: Cambridge University Press.

Mahalakshmi, G.S. and Geetha, T.V. (2009) Argument-based learning communities. *Knowledge-based Systems* 22, 316–323.

Malhotra, R. (2014) *The Position of Hinduism in America's Higher Education*. Princeton, NJ: Infinity Foundation. See http://www.infinityfoundation.com/mandala/s_es/s_es_malho_h_edu_frameset.htm. Accessed 1 April 2018.

Matilal, B.M. and Chakrabarti, A. (eds) (1994) Introduction. In B.M. Matilal and A. Chakrabarti (eds) *Knowing from Words: Western and Indian Philosophical Analysis of Understanding and Testimony* (pp. 1–22). Boston, MA: Kluwer.

Mishra, S.K. (1998) *Educational Ideas and Institutions in Ancient India (From the Earliest Times to 1206 AD with Special Reference to Mithila)*. New Delhi: Ramanand Vidya Bhawan.

Monk, A.H. (1968) *What every Hindu ought to Know*. Bangalore, India: Sahitya Sindhu

Narain, S. (1993) *Examinations in Ancient India*. New Delhi: Arya Book Depot.

Pennycook, A.D. (1989) The concept of method, interested knowledge, and the politics of language teaching. *TESOL Quarterly* 23 (4), 589–618.

Reagan, T. (2005) *Non-Western Educational Traditions: Indigenous Approaches to Educational Thought and Practice* (3rd edn). Hillsdale, NJ: Lawrence Erlbaum.

Sharma, B.K. (2013) Hinduism and TESOL: Learning, teaching and student-teacher relationships revisited. *Language and Linguistics Compass*, 7 (2), 79–90.

Sheshagiri, K.M. (2011) A cultural view of education in Hindu civilization. In Y. Zhao, J. Lei, G. Li, M.F. He, K. Okano, N. Megahed, D. Gamage and H. Ramanathan (eds) *Handbook of Asian Education: A Cultural Perspective* (pp. 529–547). New York: Routledge.

Shin, H. and Crookes, G. (2005) Exploring the possibilities for EFL critical pedagogy in Korea: A two-part case study. *Critical Inquiry in Second Language Studies: An International Journal* 2 (2), 113–136.

Spivak, G.C. (1988) *Can the Subaltern Speak?* Basingstoke: Macmillian.

Thaker, S.N. (2007) Hinduism and learning. In S.B. Marriam and Associates (eds) *Non-Western Perspectives on Learning and Knowing* (pp. 57–74). Malabar, FL: Krieger.

Upadhyaya, P. (2010) Hinduism and peace education. In E.J. Brantmeier, J. Lin and J.P. Miller (eds) *Spirituality, Religion, and Peace Education* (pp. 99–113). Charlotte, NC: Information Age.

Wong, M.S. and Canagarajah, S. (eds) (2009) *Christian and Critical English Language Educators in Dialogue: Pedagogical and Ethical Dilemmas*. New York: Routledge.

Woodruff, P. (2001) *Reverence: Renewing a Forgotten Virtue*. New York: Oxford University Press.

8 Multiple, Complex and Fluid Religious and Spiritual Influences on English Language Educators

Stephanie Vandrick

Introduction

Some second language (L2) educators/scholars are affiliated with a certain religion, whereas others do not subscribe to a particular religion but are strongly influenced in their lives and work by one or more religions or spiritual traditions, and believe that one can be spiritual and ethical without membership in a specific religion. These latter may identify as atheists, agnostics and/or humanists. They may have been shaped by the religions of their parents and by other religions, and may have developed their own spiritual and ethical identities. Even some of those who do affiliate with specific religions are also greatly influenced by other religions. Many English language teaching (ELT)/teachers of English to speakers of other languages (TESOL) educators/scholars, like many academics in other disciplines, are critical of certain aspects of religion. At the same time, because of their own teaching in various countries and/or their teaching of students from various cultures other than their own, they are perhaps even more likely than other academics to be exposed to and interested in various religious and spiritual traditions around the world.

Yet, as Bradley (2009) points out, the scant publications on spirituality and ELT are mainly about 'the raging debate on possible connections between Christian missionary activities in English teaching and imperialism', and very little research 'exists on the spiritual beliefs and classroom practices of L2 educators adhering to a variety of belief systems' (Bradley, 2009: 236). In fact, many ELT educators have a complicated relationship with religion and spirituality; this chapter explores such multiple, complex, fluid and evolving identities regarding religion and spirituality. It offers as examples, along with some context and stories from the discipline's literature, my own story and those of others in the field of ELT, of being formed by their experiences with multiple religious influences.

Here I offer three foundational assertions regarding the religious and spiritual identifications and influences of TESOL scholars. My first assertion is that English language educators can be greatly influenced by religion without subscribing to a specific religion, or without limiting themselves to one specific religion. Academics are often open to ambiguities, to overlaps, in religion and spirituality as with other topics, so it is not surprising that they are able to tolerate and even prefer states of uncertainty and to feel comfortable with undefined statuses. My second foundational assertion is that ELT educators can be spiritual without necessarily being religious. My third assertion is that those in our field of language education can be ethical without necessarily being religious. I believe that these three assertions hold true both in educators' personal lives and in their academic work and pedagogies. After a brief overview of the current context of religion in society, and then of its role in the field of ELT specifically, I will address the three assertions with support from quotes from ELT and applied linguistics educators.

Current Context of Religion in the Larger Society

In today's small world, more than ever, there is a mixing of religions and spiritual traditions. In the United States, for example, there are adherents to Native American spiritual traditions, Christianity, Judaism, Islam, Buddhism, Hinduism, Bahá'í, Wicca and more. I do not claim that these religions live together in perfect harmony, as too many incidents of discrimination and even violence belie that claim. The most obvious examples of such discrimination and violence in recent years have been against Muslims; unfortunately, Islamophobia has increased in the current environment. But for the most part, most of the time, the religions co-exist reasonably peacefully.

In the United States many people are actually more tolerant of different religions than of someone having no official religion. Although there is supposed to be separation of church and state in the United States, many feel it is essentially a Christian country. However, if someone is not Christian, but is affiliated with Judaism, Islam or another religion, this is widely considered to be better than being without any religion; sociologists Edgell, Gerteis and Hartmann, for example, state that 'increasing acceptance of religious diversity does not extend to the nonreligious' (Edgell *et al.*, 2006: 211). People who openly state that they are agnostic or atheist are stigmatized. It would be a political death wish, for example, for a person running for office to state that she or he is atheist. I believe that many Americans are in fact atheists or agnostics, but think of themselves as culturally Christian (or culturally Jewish, or culturally some other religion), and would never use the word atheist about themselves, or at least not publicly. Perhaps only academics, prominent intellectuals, journalists and such can be open about not affiliating with a religion. In their cases, they often actively question and express concerns about the effects of religion, because of the harm that religion itself, and religious strife, have often done throughout history. Or they may find that they cannot reconcile to their satisfaction the seeming conflict, in at least some cases, between faith and science. There have been several examples of non-religious intellectuals and writers producing books and other publications in the past ten years or so, to the point that some of them have been called the 'New Atheists' (e.g. Dawkins, 2006; Harris, 2005; Hitchens, 2009; Stenger, 2008).

But there are also literary and academic figures who, while declaring that they are non-believers, acknowledge that there is something more in the world than the tangible, the physical – that there is some kind of spirit or transcendence. The noted progressive writer Barbara Ehrenreich, for example, has recently published a memoir (*Living with a Wild God*, 2014) in which she describes an overwhelming, non-explainable experience, during her adolescence, of something transcendent, a kind of flame of life blazing at her. She calls herself a rationalist and an atheist, but struggles with what the experience meant. The late writer Peter Matthiessen, in his last novel, *In Paradise*, writes of a group of people visiting one of the camps of the Holocaust, who in the midst of their sadness experience 'a moment of beatitude' (Parks, 2014); one man 'feels filled with well-being, blessed, whatever "blessed" might mean to a lifelong non-believer' (quoted in Parks, 2014: 39).

Current Context of Religion in the Field of English Language Teaching

Only in the past few years have ELT educators and scholars spoken and written publicly (outside of Christian conferences and publications, of which there are many, but these are not well known to the wider TESOL professional community) about their religious beliefs and how these have influenced their teaching. The most prominent of these educators have been associated with Mary Shepard Wong, the co-editor of this book, who has also co-edited two earlier books about the overall topic (Wong & Canagarajah, 2009; Wong *et al.*, 2013), books that allowed both Christians and non-Christians to engage in dialogue. Other examples include Smith and Osborn's (2007) edited book on 'spirituality, social justice, and language learning', and Bradley's (2011) dissertation on the role of religion and spirituality in ELT pedagogy, which focuses on his own experiences and on interviews with 'nine language teachers of varying creeds (or who professed no overt spirituality)' about their 'spiritual journeys' (Bradley, 2011: iii).

It has been even rarer for non-religious educators to write specifically about their agnostic or atheist statuses. It is understandable that many, perhaps most, educators feel that their own religions or, perhaps even more, their lack thereof, are irrelevant to their teaching and scholarship. Perhaps this is true, but one's identities often find ways of influencing one's work, consciously or unconsciously. It would be hard to assert that our gender, race, social class, sexual identity, ability/disability, age and other identities do not influence our work, or that they do not influence the way we relate to others and the way others perceive us, so it seems reasonable to believe that the same is true for our religious or spiritual identities.

One ELT scholar who does write about her own experiences with religion, despite being non-religious herself, is Ushioda (2013). She states that she is 'not an adherent of the Christian faith or indeed of any religious faith' but also 'appreciate[s] the tremendous cultural value and heritage of the world's great religions, such as Christianity' (Ushioda, 2013: 223). Ushioda was exposed to Christianity through her primary and secondary education (Ushioda, 2013: 223). She sees herself as 'essentially agnostic' (Ushioda, 2013: 223). She also feels that her Christian education directly led to her interest in languages and eventually her career in (English) language education.

I too have written of beliefs and feelings similar to Ushioda's (Vandrick, 1999). And in my own classes I have occasionally been a bit taken aback and unsettled by being asked by students about my religion. Knowing how important religion is to many of them but wanting to be honest, I have usually responded by saying that I am not a practicing member of any religion, but that I grew up Christian and am influenced by that upbringing as well as by my knowledge of and connections with other religious traditions.

This new openness, limited as it is, has not been without contentious issues and discussion. In the world of ELT/TESOL scholarship there is controversy about the influences of religion on the field. Some of the leading scholars and teachers in the field over the years have been believers, usually of Christianity; those who are open about their beliefs include H. Douglas Brown, A. Suresh Canagarajah, Dana Ferris, Thomas Scovel, Don Snow and the late Earl Stevick. Some of these have at the same time been proponents of critical pedagogy and have been advocates for certain social causes. However, some other scholars have criticized Western English language teachers who get visas to go to another country to teach, but at the same time do covert missionary work on behalf of Christianity (Edge, 1996, 1997, 2003; Pennycook & Coutand-Marin, 2003; Vandrick, 2009a; Varghese & Johnston, 2007). Further, some scholars have felt that spreading English throughout the world, even without an explicitly Christian focus, is a kind of imperialist spreading of Western and Christian values and culture (e.g. Phillipson, 1992). But I must also point out that many non-religious people, including ELT educators such as myself (Vandrick, 1999, writing about my parents' contributions through their missionary work in medicine, education and other areas), also recognize the many good things that religion has done in at least some settings, such as providing education, building community and helping those in need. One example of critical ELT educators pointing out some of these good influences is a chapter by Makoni and Makoni (2009) which reminds us that some Christian missionaries in Africa were instrumental in helping to preserve some of the local languages.

With the above contexts in mind, I now focus on the three foundational assertions mentioned earlier.

Assertion 1: Influences of Spirituality on English Language Teaching Regardless of Religious Identification

Regarding the first assertion, that English language educators can be greatly influenced by religion without necessarily subscribing to a specific religion, I first offer my own story, and then those of other educators who have responded to my questions about their spiritual identifications and influences.

My spiritual journey

I share my own story as an example of someone who is not religious, but who is strongly influenced by experiences with religion and is, I like to believe, spiritual and ethical. I have written elsewhere (Vandrick, 1999, 2009b, 2013) about the huge formative influence on my life of being raised not only in a Christian family, but also more specifically as the child of Christian missionaries in India. I spent most of my childhood and early teenage years with that identity. I was steeped in Bible stories and Christian values. At the same time, while living in India, I was able to observe and learn about Hinduism and to a lesser degree Buddhism. But then when I went to college in the United States I rather quickly and easily abandoned my childhood religious beliefs and affiliation. However, I was still fascinated by religion, spirituality and philosophy, and took several classes in these areas. An especially meaningful combination of classes took place during the semester when I took one class in Buddhism and another in Existentialism, and wrote a paper comparing the two for the philosophy class. Later, when I started teaching English, I met students of various religious backgrounds and learned much from them. A few years later, in a Bahá'í ceremony, I married a Bahá'í who is practicing up to a point, but who seldom participates in activities with the Bahá'í community; I have been somewhat influenced by this religion but I have never converted or considered myself affiliated with it. I have also been influenced by the social justice mission of the Jesuit university where I have taught for most of my career, the University of San Francisco (Vandrick, 2009b). Over the years I have sometimes felt a certain longing for a religious community and practice and have explored various possibilities, but I did not feel truly connected to any of them. I didn't, and don't, have the faith required. And in most cases I also objected, and still object, to such aspects of the religion as beliefs about and their treatment of women. Yet I have been affected by all the religious and spiritual influences I have just described. And as I get older I have realized that I cannot separate out my religious background from my identity today. For example, I have written about my reflections on the connections between being raised as the child of missionaries and my choice of a career in TESOL (Vandrick, 1999, 2009b, 2013). So I consider that despite my lack of affiliation with any religion, I am influenced by all I have learned from the various religions I have been exposed to.

These influences affect my scholarship and my teaching. My scholarship has been almost entirely focused on social issues affecting the world of ELT, such as injustices related to gender, social class, race and sexual identity. There is definitely an element of advocacy in my publications. My teaching is deeply influenced by critical and feminist pedagogies. I teach my students to be critical in their reading and thinking; I also try to empower them or, more exactly, to help them empower themselves. Ways to do this include choice of readings, giving students a voice in the classroom, encouraging open discussion about important topics and making sure that I respect their views and that they respect those of their classmates. Perhaps most of all, I believe in viewing and respecting my students not just in their roles as students, but as whole persons, each of whom has her or his own history, culture, beliefs, strengths, talents, issues, problems, worries and individual circumstances.

My colleagues' spiritual journeys

Throughout the more than three decades that I have been teaching, I have read and heard stories about those in our discipline who have also been influenced by various religious and spiritual traditions, and these stories have influenced me and have influenced my writing of this chapter. To follow up on that background, I recently corresponded by email with several TESOL/applied linguistics scholars/educators whom I know through various professional connections and networks, and gathered stories of their religious identifications and influences. These colleagues were generous in sharing their thoughts and experiences about this important but often somewhat private topic. These colleagues around the United States and in other countries are, to me, examples of those who are both spiritual and ethical, but not necessarily because of specific religious affiliations. I do not identify these scholars by name; as this is a personal matter, I promised them confidentiality if I shared their stories.[1]

Complex and critical stances towards their own religious views

Scholars in this group who do identify with a specific religion often offer caveats and variations. In some cases these arise from their serious concerns about and critiques of their religions' histories and stances on social issues. One such longtime scholar/educator who is affiliated with a Christian Protestant church states that:

> I identify as Christian, but the identity issues are very complex as I am clearly a Marxist ... (like Paolo Freire) and often find that I have more in common with those who are not practicing Christians and members of other faiths. ... Christianity has too often been associated with imperialism, colonialism and racism. ... I find that I have moved from my [name of denomination] upbringing to a more inter-faith orientation. ...

Another scholar who identifies with Christianity but is influenced by other religious traditions says that she is Roman Catholic and married to a Buddhist, 'and my family draws spiritual inspiration and nourishment from and participates in formal rituals of both of these religions'. Like the first scholar above, she does not accept her religion's tenets and practices uncritically: 'I take issue with many interpretations and practices associated with Catholicism, I resist its gender divisions, and I deplore the historical role that the religion has played in bringing together English teaching and colonialism and consequently racism.'

A third scholar who is a member of a Catholic church, but describes herself as spiritual rather than religious, shares some of the same concerns as the first two. She says:

> I have never accepted the concept of the infallibility of the pope, the exclusion of women from the priesthood, nor the church's stance regarding women's rights. I have always questioned what has been done in the name of religion, catholic or otherwise, particularly involvement in the Trans-Atlantic slave trade and the genocide of indigenous peoples and cultures across every continent.

These statements demonstrate the ambivalences of these writers, and actually those of almost all the writers who responded to my questions, along with their attempts at balancing their religious beliefs with their concerns about some of the principles and practices of their religious institutions. These ongoing attempts to reconcile or at least live with contradictions often influence these educators' attitudes and practices in their teaching and writing; education, after all, is also a site of balancing various principles and practices.

Shifting, fluid and hybrid relationships with religions

The stories of scholars who are not affiliated with certain religions generally involve having been brought up in a certain religion but then leaving it as they grew into adulthood. This leaving was often a process of shift, of fluidity, rather than a sudden, dramatic departure. It also was generally not a simple matter of leaving a religion and then having no religion; it sometimes evolved into beliefs and practices that formed a sort of hybrid of various religions and spiritual influences. And as the process affected these educators' lives, it often affected their professional work, especially their teaching, as well.

Two people's responses particularly illustrate this aspect of a gradual shift, a process. One person writes that she was raised in the Episcopal (Christian) Church, and very much disliked going to church every Sunday. Her parents did not discuss religion or spirituality with her and her sister. Although she left the church when she was 18, she had wanted to do so for years before.

> I couldn't wait until I turned 18 and from that year, never went to church again. I came to see the characters in the Bible as possible once-living figures around whom wonderful stories had been constructed, but did not find myself interested in the stories, or concerned at all about heaven and hell.

She goes on to say that her sister later converted to Judaism, and she herself married and later amicably divorced a non-practicing Muslim. She states, 'I see the world's religions as one of the sources of the world's greatest conflicts and intolerance, in spite of all the exceptions'. She, like others who have left their childhood religions behind, has done so partly because of observing the wars and other instances of problems brought about by religion, and by warring religions. Unfortunately, in some cases, this strong concern partially or completely blinds people to the good that religion does, and to the fact that many believers, perhaps a large majority, do not participate in or support these negative aspects of religion as it is practiced. Although this particular educator is very open to people of all religions among her students and others, some educators could be unduly influenced by their negative feelings about religion, just as some may be unduly influenced by their own beliefs in religion; it is important that educators be very aware of their own feelings and of how they might impact their pedagogy and their interactions with students and colleagues.

Another person demonstrated a very long, slow process of shift regarding leaving his religion, with some movement back and forth along the way. He grew up with and then eventually left the Episcopal church, which he attended with his family. He even taught Sunday school classes. When he went to college he stopped going to church for about 20 years. Interestingly, though, he returned to Christianity and the Episcopal church for a period of time after that, during a troubled time in his life; in this case, he sought out and attended 'an extremely progressive church active in many political causes'. Gradually he stopped attending that church, or any church. One of the reasons for his disillusionment with religion, specifically Christianity, was his 'encounters with evangelical Christians' which provoked 'extremely negative ... emotions in me'. He remembered that as he was growing up, the religious people he knew were 'very tolerant of others' beliefs, generally', so he was dismayed by evangelical Christians he met who said that everyone had to believe as they did. Again, this educator is very open and encouraging to all his students and colleagues, but other less open educators could negatively impact students if they let their strong feelings about religion prejudice them, consciously or – more likely – unconsciously, against certain students or others they encounter in academic and other venues. On the other hand, the years of thinking and reading about the topic of religion that these educators have done leads to more awareness, more understanding and more openness in interacting with students of various backgrounds, religious and otherwise.

Some respondents recounted their relationships with the religions, or religious traditions, that they grew up with, not so much as a leave taking as a willingness to absorb and be influenced by different religious traditions as well. In effect, they have constructed their own hybrid 'religions' or belief systems from elements of various religions. For example, one person tells of her progression through several religions. She was brought up in one religion (folk ancestor worship), converted to a second one (Christianity) in high school 'due to peer influences', then to a third (Buddhism), which she felt 'that [she] could get more peace from', and now does not 'strictly follow any particular persuasion' but is 'inclined [towards] reading and learning more about Zen Buddhist thoughts'. These experiences and phases in this person's beliefs may well help her to be very accepting of the beliefs of others she encounters in the classroom and elsewhere.

As discussed above, these quotations demonstrate both the fluidity and the mixed, hybrid nature of many ELT educators' beliefs. This is perhaps not surprising considering that the field of ELT involves much contact among various cultural and religious backgrounds. Educators themselves travel, live and teach in various countries, have students from various countries and backgrounds, and teach and write about global issues and settings. Whether or not their own religious beliefs change, or combine in new configurations, they certainly are almost forced to at least become familiar with different beliefs and to respect the variety of beliefs in the world and among their colleagues and students; this in turn influences their teaching, research and service.

Assertion 2: Being Spiritual without Necessarily Being Religious

A sense of peace, transcendence and connection

Spirituality can be defined as 'the eternal human yearning to be connected with something larger than our own egos' (Palmer, 2003, as quoted in Bradley, 2009). As can be seen from some of the examples above, it is very possible for scholars to feel that they experience spirituality in their lives, whether or not they are affiliated with a specific religion. Sometimes, for those originally (and in some cases still) from Christian or Jewish traditions, this sense of spirituality is found through, as one scholar put it above, 'meditation and yoga in the Buddhist and Hindu traditions'. Others too mention their gaining spiritual sustenance through Buddhism, including Zen Buddhism. One person says that 'it seems like a lot of what is happening to me right now comes out of the Hindu tradition' despite her not knowing a lot about that religion, and further states that, as mentioned above, some of her experiences with that religion have been 'the most powerful spiritual experiences of my life'. Other spiritual influences include relatives, art and nature. One person spoke of her mother as her 'spiritual guide' who 'showed me how to live', and also said that 'from an early age I sought calm, peace, and tranquility'. Another person spoke of being inspired spiritually by the art in Catholic churches in Italy. Regarding nature, one person wrote of how spiritually renewing springtime is, with its flowers, trees, breezes and the pleasures of planting gardens; she says that at such a time, 'you know that some awesome indescribable power is at work in the universe'. Another said that although she does not 'refer to [herself] as a spiritual person, [she has] long found [herself] fascinated and awed by patterns in nature (leaves, flowers, insect and animal parts, crystals, atoms and molecules ...'. A person who called herself a secular Jew, who has pursued social justice goals in her own teaching and writing, also addresses the spiritual side: 'Recently I've explored spirituality through meditation and yoga in the Buddhist and Hindu traditions. This crossover is not uncommon among progressive Jews.' Similarly, another person was brought up as culturally Buddhist and Shinto but also attended some Christian schools; this person regarded both religions more as cultural influences than as religions whose doctrines she believed and followed.

In all of these cases, the scholars capture a feeling that there is something transcendent in our lives, something beyond the mere physical facts of life, and they experience this through religion, through philosophy, through other human beings, through art and through nature. This openness, this positivity, this sense of transcendence affects the teaching life of these educators, as they commit themselves day in, day out, year in, year out, to caring for their students not only regarding their education but regarding their wellbeing in a much wider sense.

Therapeutic aspects of spirituality

Another aspect of various influences on some scholars' spiritual beliefs and practices is the therapeutic or self-help part of certain types of religious practices. One person, who was raised by atheist parents and later had issues with addictions, started to practice meditation and later yoga with a teacher from the Hindu tradition; she went on to do work with energy through chakras, and found that it was effective in greatly reducing pain, both physical and emotional. These experiences were, for this person, extremely powerful spiritually, and in turn helped her to be a better educator. Like this person, the person who had Buddhist, Shinto and Christian cultural influences in her life now states that her 'current spiritual identification and influence is a form of Buddhism', which helped her when she had a difficult professional challenge, and 'taught me non-attachment and positive thinking'. In particular, educators who teach for many years, often in difficult circumstances, need to find ways to maintain and renew their dedication to teaching. Those who attend to their own spiritual needs are much less likely to become cynical or to burn out, which obviously impacts their students and their institutions as well.

Assertion 3: Being Ethical, without Necessarily Being Religious: A Social Justice Mission

Whether or not they focus on the issue of religion, educators have written extensively about ethics in education and related areas (for example, among many, Card, 1991; College Composition and Communication, 2001; Noddings, 1984; Nussbaum, 1999). In the case of ELT educators, there is often a strong commitment to ethics, values and morality in education (Bierling, 2007; Buzzelli & Johnston, 2002; Johnston, 2003; Johnston *et al.*, 1998; Silva, 1997). It seems to me that this is where we can observe the influences of religious traditions at their best. This can be seen in what my correspondents wrote about religious influences on their pedagogy, research and service, academic and otherwise, whether they themselves are religious or not. This particularly comes out as a strong shared belief in social justice (Hafernik *et al.*, 2002; Smith & Osborn, 2007); it is this belief that most profoundly influences and motivates these language educators' teaching. There is a focus in these educators' lives on bettering the lives of their students, as well as on advocating for, and working for, causes related to social and political issues. In the case of ELT, these causes include language rights, racial and gender inequalities, economic inequality, rights of undocumented children to education and many more. Some of this can be seen in the quotations I have already included. Others that demonstrate these focuses are as follows. One scholar writes that:

> I was raised as a secular Jew, which means we were atheists, but identified as culturally Jewish. We celebrated certain Jewish holidays, such as Passover, but above all, we were committed to social justice: civil rights and anti-war. Because of how Jews have been treated throughout history, we felt an obligation to step in when others' rights were trampled on, not just Jews' but [those of] anyone who was oppressed. We were taught not to settle in comfortably to our own privilege as whites and middle-class professionals.

This person says that a consequence of her upbringing regarding social justice was that 'vigilance about oppression was a deeply felt commitment, one that has influenced my teaching'. This person is too modest to say so herself, but much of her teaching and her scholarship is focused on critical pedagogy, and she has often helped students to analyze situations in which they are oppressed, and has helped to empower them to resist the oppression or to find positive and effective strategies to deal with it. Another person says:

> I constantly have to remind myself of why I am on the face of the earth and what my mission is. The most important indicator of my success as a teacher educator is the quality and strength of the teachers and teacher educators that I help to produce at the end of the day – these people who will go into schools and universities and make a difference for the boys and girls and teachers that they teach. My service, teaching, research and publications must speak to this mission.

Another educator/scholar writes as follows:

> During my childhood I was shaped by my parents' commitment to service and deep concerns about social justice, poverty, peace and equity, all of which were presented to me as deriving from their Catholicism. Today, both Buddhism and Catholicism impel me to fight against root causes of poverty and various forms of social and economic inequality, help me to separate English (often a symbol of wealth and opportunity) from ideologies of capitalism and greed, and make me feel responsible for working to change an inequitable global status quo. Both religions offer me philosophical ideals that I aspire to incorporate into my research and pedagogy, including non-judgmentalism, compassion, advocacy, gratitude, mindfulness and acceptance.

To illustrate more specifically how a commitment to social justice influences her pedagogy, one correspondent sums up her social justice emphasis as follows: 'The main way in which my spiritual beliefs about social justice and compassion translate into teaching is through the texts I choose and the pedagogy itself.' She goes on to give an example of a lesson in which she asks her English language learners to read a certain newspaper article that, she says:

> shatters the myth that English is required for financial success, so it has the potential to engage students in questions about the relationship between English and work in our globalized world. These are immigrant students who are constantly judged and tested for proficiency standards that are often unrealistic, given the poor education they received in urban US schools and the immigrant communities in which they live, where languages other than English are the medium of commerce and social relationships.

She has the students write response papers, which become the basis for class discussions about the issues.

Another educator, in language which is neither specifically spiritual nor specifically academic, but which spiritedly sums up the social justice focus of these educators, says that she has had 'a lifelong tendency to root for the underdog'. She goes on to explain how this applies in her pedagogy: 'This has led me to provide encouragement to struggling students, perhaps after others might have given up on them. In my work with doctoral students writing dissertations, this has been difficult at times', because of their various personal and other problems. But, she says, 'If such students seem to have the tenacity to continue' despite their problems, 'I try to support them'.

Sometimes practicing social justice in one's pedagogy has negative consequences for the educator. For example, one teacher educator has been faced with situations where she has been asked by administrators to change the grade given by a colleague who had left the university, or where her own grades were questioned as being too low. In these cases she has stood her ground because of her religious and ethical beliefs, but she was then cast by her supervisors in the role of someone who was uncooperative. On a related issue, she writes that 'as an academic, being a Christian and Catholic is the greatest challenge of my life'; her religion asks her to be humble, yet academe asks her to be competitive, to brag about accomplishments and to seek power. Her service to others is not always what is rewarded in academe, but such service is her highest goal. Other educators who have practiced social justice through their choice of controversial topics and readings have experienced resistance and sometimes negative evaluations from students.

Conclusion

As this chapter, and the stories of English language scholars and educators, illustrate, one's religious and/or spiritual identification is not a simple matter. Whether one affiliates with one specific religion, whether one affiliates with a religion mainly culturally or whether one affiliates with no religion, almost everyone is influenced by multiple religions and spiritual traditions. One's identification may be hard to classify and may shift with time. Further, one's spirituality and ethics are perhaps influenced by, but may be independent of, one's religion or lack thereof. A notable place of commonality among English language scholars – whatever their specific religious or spiritual history or affiliation – is, as mentioned above, their commitment to social justice. As one of the scholars I corresponded with put it:

> If we could bring the spiritualities of all faiths and non-faiths to academe, imagine what beautiful music we could create in building the potential of all stakeholders in an environment rich in compassion, collaborative community-building support, mutual respect and love.

Acknowledgments

I want to express my deep gratitude to the ten ELT/TESOL/applied linguistics colleagues from around the country and the world who generously shared their own stories and feelings about their religious, spiritual and ethical identifications and experiences, and about how they were influenced by these.

Notes

(1) To provide more detailed information regarding my data gathering and methodology: On one day in early 2014, I sent out an email to 14 colleagues at various universities, mostly but not all in the United States. I described the chapter I was writing for this book, and asked them if they could briefly and informally share any personal ideas, feelings and experiences regarding their own 'religious/spiritual identifications and influences'. I said that I might quote them in this chapter, but promised them confidentiality. Ten of these scholars/educators replied, five within two days and the other five within a week; some wrote briefly and some at great length. I mention the quick responses and the length to indicate that these correspondents seemed almost eager to respond and share their experiences and thoughts on the topic; I am very grateful for their generosity and openness. I have quoted from all ten of these participants.

References

Bierling, M.R. (2007) Legal and illegal immigration: Complex ethical issues for the language classroom. In D.I. Smith and T.A. Osborn (eds) *Spirituality, Social Justice, and Language Learning* (pp. 89–105). Charlotte, NC: Information Age.

Bradley, C.A. (2009) Spiritual lessons learned from a language teacher. In M.S. Wong and S. Canagarajah (eds) *Christian and Critical English Language Educators in Dialogue: Pedagogical and Ethical Dilemmas* (pp. 235–241). New York: Routledge.

Bradley, C.A. (2011) An inquiry into relationships between spirituality and language pedagogy. Unpublished doctoral dissertation, Temple University.

Buzzelli, C.A. and Johnston, B. (2002) *The Moral Dimensions of Teaching: Language, Power, and Culture in Classroom Interaction*. New York: Routledge.

Card, C. (ed.) (1991) *Feminist Ethics*. Lawrence, KS: University Press of Kansas.

College Composition and Communication (2001) Guidelines for the ethical treatment of students and student writing in composition studies. *College Composition and Communication* 53, 485–490.

Dawkins, R. (2006) *The God Delusion*. Boston, MA: Houghton Mifflin Harcourt.

Edge, J. (1996) Keeping the faith. *TESOL Matters* 6 (4), 1, 23.

Edge, J. (1997) Julian Edge responds. *TESOL Matters* 6 (6), 6.

Edge, J. (2003) Imperial troopers and servants of the Lord: A vision of TESOL for the 21st century. *TESOL Quarterly* 37 (4), 701–709.

Edgell, P., Gerteis, J. and Hartmann, D. (2006) Atheists as 'other': Moral boundaries and cultural membership in American society. *American Sociological Review* 71 (2), 211–234.

Ehrenreich, B. (2014) *Living with a Wild God*. New York: Twelve.

Hafernik, J.J., Messerschmitt, D. and Vandrick, S. (2002) *Ethical Issues for ESL Faculty: Social Justice in Practice*. Mahwah, NJ: Lawrence Erlbaum.

Harris, S. (2005) *The End of Faith: Religion, Terror, and the Future of Reason*. New York: W.W. Norton.

Hitchens, C. (2009) *God is Not Great: How Religion Poisons Everything*. New York: Twelve.

Johnston, B. (2003) *Values in English Language Teaching*. Mahwah, NJ: Lawrence Erlbaum.

Johnston, B., Juhász, A., Marken, J. and Ruiz, B.R. (1998) The ESL teacher as moral agent. *Research in the Teaching of English* 32, 161–181.

Makoni, S. and Makoni, B. (2009) English and education in Anglophone Africa: Historical and current realities. In M.S. Wong and S. Canagarajah (eds) *Christian and Critical English Language Educators in Dialogue: Pedagogical and Ethical Dilemmas* (pp. 106–119). New York: Routledge.

Noddings, N. (1984) *Caring: A Feminine Approach to Ethics and Moral Education*. Berkeley, CA: University of California Press.

Nussbaum, M.C. (1999) *Sex and Social Justice*. New York: Oxford University Press.

Parks, T. (2014) 'The ultimate koan' [Review of the book, *In Paradise*]. *New York Review* 61 (6), 37–39.

Pennycook, A. and Coutand-Marin, S. (2003) Teaching English as a missionary language (TEML). *Discourse: Studies in the Cultural Politics of Education* 24 (3), 337–353.

Phillipson, R. (1992) *Linguistic Imperialism*. Oxford: Oxford University Press.

Silva, T. (1997) On the ethical treatment of ESL writers. *TESOL Quarterly* 31 (2), 359–363.

Smith, D.I. and Osborn, T.A. (eds) (2007) *Spirituality, Social Justice, and Language Learning*. Charlotte, NC: Information Age.

Stenger, V.J. (2008) *God: The Failed Hypothesis*. New York: Prometheus.

Ushioda, E. (2013) Christian faith, motivation, and learning: Personal, social, and research perspective. In M.S. Wong, C. Kristjánsson and Z. Dörnyei (eds) *Christian Faith and English Language Teaching and Learning: Research on the Interrelationship of Religion and ELT* (pp. 223–229). New York: Routledge.

Vandrick, S. (1999) ESL and the colonial legacy: A teacher faces her 'missionary kid' past. In G. Haroian-Guerin (ed.) *The Personal Narrative: Writing Ourselves as Teachers and Scholars* (pp. 63–74). Portland, ME: Calendar Islands.

Vandrick, S. (2009a) A former 'missionary kid' responds. In M.S. Wong and S. Canagarajah (eds) *Christian and Critical English Language Educators in Dialogue: Pedagogical and Ethical Dilemmas* (pp. 141–149). New York: Routledge.

Vandrick, S. (2009b) *Interrogating Privilege: Reflections of a Second Language Educator*. Ann Arbor, MI: University of Michigan Press.

Vandrick, S. (2013) The 'colonial legacy' and 'missionary kid' memoirs. In G. Barkhuizen (ed.) *Narrative Research in Applied Linguistics* (pp. 19–40). Cambridge: Cambridge University Press.

Varghese, M. and Johnston, B. (2007) Evangelical Christians and English language teaching. *TESOL Quarterly* 41 (1), 5–31.

Wong, M.S. and Canagarajah, S. (eds) (2009) *Christian and Critical English Language Educators in Dialogue: Pedagogical and Ethical Dilemmas*. New York: Routledge.

Wong, M.S., Kristjánsson, C. and Dörnyei, Z. (eds) (2013) *Christian Faith and English Language Teaching and Learning: Research on the Interrelationship of Religion and ELT*. New York: Routledge.

9 Response to Part 2. 'Religious Faith' and 'Pedagogical Practice': Extending the Map. A Response to Brown, Sharma and Vandrick

David I. Smith

When I first started to explore research on foreign and second language learning some 25 years ago, and began to develop my own interest in the relationship between spirituality/faith/religion (each term has significant problems limiting its usefulness) and pedagogy, the messages I encountered were mixed at best. On the one hand, there was raw material in the literature from which one could construct an account of pedagogy that honored the diversity of the factors influencing it. In one then-current text, for instance, Brumfit (1984) approvingly cited Popper's view that 'understanding, whether of the natural or human world, may be tentatively arrived at through any kind of experience or intuition' (Brumfit, 1984: 11), going on to note that in pedagogy 'the origin of the idea is unimportant – it may come from fiction, or anecdote – so long as it can be argued convincingly as a source of ideas for teachers' (Brumfit, 1984: 19). Views of pedagogies as complex cultures, and then as ecologies, seemed to offer conceptual space for examining how a range of commitments, convictions and traditionings of the self might play a role in shaping classroom practice (Smith, 2009). This seemed in tension with other views of language education research as a positivist affair beholden only to the findings of linguistic and psychological sciences, views that meshed with what Brown's essay here terms 'the supposed secularity of the Western classroom' (this volume, p. 76).

Private conversations were equally mixed: I recall a conversation with an experienced evangelical Christian language educator who found the idea that faith could have anything to do with language pedagogy almost incomprehensible and another with a secular Marxist language educator who found it obvious that there must be an influence and that it would be worth exploring. Across the intervening years, my sense has often been that the relationship between faith and pedagogy is something that those who write about language teaching and learning have generally been rather poor at articulating. The problem is exacerbated by the common insulation of the scholarly literature on language learning and its intellectual sources from scholarly literatures in religious education, children's spirituality, philosophy of religion and the theology and philosophy of education, which have dwelled more extensively and with more nuance on such questions. It is encouraging to see in the essays in this section by Brown, Sharma and Vandrick fresh signs not only of a broadening of the focus beyond earnest arguments about proselytism, but also of taking seriously a range of sources of reflection.

The three essays are disparate in confessional orientation, teaching context and even topic. My own location and perspective are different again – I am Christian, culturally (and, I suspect, intellectually) British, a US citizen teaching in the American Midwest, and currently engaged primarily in teacher education after many years teaching mostly German but also some French, English as a foreign language (EFL) and Russian at various levels and in several countries. I take the task of writing a response to involve neither simply summarizing each essay nor simply adding a fourth narrative to the ones already offered. I am sure Brown, Sharma, Vandrick and any readers of this book can get along fine without my agreement or disagreement. What I hope to do is to identify some common areas of focus in the three essays and see if that helps clarify what has been said, what has not been said and what we might want to think about trying to say. Inevitably, in all of this I will be bringing my own interests to bear in ways that color my reading of what my colleagues have done.

I begin, then, from the question: If we only had these three essays to work with, what would we have learned about the relationship between 'religious faith' and 'pedagogical practice'? The essays illustrate at least five interrelated areas of possible investigation where faith[1] may play a role in the language classroom: the *texture of the self* of teacher and student, patterns of *interpersonal interaction* in the classroom, the teacher's *ethical commitments*, a broader *philosophy of life* as it sustains educational engagement, and specific *pedagogical practices*. Let us revisit briefly how each of these appears in the three essays.

The texture of the self

Brown and Vandrick both focus on the role of faith in shaping the teacher's inner self. Brown explores the mindfulness inherent in Buddhist practice, while Vandrick speaks of the personal peace and sustenance that teachers may draw from their faith and its value for warding off cynicism and burnout. This surely matters. Teaching (when not traded for the role of the by-the-numbers technician) can be peculiarly draining and challenging to one's sense of self. The self itself is often fractured, tugged not only by external stressors but by internal temptations towards judgment, anger, impatience, superiority, favoritism and the like. The quality (meaning both the excellence and the tone/texture) of teaching is affected by these factors. Various faith traditions offer practices that have as at least part of their intent the sustaining of a self that is sufficiently centered and grounded for constructive and compassionate engagement with others and with the world to be sustained. Recognition that the teacher's spirit and what sustains it are an irreducible part of the landscape of language education has been a recurring sidebar to the literature (e.g. Mendelsohn, 1999; Stevick, 1990). As all three essays note, students also come to class both with identities that include religious identities and, as Brown in particular notes, with their own spiritual struggles and needs. The question of how particular language pedagogies ignore, suppress or address the spiritual identities and needs of both teachers and students is an important one which threads through this whole conversation and calls for further attention.

Interpersonal interaction

Despite the popularity in modern liberal contexts of privatized accounts of religion and spirituality that relegate them to personal predilection and individual inner experience, such frames are inadequate here. The inner is not cleanly segregated from the outer; it is the 'outwardness' of the inner that impinges on pedagogical interactions. Brown notes that her own religious practice is 'so private and yet performed in public' (this volume, p. 77). She narrates how her own practice of mindfulness and peace seeking both orients how she interacts with students in her classroom and provokes critical reflection on those interactions. The teacher's beliefs, values, spiritual practices and realized quality of presence help generate a classroom ethos and an implicit set of norms, guiding, governing and critiquing the pattern of interactions and relationships that are established over time in the classroom. As Vandrick notes, this may become problematic in divergent ways: 'some educators could be unduly influenced by their negative feelings about religion, just as some may be unduly influenced by their own beliefs in religion' (this volume, p. 110), with either bias carrying the potential to shape a classroom ethos less welcoming to some students; the notion of 'undue' influence does not, however, exclude the possibility of constructive influence. As Sharma notes (this volume, p. 95), modeling of particular virtues and attitudes on the part of the teacher is also a relevant educational process here. One wonders how students' own faith identities and beliefs might play into the question of what teacher qualities they find worthy of emulation or conducive to learning (cf., for example, Winslow *et al.*, 2011).

Ethical commitments

Intertwined with these interactional patterns and norms is an implicit or explicit set of ethical commitments which helps tie faith to action in the world. Brown makes clear that her Buddhist practices of fostering awareness of others, peace and mindfulness are intimately related to ethical commitments concerning lying, respectful treatment of students, resistance to consumerism, and attempts to ameliorate alienation. These commitments reach out beyond the inner life into classroom choices and specific aspirations for students that begin to shape the curriculum. Sharma focuses on how the Hindu tradition speaks against pedagogical violence, calls for particular virtues in the teacher and offers resources for peace building. Vandrick adds an intriguing example of a Christian academic's spirituality fostering specific resistance to the ethos of her academic institution: 'her religion asks her to be humble, yet academe asks her to be competitive, to brag about accomplishments and to seek power. Her service to others is not always what is rewarded in academe, but such service is her highest goal' (this volume, p. 115).

This example calls to mind an encounter a few years ago with a thoughtful and articulate evangelical undergraduate student who completed every requirement of her honors program successfully except the final project, which she declined to submit after careful reflection on the grounds that formally completing the honors program would not add anything further to her learning but might foster pride and a sense of superiority over others (cf. Bratt & Holberg, 2010). Present in all three essays is a key ethical concern that focuses on how the particular religious or non-religious identities of students in the classroom are approached by educators, and the degree to which they are honored or violated. Faith may ground specific forms of ethical resistance to the lived practices of the academy, and it is not necessary to think that faith is the sole and sufficient determinant of ethics to see that it can play an active role.

Philosophy of life

The faith–ethics connection points us towards broader worldviews. The ethical commitments named in the three essays are not random principles but rather clusters rooted in larger visions of life. As Pannenberg (1984: 16) puts it, 'a particular type of piety involves not only a specific theological focus and corresponding life-styles but also a particular conception of the human world, the world of human experience'. One of Vandrick's interviewees speaks of the importance of having a sense of 'why I am on the face of the earth and what my mission is' (this volume, p. 114); such a larger sense of what life is about may predispose teachers to view not only relationships and ethics but also other kinds of questions about education in particular ways. Sharma's essay in particular explores how a faith tradition can be an active part of 'a comprehensive philosophy of spirituality, of life and of education' (this volume, p. 89), within which more particular reflections and investigations are embedded and oriented. It is interesting that an essay that critiques the unreflective dominance of Western worldviews in scholarly discussion of language education should also be one that clearly pushes back against the modern Western construal of religions as simply discrete belief systems and of spirituality as inner states locked within the autonomous self. The difficulty that the essay faces of tracing the entangled contours of the religious, the cultural, the philosophical and the historical helpfully points to the complexity of the actual landscape.

Pedagogical practices

This brings us, finally, to the topic assigned to this section of the book, 'religious faith and pedagogical practice'. As the three essays each show in their different ways, the teacher's lived self, patterns of interaction, ethical commitments and wider worldview all help to shape pedagogical practice, not only through a kind of broad, qualitative contouring, but also in terms of specific interventions. Each essay furnishes some examples. Sharma points to the larger meaning of specific food vocabulary choices in textbooks imported into Nepali schools (this volume, p. 85) (reminding me of my own efforts to navigate a French textbook exercise about 'le T-shirt' with a Pakistani student who had never worn one and was not sure what one was). Sharma also points more broadly to how a Hindu conception of life might inform 'spiritually motivated activities' (this volume, p. 98) that seek to foster ecological attentiveness and peace. Vandrick indicates that faith-informed social justice convictions can influence choice of texts, tasks assigned to students, questions raised in class and overall orientation to pedagogy (this volume, p. 114–115). Brown sketches the implicit curriculum communicated through teachers' values as they are enacted in classroom moves, how classroom rituals and stories inform student worldviews, and the specific introduction of 'experiments' that resist student distraction and materialism in ways grounded in a valuing of a certain kind of spirituality. As Brown's essay especially illustrates, the role of a particular spiritual orientation in helping shape a vision of pedagogy also implies a vision of student growth and an understanding of the potential range of student needs which can influence what the teacher feels compelled to provide as part of their teaching. All of these are instances of faith helping to shape the normative horizon within which pedagogical strategies are designed, chosen, critiqued and implemented. This all rings true to me; one would not have dreamed that it was going on from much of the professional literature on language classrooms.

Thus far, then, a rough map of the aspects of the relationship of religious faith to pedagogical practice that are engaged in the essays by Brown, Sharma and Vandrick has been presented. The faith–pedagogy matrix weaves together personal spiritual attitudes and practices, spiritually motivated aspirations concerning how to interact with others, faith-informed ethical commitments, larger worldviews that influence educational convictions, and specific adjustments to pedagogical practice in light of the above, all informed by attention to the religious or non-religious identities that students also bring to the classroom. All of the above applies to both teachers and students, and is part of the landscape they must navigate as they engage with one another's faith, different faith or lack of faith. *This is not a sparse map.* There is plenty here for further investigation that points beyond the political tramlines of some of the published discussions to date, and I hope that these essays will provide some constructive impetus towards further study.

The map is not sparse; does it need further extension? Having sketched the themes I see in the three essays, I will conclude with a few thoughts concerning ways in which the conversation might be extended.

There is an interesting interplay of identities and contexts evident in the three essays. The faith identities presented are Hindu, Buddhist and post-Christian/non-religious (plus Christian in the present chapter). The contexts are Nepal, California and Tennessee. Two of the essays, those by Sharma and Vandrick, relate religious identity in qualified ways to national and institutional contexts. Sharma addresses the relationship between Hinduism and language education in a way that focuses on the 'local spiritual traditions of ... contexts such as Nepal' and the ways in which Hinduism has deeply informed particular national histories and traditions; this is set against Western assumptions and pedagogies, with the caveat that the apparent essentialism is 'strategic' and that Hinduism is itself a Western label (this volume, p. 100). Vandrick asserts that 'many feel [the USA] is essentially a Christian country', citing the role of civil religion in American politics, while also acknowledging that within the academy the bias is much less likely to be in favor of Christianity. Reading the essays, I wonder how far the construct of a Christian West and a non-Christian non-West lingers in the background. It is interesting to note that the two Western authors here are non-religious and Buddhist. Many Christians in North America often do not experience American culture as particularly Christian in terms of its basic values as opposed to its civil rhetoric. There are, of course, also Nepali Christians. The massive shift of adherence to Christianity from the West to the Global South over the course of the past century has been widely documented (e.g. Jenkins, 2011), and the tendency of past Western histories to underrepresent non-Western Christianity is being rectified (Walls, 1996). Walls (2002: 1) somewhat provocatively commented over a decade ago that 'the most striking feature of Christianity at the beginning of the third millennium is that it is predominantly a non-Western religion'. The relationship between the assumed or actual religious identities of teachers and students and their geographical and cultural locations is not simple, nor are those locations themselves homogeneous. Care is needed with these matters going forward.

A further question concerns the degree of focus in the essays on pedagogical practices, the focus of this section. As I have noted, the three authors all point to specific ways in which faith/religion/spirituality may inform pedagogical practice. However, aside from a few brief instances, the overall focus of the essays is only occasionally on the specifics of classroom practice. I wish for more investigation that follows through more fully from broad commitments undergirding stances of compassion, humility or mindfulness to understanding *how* these inform the actual design of pedagogical tasks and curricular resources. In other words, how in particular do broad orientations of the self as fostered by faith show up in the material texture of classroom life? This is the element that has most fascinated me in my own work in language education. There are plenty of concrete questions to pursue. I have found myself interested in questions such as how the choice of images and narratives in the language classroom relates to implied conceptions of human worth and of power (Smith, 2010), or how pace, posture and repetition relate to the embodied valuing of charity and humility (Smith, 2011). Recently, theological discussions on time (Tran, 2010) and on the ways in which we (often violently) impose time schemes on one another have me reflecting in fresh ways on how I manage time in my classroom – what goes fast or slow, how students are made to move through time – and on what that means for their sense of self, on how beginnings, endings and pauses are shaped. I mention these examples simply to point out that consideration of how faith informs pedagogy can press beyond the incidental into a more systemic and concrete consideration of embodied classroom practices. In terms of understanding faith and *pedagogy*, there is a journey beyond where the present three essays arrive.

Finally, some consideration should be given to the role of faith in the scholarship that informs pedagogical practice. A passing comment by one of Vandrick's interviewees points to an element which is absent from the three essays yet forms an important part of the larger map. A Christian educator reflects, 'I identify as a Christian, but the identity issues are very complex as I am clearly a Marxist ... (like Paolo Freire) and often find that I have more in common with those who are not practicing Christians and members of other faiths' (this volume, p. 109). The ellipsis adds to the ambiguity of this statement – is the respondent invoking Freire as another example of a Christian Marxist, or is Freire only meant to illustrate the category of Marxist as opposed to Christian? Conceptions of love, hope and even resurrection, conceptions indebted to Christian discourse, helped shape Freire's educational theories (Kristjánsson, 2007). There are other instances of theorists important to second language pedagogies drawing upon theological sources. Charles Curran's counseling-learning and community language learning, and their emphasis on community, holism and the decentering of teacher authority, were rooted in an attempt to cross-fertilize Christian understandings of the Trinity, incarnation and redemption with the existentialist anthropologies of Sartre and Rogers (Curran, 1969). Bakhtin's account of language and sociolinguistic interaction, also influential in second language education circles, was influenced by views of the self and communion found in Russian Orthodox ontology (Felch & Contino, 2001; Mihailovic, 1997). Even when theories are not directly rooted in religious perspectives, their implicit commitments to particular views of matters such as human autonomy, power, conflict, truth and purpose may play a role in making them harder or easier for those scholars and educators who do have religious commitments to swallow (Wolterstorff, 1988). If we seek to understand how faith affects and informs language pedagogy, this will need to be approached not only in terms of the existential experiences of teachers but also in terms of the commitments informing the scholarly sources shaping the pedagogies they have learned. It may be wondered whether the modern scholarly habit of wielding such theoretical sources without attention to or mention of their religious influences reflects or contributes to the difficulty of theorizing how religious faith might inform language pedagogy.

There are, then, avenues not substantively explored in the three essays presented here. That is not a criticism. These are essays, not exhaustive treatments, and each is thoughtful and helpful; I am glad to have read them. The essays and this book as a whole are part of a welcome recovery of an honest naming of the faiths, practices and commitments, including 'religious' ones, that inform both scholarly and pedagogical practices. May the recovery continue.

Notes

(1) As already mentioned, the terms 'spirituality', 'faith' and 'religion' each have their limitations in terms of how well they get at the role of core beliefs and commitments in teacher identity. For the sake mainly of economy, I will stick with 'faith' for the rest of this chapter, following the section title, without thereby intending to imply, for instance, a focus on belief contents at the expense of the more experiential or traditioned factors that may be implied more strongly by 'spirituality' or 'religion' or of the role of faith-informed practices in shaping embodied action (Smith & Smith, 2011).

References

Bratt, K. and Holberg, J.L. (2010) *Christian Higher Education for the 'Best and Brightest'*. Nottingham: Stapleford Centre.

Brumfit, C. (1984) *Communicative Methodology in Language Teaching: The Roles of Fluency and Accuracy*. Cambridge: Cambridge University Press.

Curran, C.A. (1969) *Religious Values in Counseling and Psychotherapy*. New York: Sheed & Ward.
Felch, S.M. and Contino, P.J. (2001) *Bakhtin and Religion: A Feeling for Faith*. Evanston, IL: Northwestern University Press.
Jenkins, P. (2011) *The Next Christendom: The Coming of Global Christianity*. New York: Oxford University Press.
Kristjánsson, C. (2007) The word in the world: So to speak (a Freirean legacy). In D.I. Smith and T.A. Osborn (eds) *Spirituality, Social Justice, and Language Learning* (pp. 133–153). Greenwich, CT: Information Age.
Mendelsohn, D.J. (1999) *Expanding our Vision: Insights for Language Teachers*. Toronto: Oxford University Press.
Mihailovic, A. (1997) *Corporeal Words: Mikhail Bakhtin's Theology of Discourse*. Evanston, IL: Northwestern University Press.
Pannenberg, W. (1984) *Christian Spirituality and Sacramental Community*. London: Darton, Longman & Todd.
Smith, D.I. (2009) The spiritual ecology of second language pedagogy. In M.S. Wong and S. Canagarajah (eds) *Christian and Critical Language Educators in Dialogue: Pedagogical and Ethical Dilemmas* (pp. 242–254). New York and London: Routledge.
Smith, D.I. (2010) Teaching (and learning from) the White Rose. In D.M. Moss and T.A. Osborn (eds) *Critical Essays on Resistance in Education* (pp. 67–82). New York: Peter Lang.
Smith, D.I. (2011) Reading practices and Christian pedagogy: Enacting charity with texts. In D.I. Smith and J.K.A. Smith (eds) *Teaching and Christian Practices: Reshaping Faith and Learning* (pp. 43–60). Grand Rapids, MI: Eerdmans.
Smith, D.I. and Smith, J.K.A. (2011) *Teaching and Christian Practices: Reshaping Faith and Learning*. Grand Rapids: Eerdmans.
Stevick, E.W. (1990) *Humanism in Language Teaching: A Critical Perspective*. Oxford: Oxford University Press.
Tran, J. (2010) *The Vietnam War and Theologies of Memory: Time and Eternity in the Far Country*. Oxford: Wiley-Blackwell.
Walls, A.F. (1996) *The Missionary Movement in Christian History: Studies in the Transmission of Faith*. Maryknoll, NY: Orbis.
Walls, A.F. (2002) Eusebius tries again: The task of reconceiving and re-visioning the study of Christian history. In W.R. Shenk (ed.) *Enlarging the Story: Perspectives on Writing World Christian History* (pp. 1–21). Maryknoll, NY: Orbis.
Winslow, M.W., Staver, J.R. and Scharmann, L.C. (2011) Evolution and personal religious belief: Christian university biology-related majors' search for reconciliation. *Journal of Research in Science Teaching* 48 (9), 1026–1049.
Wolterstorff, N. (1988) *Reason within the Bounds of Religion*. Grand Rapids, MI: Eerdmans.

Part 3

Religious Faith and the Language Learning Context

10 Language and Religion in the Construction of the Lebanese Identity

Kassim Shaaban

Introduction

Lebanon, a small country at the crossroads between East and West, has always been a major player on the political and cultural scene in the Arab Middle East region, a role not warranted by its size or its resources. Lebanon has done this through the sheer determination of its population to be distinguished from their neighbors, mainly by the long tradition of religious and linguistic freedom and diversity and the pioneering role of Lebanese intellectuals in education, journalism, literature, religious coexistence and tolerance, political and social awareness, and freedom of self-expression in words and actions. Since the mid-19th century, religious pluralism and linguistic diversity have been critical factors in the development of Lebanon's unique character and identity. While, for most contexts, linguistic analysis is the major method for examining social identity formation, in the case of Lebanon language issues intersect with key moments of cultural, sociopolitical and religious change (Womack, 2012).

Religious diversity is one of the main hallmarks of Lebanon. There are 18 different religious sects in the country recognized by the Lebanese government and distributed over two major religions: Islam and Christianity. The most influential of the sects that have played major roles in the country's history are Maronite-Catholic and Greek Orthodox Christians; and Sunni, Shia and Druze Muslims. Members of these religious communities have historically placed their allegiance to their communal groups ahead of their allegiance to the country. This situation has encouraged foreign powers that share the same faith with these groups to interfere in Lebanese affairs under the pretense of preventing persecution of religious minorities. In fact, the continuous attempts of the communal groups to maintain and nurture their sectarian identities, coupled with their continued alliances with outside forces, have allowed sectarianism to play a decisive role in the lives of the Lebanese people and to continue to act as the principal determinant of their sociocultural communities and identities (Hage, 2005).

Political-sectarian alliances between Lebanese communities and foreign powers started in the 19th century with the coming of Russian, European and American missionaries. From the start, these missionaries turned to education to work their way into the hearts of the locals. With the basic allegiances between the outside powers behind these missions and the Lebanese religious communities secured (France and Italy with the Maronite-Catholics, Russia with the Greek Orthodox, England with the Druze, Turkey with the Muslims, Americans with newly converted Protestants), the missionaries engaged in an educational rivalry which took the form of printing books, encouraging educated locals to establish newspapers and to read and write literature and establishing schools and institutions of higher education. In these schools and universities the language of the missionaries became the main language of instruction. Thus, religious affiliation was strengthened by the development of linguistic allegiance. This phenomenon is being repeated nowadays as the rift between the various Lebanese religious groups increases. The Shia Muslims who share faith with Iran have started, as of 2008, teaching Persian in their schools at the rate of two hours a week in Grades 6 through 9. Although, on the surface, the introduction of Persian could be argued for on the basis of cultural and vocational benefits, Rowell (2013) notes that 'critics argue the move is viewed by many Lebanese as a political endeavor to expand the Islamic Republic's influence in Lebanon, particularly within the Shiite community'.

In multi-faith, multilingual Lebanon, religion and language are often used in times of communal conflicts as prominent idioms 'with which to articulate' conflicting visions of national identity and of the political system that would embody that vision (Corstange, 2012). Such visions and the ensuing conflicts tend to weaken national bonds and strengthen sectarian feelings and communal group identity. For example, during the two civil wars of 1958 and 1975–1990, some Christians denied their Arab heritage and tried to invoke a Phoenician heritage in their attempt to carve out a separate identity, while the Muslims became more attached to their Arab roots. Furthermore, at times Christians called for the adoption of the vernacular (spoken Lebanese Arabic variety) as an official language that reflects the Assyrian linguistic heritage, and at other times called for the adoption of French as a national language based on the common history of the Lebanese with the French (Hage, 2005). In that sense, both Arabic and French became part of the wider social and political conflict in the country. So what started in 1975 as a political conflict over the presence of armed Palestinians in Lebanon turned first into a religious sectarian conflict and was later extended to become an ethnolinguistic conflict.

This chapter discusses the interactions among politics, religion and language in the formation of a Lebanese national identity. It addresses issues of language policy in relation to communal identity and explores the reasons behind the failure of Lebanese communities to construct a unifying national identity after 70 years of independence. Furthermore, the chapter addresses the issue of how religion affects foreign language choice and teaching.

Theoretical Framework

The main theoretical framework used is the notion of ethnolinguistic vitality, which is often defined as what 'makes a group likely to behave as a distinctive and active collective entity in intergroup situations' (Giles *et al.*, 1977: 308). The theory maintains that language plays a major role in ethnic and intergroup relations in multilingual settings. Ehala (2010) argues that vitality manifests itself as group members' readiness to participate in collective action, a readiness created by shared language, shared religious faith, or both.

One approach to the study of language vitality and language maintenance is the core value theory developed by Smolicz through his studies of multilingualism in Australia. Smolicz and Secombe (1985: 11) define the term 'core values' as 'those values that are regarded as forming the most fundamental components or heartland of a group's culture, and act as identifying values which are symbolic of the group and its membership'. Having a specific set of values in common with others, cherishing and defending them, is an indication of belongingness to a group, whereas rejecting these values amounts to potential exclusion from the group. Smolicz (1992) differentiates between general values and core values, explaining that general values could be adapted or changed without causing any harm to the stability, coherence and survival of the group, whereas 'other aspects of culture are of such fundamental importance for its continued viability and integrity that they can be regarded as the pivots around which the whole social and identificational system of the group is organized' (Smolicz, 1992: 279).

Minority groups that feel threatened and insecure in their wider societies usually attach themselves to the core value of indigenous language and, in many contexts, the core value of religious sect, because of the strong connection that exists between group identity and a native tongue and/or religious affiliation (May, 2003; Tannenbaum, 2009). When members of a group perceive language as their primary core value, they will resort to all possible means to ensure its maintenance (Gogonas, 2011; Smolicz, 1992; Smolicz & Secombe, 1985). In addition, when language is closely intertwined with another potent core value, such as religion, the connection between people's perceptions and actual maintenance efforts and results could be much higher.

Another theoretical approach brought to bear on this chapter is that of language and identity, with emphasis on teachers' religious identity as a major contextual factor in second language (L2) acquisition (Lightbown & Spada, 1993; Norton-Peirce, 1995; Wong *et al.*, 2013).

Review of the Literature

Spolsky (2003) pointed out that the literature on the relation between language and religion has not been adequately explored. He traced the emergence of interest in this connection to the works of Cooper (1989), Ferguson (1982), Kaplan and Baldauf (1997), Sawyer (2001) and Schiffman (1996) and concluded by calling on sociolinguists to explore the topic further. One of the earliest studies exploring the relation between language and religion is that of Ferguson (1982), in which he claimed that religion is a major factor in language spread, language change and language endangerment. He discussed aspects of interaction between religion and sociolinguistics, such as changes in orthography, as in the adoption of Arabic script by Persian and Urdu; language shift as in the abandonment of Syriac in favor of Arabic in Eastern Mediterranean countries; and borrowings which take place whenever two languages come into contact. Regarding orthographic changes, Ferguson (1982: 95) stated: 'The distribution of major types of writing systems in the world correlates more closely with the distribution of the world's major religions than with genetic or typological classifications of languages'.

Cooper (1989) discussed language choices made by religions, as in the case of Islam and Judaism, which maintain their sacred texts only in the original language. Similarly, Sawyer (2001: 321) highlighted the fact that the Qur'an has to be read in Arabic because 'translation of the Qur'an is officially prohibited'. Schiffman (1996) discussed how religion-motivated political changes could result in language splits as in the case of Hindi-Urdu and Serbo-Croatian.

Other studies carried out in a variety of sociolinguistic contexts have explored the connection between religion and language in the domains of language variation, shift, maintenance, and policy and planning. Haugen (1953) examined the link between religious affiliation, identity and language shift among Norwegians in America. Fishman (1991) also discussed the way in which religious factors interact with processes of language shift and maintenance in contexts of immigration. De Kadt (2002) investigated the maintenance by the Natal Germans of their unique German identity or 'tradition of the forefathers' within a South African landscape for so many years. She concluded that the four factors that have contributed most to the survival of the Natal German ethnic group are first language, then religion, cultural mores and values (de Kadt, 2002: 150). Florey (1993) reported that speakers of Alune, an indigenous language of Western Seram in Indonesia, although having converted to Christianity, do not use Christian names. Instead, they use Alune personal naming practices as a means of adhering to the Alune language and to ancestral practices in an era of rapid social and cultural change. Wherritt (1985) found that as soon as the Portuguese left Goa in India, the use of the Portuguese language among the local population weakened. However, the language still survives among churchgoing, older Catholics, a fact that demonstrates the relation between religion and language maintenance.

Furthermore, studies dealing with the linguistic aspects of colonialism have discussed the role of religion as a motivating factor in the activities of missionaries all over the globe in the education of local populations. It also discussed how language and religion could serve as rallying points for the natives to liberate themselves from colonialism – as in the case of Algeria, where the people united around Islam and the Arabic language (Suleiman, 2003). Kaplan and Baldauf (1997) discussed the often-negative impact of language spread that may accompany religious spread on language ecology, on the future of other languages, and on their speakers' sense of identity and wellbeing.

More recently, there has been resurging interest in exploring the sociolinguistic aspects of the relation between language and religion, from the perspectives of the effect of each one on the other and their role in identity formation and language policy (Spolsky, 2003). Omoniyi and Fishman (2006) called for establishing the sociology of language and religion as a new field of study with a theoretical home base in both sociology and the sociology of language. Since then, studies have been appearing in which authors have examined the relation between language, religion and other sociolinguistic factors (Mukherjee, 2013; Omoniyi, 2010; Spolsky, 2009).

Other studies explored the role of core values in language maintenance. Gogonas (2011) investigated patterns of language use within households of Egyptians living in Greece. He reported that there was a language shift to Greek among adolescents of the Coptic religion. In contrast, Muslim informants maintained the use of their native language, Arabic. Gogonas (2011) concluded that religious practice led Muslims and Copts to view Arabic and Coptic, respectively, as core values for their identity. Similarly, Tannenbaum (2009) studied language maintenance among members of three minority groups in Israel (Arabs, Ethiopians and Russians). His analysis of collected memoirs revealed that the native language has functioned as a core value for all of them. Israeli Arabs viewed Arabic as a symbol of national identity and of their resistance to the hegemony of Hebrew; immigrants from the former Soviet Union emphasized the maintenance of Russian in early literacy and in preserving their native culture; and participants from the Ethiopian group viewed Amharic as the means for maintaining values they cherish – family relations and respect for their elders.

More recently, many scholars have shown interest in investigating the impact of teachers' religious beliefs and spirituality on the dynamics of interaction in the English as a second language (ESL) classroom (Baurain, 2013; Bradley, 2005; Glanzer & Talbert, 2005; Schoonmaker, 2009;

Shaaban & Ghaith, 2003; White, 2010). This interest started with studies on Christian teachers (Green, 2010; Snow, 2001; Varghese & Johnston, 2007; Wong *et al.*, 2013). Religious beliefs, according to Baurain (2013: 1), are 'often at the core of who we are, what we do, how we perceive ourselves and others, and how we envision and pursue purpose, relationships, moral goodness, and overall well-being'. Stevick (1990) considers religious beliefs as deep-seated ideas and commitments that define people and determine their actions.

The roots of the debate about religion in the ESL classroom can be traced back to debates on related issues which had engaged the profession since the 1990s within the context of views of education as a process of pedagogical transformation and the belief that the ESL classroom provides a suitable venue for promoting awareness of global issues such as the environment, peace, character and morality (Ghaith & Shaaban, 1994; Morgan & Vandrick, 2009; Shaaban, 2005; Smith & Osborn, 2007). ESL scholars remain engaged in debate about the extent to which the religious affiliation of the school and the religious faith of the teacher should be allowed to impact classroom practices (Edge, 2003; Griffith, 2004; Westwood, 2014; Wong & Canagarajah, 2009).

Smith and Osborn (2007) addressed the role of teachers' religious beliefs in language education in a pioneering study that suggested that spirituality infiltrates the sociocultural and institutional situation in which the acquisition of an L2 takes place. Other studies suggested that religious beliefs are part of teachers' characters and affect their knowledge, interactions, attitudes and practices in the classroom (Baurain, 2013; Green, 2010; White, 2010). Baurain (2013: 27) believes that 'elements of [a teacher's] faith might affect classroom decision-making, relationships with students, professional identity and development, and overall pedagogy'.

A study by Glanzer and Talbert (2005), which surveyed the opinions of 58 education students in a Christian university, showed that most respondents do not believe that their beliefs affect their teaching methods. However, a study by Varghese and Johnston (2007), which surveyed the opinions of ten English student teachers, showed that most of the student teachers viewed their teaching as a means of 'planting seeds so that others would grow curious and eventually find within themselves the need to learn and experience more about Christianity' (Varghese & Johnston, 2007: 25). Varghese and Johnston note further that, for most of the student teachers, conversion of non-Christians to Christianity was part of their mission as teachers.

Similar findings were reported in Baurain (2013), where teachers in the study expressed the view that their religious beliefs affect the way they teach, but unlike the participants in the study by Varghese and Johnston (2007), they did not believe that their educational mission was to convert others to Christianity. They felt that their faith makes them better professionals and that their religious values fuel their relationships with their students, especially the values of respect and caring.

Complexity of Lebanese Identity

Brief political history

It is very hard for anyone to begin to understand the complexity and uniqueness of the national identity construct in Lebanon without having a close look at the historical events that precipitated the non-ending identity crisis of the Lebanese.

The issue goes back in history to the time when Muslim Arabs came to Lebanon. At the time, Lebanon's population was mainly of Phoenician, Assyrian or Arab origin; the dominant language was Syriac; and the dominant religion was Christianity. When the Arabs took Lebanon and the rest of the Eastern Mediterranean region from the Byzantines, they did not impose Islam on the local population and 'did not do away with their heritage' (Naiden & Harl, 2009). In return, most Lebanese abandoned their native tongues and adopted Arabic as their language, except for the Maronites who continued to use Syriac into the 13th century. Since then, Arab–Maronite relations have been governed by mutual suspicion, mistrust and accommodation. The Maronites' fiercely independent tendencies set them in conflict with the Umayyad, the Abbasid and the Ottoman caliphates. Their siding with the Crusaders did not help much.

Under the Ottomans, Lebanon's mountain regions were given semi-autonomy. During this period, the first semi-independent Lebanese political entity came into existence during the reign of Emir Fakhreddine II – a Sunni Muslim who was able to unite all the Lebanese sects behind him, build modern infrastructure, put together a strong multi-faith army and defeat the Sultanate army in 1623. However, this dream-turned-into-reality of a sovereign, united and independent Lebanon ended when the Sultanate army defeated Fakhreddine in 1635 and executed him (Abu Husayn, 2004).

As the Ottoman Empire started weakening in the 19th century, European intervention in its affairs increased considerably. The French and the British were seeking to spread their influence in the region through nourishing special relations with local communities. The French pledged their support to the Maronites and the British built good relations with the Druze.

Mounting tensions between the Lebanese communities supported by outside powers broke into violence several times. The worst conflict took place in 1840 between the Maronites and the Druze and lasted for 20 years, culminating in 1860 with a massacre of about 10,000 people. After that, the Ottomans re-imposed their direct authority and, with the help of France, introduced the Mutasarrifiyya system, whereby each group ran its own affairs under the Ottoman rule. That system was the precursor of the system of confessionalism and sectarianism that was to be the system of government starting in 1920 with the establishment of Greater Lebanon and continuing in slightly modified forms until the present.

In the second half of the 19th century, Protestant and Jesuit missionaries came to Lebanon from America, France, England, Italy, Russia, Denmark and Germany, allying themselves with the Christian Lebanese who shared or accepted their faith and using education as the main tool for reaching people. Muslims resorted to the Ottoman Empire, which helped establish the first public school education system in Lebanon; furthermore, Muslims and Christians established their own private educational institutions, modeled after French schools (Bashshur, 1978; Hitti, 1956; Salibi, 1988).

At the end of WWI, Lebanon was placed under French mandate in accordance with the 1916 Sykes–Picot Agreement. The French set to work immediately, establishing Greater Lebanon in 1920. The new country had its own government, parliament and institutions along the French model of governance. The first Lebanese constitution was issued in 1926. The political system was a consociational, confessional one based on the proportional representation of the various religious communities in administration, with the top jobs going to the Maronites.

The National Pact, which was worked out by all the communal groups in Lebanon leading to its independence from France in 1943, maintained the consociational system. Political representation followed a 6:5 formula in favor of Christians in the parliament and cabinet posts; the positions of heads of army, general security and intelligence services all went to Maronites. The President was to be a Maronite Christian, the Speaker of the Parliament a Shia Muslim and the Prime Minister a Sunni Muslim.

Since the 1933 census, which showed a Christian majority (51.2%), there has been a major demographic shift, although not officially documented or verified, in which the population figures changed drastically in favor of Muslims. The latest overall picture for Lebanese who are registered in the country stands at 61.2% for Muslims and 38.2% for Christians (Lebanese Information Center, 2013).

Based on demographic changes, Muslim leaders asked for an adjustment of the ratios of representation. The political debates that ensued tore the country apart and, in 1958, broke into clashes between Christians and Muslims. However, a more serious rift between the two groups came in 1975, fueled by the armed presence of Palestinians, resulted in a destructive 15-year civil war that left the country and all its institutions in shambles and handed the country to the Syrians, who entered the country as a temporary Arab deterrent force but did not leave until 2005.

With the help of global and regional powers, the Lebanese groups met in the City of Taif in Saudi Arabia in 1989 and reached an agreement on a new constitution, which came to be known as the Taif Accord. The

Accord replaced the old power-sharing formula of 6:5 in favor of Christians with a 50:50 one regardless of numbers. Furthermore, taking into consideration the causes of the war and the suffering it had caused, the Accord set the goal of gradual abandonment of sectarianism as a vital national priority and encouraged the establishment of secular institutions. The new constitution has been in place since 1990 and no serious challenges have been raised against it since then, although dissenting voices speak out from time to time.

The tribulations of constructing a Lebanese national identity

A communal identity is expressed in Lebanon in many forms: shared beliefs and attitudes towards self and others; largely homogeneous ethnic and religious mountain villages and neighborhoods within the cities; and seeking outside support for communal political stands. All these have played out to disastrous effect during and after the 1975–1990 civil war. The practice of sect-based power sharing has proved beyond any doubt that, in Lebanon, 'one's sect is almost equivalent to one's nation' (Turkmen-Dervisoglu, 2012: 67). Every sect has the right to regulate its own rituals (wedding, divorce, baptism) according to its own religious beliefs, and this 'autonomy' makes the formation of a broad national identity much harder. Furthermore, the stratified structure of the current education system, where private, religion-based schools hold the upper hand in terms of quality and number of students, also helps perpetuate sectarian autonomy as a primary tool in shaping people's identities and feeding prejudices towards other sects (Muhanna, 2010). Although the major Lebanese religious communities are not ethnically different from one another, the heterogeneity of these groups leads people to believe that 'Lebanon represents the microcosmic impossibility of a monolithic identity' (Carpi, 2013: 98).

Sectarianism permeates every aspect of the lives of the Lebanese people, from daily social interaction – where any conversant tries before getting into any deep discussions to identify the sectarian identity of the other – to mass media, sports, language(s) used, and schooling. Whether one calls it confessionalism, sectarianism, communalism or any other name, the phenomenon of placing loyalty to the religious group ahead of allegiance to the state is so deeply entrenched in the psyche and everyday practices of the Lebanese that many scholars have described Lebanon as a failing state, on account of the failure of its consociationalist system of government to create a national identity and to prevent inter-sectarian conflicts (Crighton & MacIver, 1991; El-Khazen, 2000; Hudson, 1997; Picard, 1996; Salibi, 1971). Abraham (2008: 176) believes that 'Lebanon's communal organization had produced an identity problem in the tiny republic'. He adds that communal groups in Lebanon 'act as independent mini-nations within a larger national entity called Lebanon making it very difficult for a citizen to be "just Lebanese"' (Abraham, 2008: 176).

In light of the above, the challenge for Lebanon 'is how one goes about building a viable, democratic, secular state that is more inclusive than any intrastate grouping, be it ethnic, tribal or religious' (Muhanna, 2010: 1).

Perceptions of intergroup relations

Moaddel (2008) conducted a survey administered to a cross-sectional sample of Lebanese to assess their perceptions of intergroup relations and the future of Lebanon. Results of the survey showed that 'feelings of insecurity remain quite high among all religious groups in Lebanon. Across the board, about 75% agreed that life in Lebanon these days is dangerous and unpredictable' (Moaddel, 2008: 2). The various sects expressed their trust in their own kind only, and little or no trust of other sects, a situation that has created 'a strong sense of group solidarity and weak inter-group relations' (Moaddel, 2008: 2). Christian sects trust other Christian sects more than they trust Muslim sects; Maronites trust Christians (31–57%) more than Muslims (10–17%); Druze trust Muslims (29–84%) more than they do Christians (8–9%); Sunnis have an almost equal level of trust of other Muslim and Christian sects (23–82% for Muslims and 29–30% for Christians); and Shia have the least trust of other Muslim sects (9–16%) and a slightly higher trust of Christians (19–20%). This reflects the fact that the current struggle is between Sunnis and Shiites, with Christians divided in alliances. It is obvious from these figures that, years after the Taif Accord has been put into effect, the Lebanese are still afraid of one another and look towards those who are partners in faith for support and solidarity, making religion the major core value for all the Lebanese.

The percentage of the respondents who strongly agreed that 'Lebanon would be a better place if religion and politics are separated' is 38% for Shias, 36% for Sunnis and 63% for the Druze and Christians. Support for secular politics is thus much higher among the Druze and Christians than it is among the Shias and Sunnis. Furthermore, between 61% and 62% of the Shias and Sunnis described themselves as Lebanese above all; this figure was 96% for the Druze and 71% for Christians.

A study conducted not long after Moaddel's had slightly more optimistic findings. In a survey conducted by Fahed (2009) at Notre Dame University, a Catholic-affiliated university that caters to all Lebanese communities, 67% of the participants felt that their national belongingness and identity comes first and, as such, it should protect their religious identity. Similarly, a poll conducted in 2010 by the firm Information International showed that 58% of people surveyed were in favor of abolishing confessionalism: 75% of Muslims approved the movement towards a secular state, but only 35% of Christians did. These figures reflect the mistrust and fear that Christians exhibit towards their compatriots and towards their own role in such a structure (Turkmen-Dervisoglu, 2012). The discrepancy among the figures presented in these three studies could be explained by the nature of the sample populations. Nevertheless, there remains an overall indication that, after all the years of conflict, people may be willing to put their national interests ahead of their communal feelings.

Lebanese identity maintenance

The maintenance of distinct communal identities in Lebanon has been carried with the Lebanese immigrant communities to their new homes around the world. Although the same issues that divide the Lebanese at home seem to separate the various religious groups abroad, these issues do not come to the surface; the various communities put on a semblance of cooperation and unity and show pride in their Lebanese heritage. The role of religious institutions, operating separately or in unison, in creating and maintaining an intra- and intercommunal sense of identity among the Lebanese immigrants cannot be overestimated. Thus, in Brazil, for example, the role of the religious institutions is essential 'in the maintenance of ethnic identity, through actions such as conducting services or sermons in Arabic, offering Arabic language courses, inviting dignitaries from other Syrian-Lebanese religious groups to attend important socio-religious functions, and preserving, to varying extents, their Eastern Christian or Muslim liturgical traditions' (Pitts, 2006: 67).

However, the different religious groups view the issue of maintenance of the Lebanese identity among immigrants to Brazil from slightly different perspectives: Muslims tend to strongly emphasize the Arab cultural and linguistic identity; the Orthodox promote Lebanese 'culture and identity to a greater extent than the Eastern Catholic churches; and ... the Maronites are much less actively involved in the maintenance of ... Lebanese identity, primarily because as Catholics, many of them identify more strongly with a general Catholic religious tradition than with their Syrian-Lebanese ethnic tradition' (Pitts, 2006: 69). It is important to emphasize that the Lebanese immigrants try as far as they can to maintain the Arabic language and think of it as the basis of their identity.

Language, religion and politics

Engaged in fierce competition for political advantage, the Lebanese communal groups have produced conflicting narratives of identity and nationhood that have marked the history of modern Lebanon. More specifically, throughout the 19th and 20th centuries, the major Lebanese religious communities have all been involved at one time or another in violent conflicts and have suffered heavy physical, psychological and material losses in their attempts to strengthen their political position vis-à-vis other communities and to attain a measure of security and a sense of identity for their communities.

Religion-and-language-in-the-service-of-politics or 'politicized language and religion' constituted the strongest link within the Lebanese groups and between them and the foreign powers that supported them. These associations have generated tensions and triggered linguistic and political decisions intended to fortify communal identities. For example, at the time of the establishment of Greater Lebanon in 1920, Muslims felt that their Arab identity as Arabs was under attack by the French and their Christian allies who wanted to spread French culture, French language and French education, causing them to show more attachment to Arabic (Bashshur, 1978; Suleiman, 2003). Similarly, in the mid-20th century, Muslim espousal of the idea of Arab nationalism only served to reinforce Christian religious identity in general and to develop doubts about their earlier championing of Arabic as the language of national identity in the face of Ottoman Turks.

The conflict of 1958, which pitted Christians against Muslims, was a reflection of the regional political and linguistic struggle between Arab nationalists and pro-Western forces. Similarly, the militarized Palestinian presence in Lebanon, especially in 1970 after the Palestinian Liberation Organization was kicked out of Jordan, created an unprecedented sense of insecurity and fear among Christians, especially after the Muslims seemed eager to use the Palestinians to weaken the Christian domination of the country. The 1975–1990 civil war put an end to prosperity, national unity and a unified identity, and created an atmosphere of betrayal, mistrust and fear in all communities. Once again, the Lebanese parties in general, and the Christian parties in particular, resorted to religion and language, in this case French, as a means of rallying their communities around their cause. Language issues did not trigger the social, political and military conflicts among the Lebanese, but such issues were tools used in the struggle. Wiegand (1997) argued that the Lebanese elite exploited nascent religious, linguistic, ancestral and national identity issues for their own purposes. She stated that '[the] Lebanese state's gradual disintegration to the point of civil war exemplifies how intensification and manipulation of cultural identity weakened national identity and solidarity among religious groups' (Wiegand, 1997: 243).

The Taif Accord brought some hope to the Lebanese that they can build a true state around common goals agreed upon by most Lebanese communal groups. However, under Syrian pressure, the implementation was slow and disorganized, leaving Sunnis and many Christians feeling betrayed, insecure and mistrustful of their compatriots. Once again, the Lebanese withdrew into their communal shells in an attempt to build in-group solidarity for preservation purposes. In fact, the linguistic landscape and linguistic attitudes have changed with changes in politics. Language choice ceased to be an issue of contention as all Lebanese have opted for multilingualism, where all languages operating in Lebanon seem to have developed their own domains of use, which are separate from the domains of the other languages, although they overlap in some functions. The Lebanese have also learned to accept diglossia, which, according to Ferguson (1959), refers to the existence side by side of two varieties of the same language, a standard formal one and a spoken informal one. The former is referred to as high variety H (Modern Standard Arabic), used in writing and in formal speaking, and the latter is known as low variety L (Colloquial Lebanese Arabic), used in everyday communication. The two varieties overlap in many functions such as singing, news commentaries and news reports, theater and the like. Thus, although all groups share a mother tongue, Arabic, each group espouses one or more foreign languages to create its own distinctive identity. The issue is not that French dominates among Christians and English among Muslims, but rather the way each group values foreign languages. Francophone Christians value French for its cultural value, and many of them see themselves as part of the culture of the West. Muslims, on the other hand, attach themselves to Arabic and consider it sacred; they learn foreign languages, French or English, for their practicality and not for their cultural value. Recently, the Shia Muslims have been interested in learning French as a sign of improving ties with the French (Esseili, 2011), and they have also introduced Persian as a third language as a form of assertion of their sectarian identity. Likewise, Francophone Christians have added English for its role in helping people obtain employment that is more lucrative. What unifies the Lebanese linguistically is not the Arabic language, but rather multilingualism whose base is Arabic and at least one foreign language, a *multilingualism motivated by political and economic interests*.

The Jesuit intellectual Father Salim Abou believes that Lebanon could be a linguistic and cultural bridge between East and West and between Christianity and Islam, and that multilingualism could be one of the essential elements for building that bridge; he also believes that foreign languages become like the native language, part of the Lebanese linguistic identity (Fernandez, 2009: 22–23).

Religious faith and foreign language education

The Lebanese, Muslims and Christians alike have always recognized the positive impact of religious faith on foreign language education; to them, language teaching is an act of faith. To Christians, foreign language teaching is an act of love that opens the gate to another culture and helps spread the word of God. To Muslims, it is a means of gaining knowledge from others and learning to keep their harm away, as the Prophet is quoted to have said. In fact, religion-affiliated schools constitute the bulk of quality private education in Lebanon. These schools, as expected, try to develop their students' knowledge, but they additionally focus on shaping their students' character, identity, values and morality.

In fulfillment of a research paper requirement for a course on language acquisition I teach, Iliovits (2014) conducted a study in which she held interviews with six English language teachers in three Lebanese schools to investigate the impact of teachers' religious beliefs on their ESL teaching practices. The six teachers were two Sunni Muslims, two Shia Muslims and two Catholic Christians, who were teaching at three prestigious religion-based schools. They were interviewed with the purposes of exploring the effect of their faith on their attitude towards English and other languages, identifying what role their religious beliefs have in their interaction with students in the classroom and examining how these beliefs affect teachers' curricular choices and teaching methods.

The findings of the study by Iliovits (2014) show that all the ESL teachers interviewed showed a highly positive attitude to English, stressing its global spread and utility in today's job market in comparison to Arabic and French. She noted that Muslim Sunni and Shia teachers were more likely than Christian teachers to have their attitudes driven by religious beliefs. On the other hand, the study found that, while Muslim teachers spoke of focusing mainly on developing their students' knowledge and linguistic skills as their top priority, Christian teachers emphasized the goal of 'spreading the word of God'. Furthermore, those who are religiously committed (four out of six) exhibited the tendency to be more intensely engaged with their students and to use learner-centered pedagogical teaching strategies such as cooperative and active learning, problem solving and other critical thinking activities. This is in line with the findings of Lindholm and Astin (2008).

The study also showed that three of the teachers, knowing that the majority of their students share their faith, invoked religion to promote or discourage certain behaviors, using expressions like 'God hates cheaters' and 'Cheating is not Christian'. The others resorted to emphasizing that cheating is simply immoral. All the teachers seemed to accept the use of religious references and points of view to explain concepts or to argue for a point of view, when debating controversial topics like abortion, euthanasia and the environment. However, only the two Shia teachers stated that they use religious texts in their classes; two others (one Sunni and one Christian) were not opposed to the idea but never used it, and the last two were totally against using religious texts.

The study by Iliovits (2014) demonstrates clearly that ESL teachers differ in their classroom practices, but it is very difficult to attribute that to religious beliefs alone. Furthermore, the small size of the sample would make it difficult to make sweeping generalizations.

Core values of Lebanese society

All Lebanese groups, despite their many differences, are united in their perception of the role of religion in the running of everyday affairs; they prefer keeping the status quo in jurisdiction in personal matters (marriage, divorce, inheritance, adoption), refusing to accept civil marriage and other aspects of secularism despite their claims of supporting moves towards secularism (Moaddel, 2008). This leads us to believe that religion constitutes the major Lebanese identity core value that politicians resort to for rallying support for their political stands. However, religion alone was not considered enough as a basis of national identity in a country that has a diversity of religious affiliation. For this reason, the Lebanese looked for language as a possible core value for an identity that supersedes their communal identities. But what language was to be chosen: Arabic, which the Maronites feared because of its connection to Islam and Arab nationalism; Syriac, the historical language of Lebanon that ceased to exist except in church sermons; French, the language of the ex-colonizer; or Lebanese Arabic, the uncodified vernacular which is the language of everyday communication? In fact, the Lebanese have reached an informal consensus that the uncontested linguistic basis of Lebanese identity is not a single language but a diversity of languages in the form of bilingualism or multilingualism, making it a major trait of the Lebanese identity and a core value of that identity. However, within that consensus, Arabic remains the identity symbol for all; French is valuable personally and culturally for those with historical ties to the language; English is adopted for its advantages as a global language of communication and employment; Armenian and Kurdish are as vital as Arabic for the ethnic groups that speak them; Persian, the newest language on the scene, is a confirmation of religious identity for the Shia; and Syriac, the language of Lebanon before the coming of the Arabs, is still used for religious sermons, along with formal and informal varieties of Arabic. For Sunnis, Arabic serves as the symbol of their Lebanese Arab identity as well as a symbol of their belongingness to a larger entity, the Islamic nation (Fishman, 1991).

For the Lebanese diaspora, both language and religion seem to be two core values, with Arabic being the unifying factor between Muslims and Christians in their new countries. Pitts (2006) highlighted the role the Arabic language has played in creating and maintaining a sense of identity among Lebanese immigrants in Brazil. He reported that the Arab ethnic identity had been maintained '… through actions such as conducting services or sermons in Arabic, offering Arabic language courses, inviting dignitaries from other Syrian-Lebanese religious groups to attend important socio-religious functions' (Pitts, 2006: 67).

Shifts in identity narratives in Lebanon

Zakharia (2009) and Carpi (2013) reported a shift in the perception of the Lebanese of the bases of their national identity, whereby the new generation of young Lebanese seem to think of Arabic as the symbol of their national identity. Such a shift has also been reported by John Joseph

(2006), who describes how his Christian cousin in Lebanon consciously shifted her perception of her identity from an Arab to a French one in protest at what was happening in the country. In this sense, people could have different identities and these identities vary according to contextual factors. The Lebanese identity narrative is being continuously reconstructed by its components.

In the dynamic representation of identity, the Lebanese have to live with different identities. Within Lebanon, they are stuck with their communal religious identity that acts as a buffer against threats coming from other communities. Outside Lebanon and the Arab world, they are seen as Arabs, and in the Arab world, they are seen as Lebanese. It is an indication of the existence of distinct but overlapping identities. And all Lebanese are proud of the different labels they get because it makes them feel unique in one way or another. For example, the use of French or English in everyday communication among some middle-class, educated Lebanese is a form of identification and solidarity with a perceived advanced Western culture and a symbol of their being cultured and educated.

Another clear example of the shift in identity narratives is the way Maronites have looked at language in relation to identity. During the final days of the Ottoman Empire, they – more than their Muslim compatriots – actively championed the cause of Arabic as the language of liberation from the Turks (Suleiman, 1996). However, with the rise of Arab nationalism, they shunned Standard Arabic as the tool with which Muslims were trying to integrate them into the Islamic community and rob them of their distinctness (Suleiman, 1996). Consequently, Christians reacted by embracing foreign languages, especially French and the French culture that came with it. Muslims, on the other hand, considered Standard Arabic the forbearer of the Muslim-Arab culture and a major pillar of Arab nationalism. This ideological conflict between Christians and Muslims found expression in many educational and linguistic battles concerning the medium of instruction at school and college (Suleiman, 1996). The situation has been settled by adopting the use of foreign languages in professional, scientific and technical subjects by all communities concerned.

Conclusion

It is true that two of the world's largest religions, Christianity and Islam, and the many sects that have branched from them, have co-existed in Lebanon for a long time. But it is also true that such a coexistence has not always been a peaceful one. While some people find this religious diversity admirable, others see in it the roots of past conflicts and the source of potential future conflicts. Prior to 1975, Lebanon was often thought of as an almost successful balance among different communities and interests. In 1975, a disastrous civil war started; the general impression of some outside observers and journalists was that it was a war between Rightists and Leftists or a war between Christians and Muslims. The actual situation on the ground was far from that and much more complex, involving ephemeral, shifting alliances between sects and factions who often cross sectarian boundaries.

More than any other country in the Middle East region, Lebanon has been worn out by inner conflicts that have underscored the ineffectiveness and instability of consociationalism. At the root of these conflicts are contradictory narratives of identity and nationhood that invoke sectarian affiliation and indigenous communal languages, real or imagined, as the foundations of the Lebanese individual, societal and cultural identity. While such narratives have served as rallying grounds for the construction of distinct communal identities, they have failed to bring these communities to agree on a unifying national identity. The political system has failed to guarantee Lebanese unity, sovereignty and independence.

This chapter has demonstrated the dangers of putting religious affiliation ahead of national identification and of promoting communal interests at the expense of national welfare. It has also highlighted the failure of consociationalism to create a viable, sovereign state. Lebanese people feel their path is a minefield that could blow up at any minute. To make things right, there needs to be the development of a social and national identity that maintains a delicate balance between three language-related identities where language could be: a symbol of politico-religious affiliation; a tool of economic development and advancement; and a solid foundation for national identity. It is my firm belief that this balance cannot be achieved and maintained through dependence on one language alone, be it the native tongue or a foreign language; only multilingualism will do.

References

Abraham, A.J. (2008) *Lebanon in Modern Times*. Lanham, MD: University Press of America.

Abu Husayn, A.R. (2004) *The View from Istanbul: Ottoman Lebanon and the Druze Emirate*. London: I.B. Tauris.

Bashshur, M. (1978) *The Structure of the Lebanese Educational System* (in Arabic). Beirut: Center for Educational Research and Development.

Baurain, B. (2013) Religious faith, teacher knowledge, and overseas Christian ESOL teachers. Unpublished doctoral dissertation, University of Nebraska.

Bradley, C. (2005) Spirituality and L2 pedagogy: Toward a research agenda. *Journal of Engaged Pedagogy* 4 (1), 26–38.

Carpi, E. (2013) Lebanon and its linguistic wandering: On the road to language de-essentialization. *Communication and Culture Online, Special Issue* 1, 96–115.

Cooper, R.L. (1989) *Language Planning and Social Change*. Cambridge: Cambridge University Press.

Corstange, D. (2012) Religion, pluralism, and iconography in the public sphere: Theory and evidence from Lebanon. *World Politics* 64 (1), 116–160.

Crighton, E. and MacIver, M.A. (1991) The evolution of protracted ethnic conflict: Group dominance and political underdevelopment in Northern Ireland and Lebanon. *Comparative Politics* 23 (2), 127–142.
de Kadt, E. (2002) German speakers in South Africa. In R. Mesthrie (ed.) *Language in South Africa*. Cambridge: Cambridge University Press.
Edge, J. (2003) Imperial troopers and servants of the Lord: A vision of TESOL in the 21st century. *TESOL Quarterly* 37, 701–709.
Ehala, M. (2010) Refining the notion of ethnolinguistic vitality. *International Journal of Multilingualism* 7 (4), 363–378.
El-Khazen, F. (2000) *The Breakdown of the State in Lebanon 1967–1976*. Cambridge, MA: Harvard University Press.
Esseili, F. (2011) English in Lebanon: Implications for national identity and language policy. Unpublished doctoral dissertation, Purdue University.
Fahed, Z. (2009) How the Catholic Church views the political community? *Politics and Religion Journal* 1 (3), 99–110.
Ferguson, C.A. (1959) Diglossia: Language in culture and society. *Word* 15 (2), 325–340.
Ferguson, C.A. (1982) Religious factors in language spread. In R.L. Cooper (ed.) *Language Spread: Studies in Diffusion and Social Change* (pp. 95–106). Bloomington, IN: Indiana University Press.
Fernandez, M.A. (2009) National, linguistic, and religious identity of Lebanese Maronite Christians through their Arabic fictional texts during the period of the French Mandate in Lebanon. Unpublished PhD dissertation, Georgetown University.
Fishman, J.A. (1991) *Reversing Language Shift*. Clevedon: Multilingual Matters.
Florey, M.J. (1993) The reinterpretation of knowledge and its role in the process of language obsolescence. *Oceanic Linguistics* 32, 295–309.
Ghaith, G. and Shaaban, K. (1994) Peace education in the ESL/EFL classroom: A framework for curriculum and instruction. *TESL Reporter* 27 (2), 55–62.
Giles, H., Bourhis, R.Y. and Taylor, D.M. (1977) Towards a theory of language in ethnic group relations. In H. Giles (ed.) *Language, Ethnicity, and Intergroup Relations* (pp. 307–348). New York: Academic Press.
Glanzer, P. and Talbert, T. (2005) The impact and implications of faith or worldview in the classroom: The priority and importance of character. *Journal of Research in Character Education* 3 (1), 25–42.
Gogonas, N. (2011) Religion as a core value in language maintenance: Arabic speakers in Greece. *International Migration* 50 (2), 113–129.
Green, E. (2010) What would Jesus do now in the classroom? The CREATE Research Project. *Journal of Beliefs & Values* 31, 349–352.
Griffith, J. (2004) Unless a grain of wheat .... *TESOL Quarterly* 38, 714–716.
Hage, G. (2005) Maronite white self-racialization as identity fetishism: Capitalism and the experience of colonial whiteness. In K. Murji and J. Solomos (eds) *Racialization: Studies in Theory and Practice*. Oxford: Oxford University Press.
Haugen, E. (1953) *The Norwegian Language in America: A Study in Bilingual Behavior*. Philadelphia, PA: University of Pennsylvania Press.
Hitti, P. (1956) *Lebanon in History*. New York: St. Martin's Press.
Hudson, M. (1997) Trying again: Power-sharing in post-civil war Lebanon. *International Negotiations* 2, 102–122.
Iliovits, M. (2014) Effect of a teacher's religious beliefs on the teaching of ESL. Unpublished paper for English 345 Language Acquisition, American University of Beirut.
Joseph, J.E. (2006) The shifting roles of languages in Lebanese Christian and Muslim identities. In T. Omoniyi and J.A. Fishman (eds) *Explorations in the Sociology of Language and Religion* (pp. 165–179). Amsterdam: John Benjamins.
Kaplan, R.B. and Baldauf, R.B. (1997) *Language Planning: From Practice to Theory*. Clevedon: Multilingual Matters.

Lebanese Information Center (2013) *The Lebanese Demographic Reality*. Beirut: Lebanese Information Center.

Lightbown, P. and Spada, N. (1993) *How Languages Are Learned*. Oxford: Oxford University Press.

Lindholm, J.A. and Astin, H.S. (2008) Spirituality and pedagogy: Faculty's spirituality and use of student-centered approaches to undergraduate teaching. *Review of Higher Education* 31 (2), 185–207.

May, S. (2003) Rearticulating the case for minority language rights. *Current Issues in Language Planning* 4 (2), 95–125.

Moaddel, M. (2008) Ethnicity and Values among the Lebanese Public: Findings from a Values Survey. Ann Arbor, MI: Population Studies Center, University of Michigan. See https://www.psc.isr.umich.edu/research/tmp/moaddel_lebanese_survey_pr_jan08.pdf (accessed 3 May, 2018).

Morgan, B. and Vandrick, S. (2009) Imagining a peace curriculum: What second language education brings to the table. *Peace & Change* 34, 510–532.

Muhanna, E. (2010) The end of political confessionalism in Lebanon? *The National*, 31 October. See http//www.the national.ae/news/worldwide/the-end-of-political-confessionalism-in-lebanon? (accessed 3 May, 2018)

Mukherjee, S. (2013) Reading language and religion together. *International Journal of the Sociology of Language* 200, 1–6.

Naiden, F.S. and Harl, K.W. (2009) Adieu to Lebanon. *Historically Speaking* 10 (2), 24–26.

Norton-Peirce, B.N. (1995) Social identity, investment, and language learning. *TESOL Quarterly* 29 (1), 9–31.

Omoniyi, T. (2010) *The Sociology of Language and Religion: Change, Conflict and Accommodation*. Basingstoke: Macmillan.

Omoniyi, T. and Fishman, J. (eds) (2006) *Explorations in the Sociology of Language and Religion*. Amsterdam: John Benjamins.

Picard, E. (1996) *Lebanon a Shattered Country: Myths and Realities of the Wars in Lebanon*. New York: Holmes & Meier.

Pitts, M.B., Jr. (2006) Forging ethnic identity through faith: Religion and the Syrian-Lebanese community in Sao Paulo. Unpublished MA thesis, Vanderbilt University.

Rowell, A. (2013) The Persian conversion? *NOW*, 15 October. See https://defence.pk/pdf/threads/the-persian-conversion.283356/ (accessed 3 May, 2018).

Salibi, K. (1971) The Lebanese identity. *Journal of Contemporary History* 6, 76–86.

Salibi, K. (1988) *A House of Many Mansions*. Berkeley, CA: University of California Press.

Sawyer, J.F.A. (2001) Religion and the study of language. In J.F.A Sawyer, J.M.Y. Simpson and R.E. Asher (eds) *Concise Encyclopedia of Language and Religion* (pp. 322–326). Amsterdam: Elsevier.

Schiffman, H.E. (1996) *Linguistic Culture and Language Policy*. London: Routledge.

Schoonmaker, F. (2009) Only those who see take off their shoes: Seeing the classroom as a spiritual space. *Teachers College Record* 111, 2713–2731.

Shaaban, K. (2005) A tentative framework for incorporating moral education into the ESL/EFL classroom. *Language, Culture and Curriculum* 18 (1), 201–217.

Shaaban, K. and Ghaith, G. (2003) Effects of religion, first foreign language, and gender on the perception of the utility of language. *Journal of Language, Identity, & Education* 2 (1), 53–77.

Smith, D.I. and Osborn, T.A. (eds) (2007) *Spirituality, Social Justice, and Language Learning*. Charlotte, NC: Information Age.

Smolicz, J.J. (1992) Minority languages as core values of ethnic cultures: A study of maintenance and erosion of Polish, Welsh, and Chinese languages in Australia. In W. Fase,

K. Jaspaert and S. Kroon (eds) *Maintenance and Loss of Minority Language* (pp. 277–305). Amsterdam: John Benjamins.

Smolicz, J.J. and Secombe, M.J. (1985) Community languages, core values and cultural maintenance. In M. Clyne (ed.) *Australia, Meeting Place of Languages.* Canberra: Pacific Linguistics, Australian National University.

Snow, D. (2001) *English Teaching as Christian Mission: An Applied Theology.* Scottdale, PA: Herald Press.

Spolsky, B. (2003) Religion as a site of language contact. *Annual Review of Applied Linguistics* 23, 81–94.

Spolsky, B. (2009) *Language Management.* Cambridge: Cambridge University Press.

Stevick, E. (1990) *Humanism in Language Teaching: A Critical Perspective.* Oxford: Oxford University Press.

Suleiman, Y. (ed.) (1996) *Language and Identity in the Middle East and North Africa.* London: Curzon Press.

Suleiman, Y. (2003) *The Arabic Language and National Identity: A Study in Ideology.* Washington, DC: Georgetown University Press.

Tannenbaum, M. (2009) What's in a language? Language as a core value of minorities in Israel. *Journal of Ethnic and Migration Studies* 35 (6), 977–995.

Turkmen-Dervisoglu, G. (2012) Lebanon: Parody of a nation?: A closer look at Lebanese confessionalism. *Yale Review of International Studies* 2 (1), 61–71.

Varghese, M. and Johnston, B. (2007) Evangelical Christians and English language teaching. *TESOL Quarterly* 41, 5–31.

Westwood, M.K. (2014) Addressing reconciliation in the ESL classroom. *International Journal of Christianity & English Language Teaching* 1, 82–92.

Wherritt, I. (1985) Portuguese language use and the Catholic Church in Goa, India. *Southwest Journal of Linguistics* 8, 60–75.

White, K.R. (2010) Asking sacred questions: Understanding religion's impact on teacher belief and action. *Religion & Education* 37 (1), 40–59.

Wiegand, K.E. (1997) Religious, ancestral, and national identity: Political use and abuse in Lebanon. Unpublished MA thesis, American University (Washington).

Womack, D.F. (2012) Lubnani, Libanais, Lebanese: Missionary education, language policy and identity formation in modern Lebanon. *Studies in World Christianity* 18 (1), 4–20.

Wong, M.S. and Canagarajah, S. (eds) (2009) *Christian and Critical English Language Educators in Dialogue: Pedagogical and Ethical Dilemmas.* New York: Routledge.

Wong, M.S., Kristjánsson, C. and Dörnyei, Z. (eds) (2013) *Christian Faith and English Language Teaching and Learning: Research on the Interrelationship of Religion and ELT.* New York: Routledge.

Zakharia, Z. (2009) Positioning Arabic in schools: Language policy, national identity, and development in contemporary Lebanon. In F. Vavrus and L. Bartlett (eds) *Critical Approaches to Comparative Education: Vertical Case Studies from Africa, Europe, the Middle East, and the Americas* (pp. 215–231). New York: Palgrave Macmillan.

11 Teachers' Perceptions of the Interface between Religious Values and Language Pedagogy in Egypt

Deena Boraie, Atta Gebril and Raafat Gabriel

Introduction

Religion has played a central role in life in Egypt from antiquity up to the present day. Egypt is predominantly Muslim, making up 90% of the population, while Christians constitute 10% of Egyptians (*World Factbook*, 2013–2014). Egypt's 2014 constitution guarantees freedom of religion and stipulates that Islam is the religion of the state. Sharia is the main source of legislation, but allowing Christians and Jews to have their own personal laws such as family statutes based on their own religious rules. The majority of Egyptian Christians belong to the Coptic Orthodox Church. Egyptian Christians live all over Egypt and are integrated in all sectors of life within the country. They are not confined to specific cities or neighborhoods.

Two of the authors of this chapter are Muslim and one is a Christian Copt. Religion is deeply embedded in our lives and is evident in our choices and decisions, yet it is not overtly discussed, particularly between Muslims and Christians. Our interest in the relationship between faith and the teaching and learning of English arose from the changes that occurred in Egypt's political context when the Muslim Brotherhood came to power in 2012. In spite of the shared history and culture between Muslims and Christians, tensions and divisions developed between the Muslim and Christian communities. During that time, religion was on our mind and intense discussions about the use and abuse of religion took place at all levels of society and among the three of us. In this context, as colleagues coming from different religious backgrounds and experiences working in the American University in Cairo (AUC), we developed a strong professional interest in exploring possible links between religion and language pedagogy, spurred by an invitation to contribute a chapter to this book. We turned to the available research on English language teachers' pedagogical beliefs and faith and discovered that no research had been carried out in an Arab-Islamic culture such as Egypt. Only one Egyptian researcher (Mansour, 2008, 2009, 2011, 2013) has conducted several studies showing how the personal religious beliefs of Egyptian science teachers have shaped their teaching beliefs and practices. Although it was not clearly indicated, Mansour's research focused on Muslim science teachers and there was no indication that Christian science teachers were included in his studies. Building on this line of research, the current study explores the views of both Muslim and Christian English language teachers regarding the relationship between faith and teaching/learning English in Egypt.

Religion and language in Egypt

There are mixed views about the relationship between religion and language in Egypt and other Arab countries. One view is that Arabic is seen to be crucial to Islam and intrinsically linked to the faith of Muslims. Another view is that Christianity is associated with English and that Egyptian Christians would have more positive attitudes towards English compared to Arabic. A study conducted by Shaaban and Ghaith (2003), investigating the attitudes of Lebanese college students towards the utility of Arabic, English and French, supported these two views. Their results showed that Muslim students viewed the utility of the Arabic language more favorably than Christian students and 'Christian students viewed the role of the FL in social life in Lebanon more favorably than Muslim students did' (Shaaban & Ghaith, 2003: 69). Shaaban and Ghaith attributed this difference in linguistic attitudes between Muslim and Christian students to the presence of foreign missionaries in Lebanon who established missionary schools. Christians attending these schools acquired good English language skills and subsequently obtained good jobs, an opportunity denied to most Muslims and Christian sects other than Protestants, Catholics and Maronites.

On examining the history of religion and language in Egypt and the nature of Arabic, the language context is much more complicated than the views described above. There are actually three main varieties of Arabic: classical Arabic, modern standard Arabic (MSA) and colloquial Arabic. Classical Arabic is the language of the Qur'an and is viewed as the purest or even divine form of the language. Classical Arabic is used to recite, read and write verses from the Qur'an and their interpretations. Most Muslims in the world are not Arabs and live outside the Arabic-speaking countries. Those Muslims use classical Arabic for their prayers (oral) and reading the Qur'an and Islamic texts, although classical Arabic is not their mother tongue. MSA, which is a simplified version of classical Arabic, is the language used by most educated speakers orally and in writing in Egypt and the Arab world, the media and most of the printed publications in Arabic. All Egyptians, both Muslim and Christian, study MSA in public and private schools and universities. Egyptian colloquial Arabic, a spoken variety, is used on a daily basis by all Egyptians as well, regardless of their religious affiliation. Colloquial Arabic is the mother tongue of Egyptian Muslims and Christians. With the advent of social media the linguistic landscape has changed, and now many Egyptians exchange messages on Facebook and Twitter writing using a mixture of MSA and colloquial Arabic. In fact, in the Coptic Church all the sermons are in MSA interspersed with some colloquial Arabic. Until the Arabs conquered Egypt in the 7th century, Coptic was the language of the Christian population and the church. By the end of the 12th century, MSA became the main written language of the church and Coptic became a classical language mastered by very few people (Rubenson, 1996).

There is a strong connection between the work of missionaries in different parts of the world and the teaching of English (Varghese & Johnston, 2007; Wong & Canagarajah, 2009), which most likely explains why there is a misperception that Egyptian Christians are viewed as identifying with English and having more positive attitudes towards English than Arabic. American Evangelical Presbyterian missionaries came to Egypt in 1854 and from then until decolonization in 1952 they did considerable community work such as opening schools, libraries and medical centers as well as literacy campaigns to promote Bible reading (Sharkey, 2008). The missionaries promoted evangelization and American culture; however, '... despite a century of work among Egypt's Muslim majority and indigenous Coptic Christian minority, they gained few converts' (Sharkey, 2008: 1). By the 1930s, there was an anti-missionary backlash and Muslim nationalists perceived them as a threat, causing dividing lines between Muslim and Christian communities. By the late 1930s, the Coptic Orthodox Church had become very active and the Egyptian Coptic Christians resisted being converted into the Evangelical Church.

In summary, Arabic is the official language of Egypt and is spoken by both Muslims and Christians and is used in all aspects of life. The following section discusses the role and status of the English language.

The current status of the English language in Egypt

Since the British occupation of Egypt from 1882 until 1952, the English language slowly grew in influence, taking over other popular European languages such as French. The importance of English was emphasized by the colonizers to the extent that 'between the two World Wars, colonial policy attempted to subvert the status of Arabic under that of English' (Lewko, 2012: 29). After the 1952 revolution led by Nasser, overthrowing the monarchy and marking the end of British colonial rule, Arabic became the official language of Egypt. Throughout the Nasser years, the status of Arabic was elevated in reaction to colonialism, and the learning of English was not given as much importance.

The introduction of English as a subject in a specific grade in the school curriculum reflects the importance given to the language. During the Nasser years, English was only taught starting from Grade 7 in all public schools. This changed during the Sadat years and today the learning of English has once again gained prominence. In the fall of 1994 English as a foreign language (EFL) was introduced into Grade 3 and in the fall of 2003 English was introduced in Grade 1. Now English is a compulsory subject for all students in Egypt in both public and private schools. The reasons given by the Ministry of Education for the early introduction of English are to enable children to study science and technology in English, to provide children with an expanded worldview and to satisfy the English language needs of the workplace as Egypt enters a more global economy (Saad, 2003).

Today the demand for studying and mastering English is high. Although there is no explicit language policy, schools and universities give priority to English as there is a 'strong link between English and what is considered to be a good education in Egypt' (Ramaswami *et al.*, 2012: 150). English is considered to be very important; it opens up opportunities in higher education, employment and career achievement and allows for social mobility. English is the medium of instruction in many universities including the colleges of medicine, engineering, science and agriculture. English language proficiency is a requirement for students to register for graduate studies in many university programs. There is also a strong correlation between socio-economic class and proficiency in English. In Egypt 'the average salary gap between non-English speakers and English speakers is around 70–80%' (Ramaswami *et al.*, 2012: 124). Thus, the perception is that English skills are necessary in order to obtain a good job or to travel overseas and work abroad.

Interestingly, in spite of the fact that English is taught from Grade 1 as a school subject in all public and private schools in Egypt, bilingualism is largely absent. This reflects a problem with the low quality of English language education provided in most public and private schools and universities. There are ongoing efforts by the government to improve the standard of English language teaching and learning, moving to a more interactive skills-based approach. In light of the importance and role of English in Egypt, thousands of adults enroll annually in EFL evening classes in private language schools and centers, keen to improve their language proficiency in order to be able to compete in the job market and find employment.

On examining the history, it is clear that there is a relationship between religion and language in Egypt and the role and importance of English is also evident. Furthermore, recent research has established the interconnectedness between faith and English language teaching (ELT; Behnam & Mozaheb, 2013; Varghese & Johnston, 2007; Wong *et al.*, 2013). On examining the literature, there is little research on the relationship, if any, between English instruction and faith in Egypt. Thus, the purpose of this study is to contribute to addressing this gap by investigating the relationship between the religious beliefs of Egyptian EFL teachers and their beliefs about the teaching and learning of English as well their attitudes towards Arabic and English. The following section discusses the definitions of the two main constructs we investigated: beliefs about the teaching and learning of English, including religious beliefs, and attitudes towards English and Arabic.

Teacher Beliefs

Beliefs are defined by Richardson (as cited in Altan, 2012: 481) as 'psychologically held understandings, premises, or propositions about the world that are felt to be true'. Beliefs include assumptions, perceptions, pedagogical knowledge, preconceived opinions or ideas, mental models, conceptions and misconceptions about language teaching and learning (Gabillon, 2012; Nguyen, 2013). Although beliefs are a very important construct, they are difficult to define. According to Pajares (1992), beliefs are a 'messy construct' and are somewhat problematic to investigate empirically. He also argued that we cannot discuss beliefs separately from a belief system. Research on teaching and learning within a social constructivist framework emphasizes that the culture and the context must be taken into account. Beliefs should be investigated in a sociocultural context and thus they are not context free (Mansour, 2013). Mansour (2008: 1608) defines personal religious beliefs (PRBs) as 'the views, opinions, attitudes and knowledge constructed by a person through interaction with his/her sociocultural context through his/her life history and interpreted as having their origins in religion'. Mansour proposed a PRB model to explain the interaction between teachers' personal religious beliefs, their experiences, pedagogical beliefs, identity and practices. Mansour's study showed that science teachers' beliefs about teaching and learning were 'strongly shaped by their personal religious beliefs derived from the values and instructions inherent in the religion' (Mansour, 2008: 1623). He also predicted that teachers with particular PRBs are more likely to interpret an experience differently through the lens of their religion compared to teachers without these PRBs.

Therefore, a language teacher's belief system consists of different kinds of beliefs including religious beliefs. For the purpose of our study, teacher beliefs are teachers' views of their own approaches to teaching and learning English and the research focus is on exploring and understanding the sociocultural mediator of religion on these beliefs. We are 'concerned with the influence of teachers' understanding and interpretation of religious principles on the teaching and/or learning' (Mansour, 2008: 1608) of English.

Attitudes towards English and Arabic

Generally, an attitude is defined as a 'disposition to react favorably or unfavorably to a class of objects' (Sarnoff, 1970: 279). Garrett (2010: 20) offered a relatively similar definition that emphasizes the stability of attitudes: an attitude is 'an evaluative orientation to a social object ... seen as having a degree of stability that allows it to be identified'. Although we are not usually conscious of our language attitudes, they can shape our perceptions of and reactions to certain people or social events. In this study attitudes are defined as the evaluative orientations of EFL teachers towards English and Arabic.

Referring back to our earlier description of the linguistic landscape in Egypt, it 'can leave one with an ambiguous place of English in Egypt', which reflects a colonial history and is related to socio-economic differences (Lewko, 2012: 22). Attitudes towards English are also related to native-speaker norms of using English such as accent and pronunciation, as well as perceptions regarding whether or not English is seen as a threat to the native language and local culture. The current study attempts to look into issues related to the attitudes Muslim and Christian teachers have towards both English and Arabic and how this variable is affected by religious affiliation.

Research questions

(1) What, if any, is the relationship between religion and beliefs about the teaching and learning of English as perceived by Muslim and Christian English language teachers in Egypt?
(2) What, if any, is the relationship between religion and attitudes towards Arabic and English as perceived by Muslim and Christian English language teachers in Egypt?

Methods

Given the nature of the research questions, this is a qualitative study. The data were collected based on interviews and analyzed using qualitative thematic analysis. Because there is limited research available in this context regarding religious beliefs and English language teaching and learning, an inductive approach is adopted to extract categories and themes from the interview data.

Participants

Participants in this study are part-time instructors in a languages department housed in the School of Continuing Education (SCE) at the AUC, which offers a wide range of continuing education and training programs including English. The EFL programs include general English, conversational English, test preparation courses and English for specific purposes (ESP). Examples of ESP courses include business English, legal English, academic English and English for religious purposes. The school has set standards for recruiting high-quality instructors to ensure delivery of high-quality EFL programs. All instructors are required to have an advanced level of English proficiency (Level C1 on the Common European Framework Reference scale) as well as teaching certification from an accredited educational/training institution. These part-time instructors have diverse backgrounds and come from a wide range of teaching contexts such as teaching at schools, universities or private language centers. A total of eight participants were purposively selected for interview, taking into consideration the variables of religion and gender. Four Muslim (two male and two female) and four Christian (two male and two female) instructors were selected for the interview who displayed evidence of being devout believers. The following is a detailed description of the background of the eight interviewees (pseudonyms are used in this study instead of their real names).

Eman

Eman currently works as a full-time EFL instructor in an Islamic school in Cairo and as a part-time EFL instructor at SCE, AUC. She is both an experienced and certified EFL teacher and has been working at prestigious language schools in Cairo for over 20 years. Eman obtained a BA in English arts and education from the Faculty of Education, Ain Shams University in Cairo. In 2010 she completed the Fundamentals of English Language Teaching (FELT) certificate at SCE. In 2013 Eman earned a certificate in teaching English as a second language for IGCSE from Cambridge University.

Father Joseph

Father Joseph graduated from the Faculty of Education, English department in 1993; since then, teaching English has been his career except for the last couple of years. He taught English to teenagers for 17 years and served as Deputy Principal at a language school for two years. Meanwhile, he worked as a part-time EFL teacher at AUC for six years and conducted teacher training for mathematics and science teachers. In May 2012 Father Joseph became a Coptic priest and in August 2014 he became the secretary of the Coptic Pope for the Diaspora, where he uses English almost daily to communicate with Copts all over the world as well as to communicate with embassies and international organizations.

Salem

Since he graduated in 1995 from the Faculty of Alsun (languages), English department of Ain Shams University, Salem has been working as a full-time EFL teacher in four language schools in Cairo. After earning his FELT certificate in 2011, he joined SCE, AUC as a part-time EFL instructor. Salem is keen on his professional development as an EFL instructor and attends EFL conferences, seminars and workshops regularly.

Sadek

Sadek is a full-time administrator at SCE, AUC. He has more than 15 years of experience in the field of EFL teaching, teacher training, assessment and administration. Sadek earned his MA in teaching English to students of other languages (TESOL) in 2002 from AUC and obtained the Preliminary Certificate in teaching EFL for adults in 1997. In 1997 he earned a Diploma in applied linguistics and in 1995 he completed his BA in English literature from the Faculty of Arts, Cairo University.

John

John has been a part-time EFL instructor at SCE since 2010. He has 17 years of experience in EFL as a teacher, lecturer and certified examiner in various institutions in Egypt and Libya. John is multilingual as he speaks Arabic, English, French, Italian, Greek, Spanish and Russian. He also teaches exceptional learners such as visually and hearing impaired learners. John uses Egyptian and international sign language and is involved in a lot of voluntary work. After earning his GCE in London, he completed his BA in English literature at Al-Fateh University in Tripoli, Libya and an MA in comparative literature at AUC.

Rita

Rita has been a part-time EFL teacher at SCE for over ten years and has taught a variety of general English and ESP courses. She is also a freelance translator for the Evangelical church in Egypt. Rita earned her MA in comparative and international education in 2014 and a Professional Educator Diploma in leadership in 2013 from the Graduate School of Education at AUC. Rita earned her BA in English literature from the Faculty of Arts, Cairo University in 1984. After doing several administrative jobs in various businesses, Rita changed careers and started teaching English, which she loves doing.

Rahma

Rahma is an English language teacher who has been teaching English for 15 years. She has taught different age groups and different proficiency levels in various institutions. Rahma obtained an MA in TESOL from AUC in 2011. She has volunteered to teach Arabic literacy classes for women.

Sister Safaa

Sister Safaa is a consecrated deaconess in the Egyptian Coptic Orthodox Church and does several part-time jobs in the fields of ELT, simultaneous translation, graphics and community service. She has been a part-time EFL teacher in church organizations for 12 years and joined SCE after earning the FELT certificate in 2014. Sister Safaa runs and teaches at a church-run nursery and regularly represents the church at conferences and retreats. After obtaining her GCE in Dubai, Sister Safaa completed her BSc in dentistry from Cairo University. She also earned five certificates in translation and five others in theology.

Data Collection

The interview questions were prepared by the researchers in advance, based on the previous literature. Teachers were asked directly about how their religion and religious beliefs affect: their views about the importance of English language in Egypt; their choice of teaching as a career; the purpose of teaching and learning English; their role as a teacher; their view of an effective English language curriculum; their teaching methodology; teaching materials used; topics commonly discussed or avoided in class; classroom teaching activities including pair and group work in classes with male and female students; their assessment practices and ways of ensuring fairness in assessing their students; their views about integrating local and international culture in the classroom; the strategies used to motivate their students in class; the role of their students in class; and the values they would like to nurture in their students. Participants were also asked about whether they thought there are differences between devout Muslim and Christian teachers compared to Muslim and Christian teachers who do not observe religious practices. As for the second question, teachers were asked about their perceptions of the importance of Arabic and English and how both languages affect national identity.

Data Analysis

Data were analyzed following a qualitative methodology to identify categories, emerging patterns and themes about the participants' PRBs and their relationships to language pedagogy as well as their linguistic attitudes. The eight transcripts were analyzed inductively with no a priori assumptions, aiming to identify and describe patterns found as reported by the respondents and then seek to understand and explain these patterns. An iterative and reflexive process was followed, involving developing themes from the data and then examining the data once again to find out whether these themes are representative or applicable.

Results

The results are presented in view of the two research questions.

RQ1: What, if any, is the relationship between religion and beliefs about the teaching and learning of English as perceived by Muslim and Christian English language teachers in Egypt?

This question attempted to investigate the relationship between faith beliefs about the teaching and learning of English. Overall, the results showed a strong relationship between religion and beliefs held about the teaching and learning of English by both Egyptian Muslim and Christian teachers. It also shows a strong link between religion and teaching practices in the classroom. The following eight themes emerged from the interviews which illustrate how religion is represented in the teaching of English and in the ELT classroom in Egypt by both Muslim and Christian teachers.

Religion is intertwined in how they view their role as teachers

All eight teachers agreed that religion is manifested strongly in their roles as teachers. Several different views of their role were expressed: a messenger, a servant leader, a serving teacher, imparting knowledge and representing Christ in a good way. The Christian teachers used constructs and concepts that are commonly used in Christian servant leadership literature (Patterson, 2003). They used the construct of servant leadership (Johnson & Vishwanath, 2011), meaning that they reflect love, humility, empowerment, trust and altruism through their work as teachers and perceive their role as their function as messengers and ambassadors of Christ. Muslim teachers also used the term messengers to describe their role as teachers.

Rita sees her role as a leader in class who is to instill certain values through language. For her, Jesus was a great leader and her role model as a servant leader (Patterson, 2003). She stated that in Egypt teachers have only one style of leadership and there is no democracy in the class in its full meaning. It is the teacher who decides upon the curriculum and tests, and the learner does not have the right to object, to change or to modify. She believes there is flexibility to some extent at AUC for a teacher to be a leader.

Rahma believes that teaching is a message and that she is a role model for people, inspiring and influencing students. According to her, learning itself is one of the pillars of religion and we are meant to learn and to know more about different people and different cultures. She noted that the Prophet Mohamed (pbuh) encouraged people to learn different languages.

Salem believes that his role is to spread love and peace through teaching. The purpose is not to earn money but to be a messenger to teach people and not only language. He realizes that he will not change the world or the school system but he feels that he has to at least try to change the part he is in – his class, hoping that it might spread.

Safaa views herself as a serving teacher. She stated that '... students are the people of God, put it in another way they are the children of God. If [she is] serving them, I am serving god.' Safaa views teaching as an altruistic calling which is also related to the construct of servant leadership (Johnson & Vishwanath, 2011).

John stated that teaching is linked to his faith; to him it is the joy of imparting knowledge to someone, the joy of making someone richer because they have spent some time with you. Because most of his students are Muslim, he always feels the responsibility of representing Christ in a good way. He noted that there is a very fine line between acting for Christ and truly representing him. He would not be extra sweet with his students because he is a Christian.

It is interesting to note that both Christian and Muslim teachers mentioned concepts related to servant leadership and service. Teachers are seen as leaders taking students on a journey of learning (Johnson & Vishwanath, 2011).

Teachers care for the spiritual wellbeing of their students

All participants noted that Muslim and Christian teachers teach English as well as nurture values. They believe that they should do more than just teach English and should help students to become more self-aware and teach them ethics and good behavior in general.

John cares a lot about his students and stated that he always prays for them. He believes that prayer impacts people's lives and that prayer moves things. When his students are feeling down for whatever reason, he prays for them. He prefers to talk to God about people instead of talking to people about God.

Eman does not see herself as just an English teacher and she tries to direct her students onto the right track. She believes that her track is the right, track not because it is hers, but because it is what she learned from the religious books and from her teachers. She is keen to have a good relationship with all her students, especially her Christian students, and would not go deeply into matters that would annoy or disturb them.

Salem sets some rules to follow at the beginning of each course. He believes God has taught us everything that is right. So in teaching these values, 'I satisfy God and whatever these people do after that will return to me; God will reward me for that ...'.

Rita focuses on nurturing the values of teaching students how to be responsible and to be conscientious by raising their awareness. She also focuses on love for lifelong learning and helps them become self-learners and self-motivated, concepts many of her students had never heard of before.

Religion drives the choice of teaching materials and topics in the language classroom

All teachers except Sadek stated that they view the curriculum and the teaching materials they choose through a lens colored by religion. Religion affects whether or not they will use songs in class as well as being careful in choosing photographs. It is clear from the interviews that religion also influences the topics that teachers will avoid or focus on in class.

Father Joseph chooses texts to be used in class that have a good purpose and teach the audience something such as friendship or helping the needy. He avoids topics that are against religion or are taboo or sensitive to Egyptians, such as living together or having children before marriage, comparison between religions, sex and politics.

Rita chooses topics that she is comfortable with, such as friendship and gender issues. Topics such as atheism or homosexuality are not taboos for her.

Eman's religious beliefs affect the way she chooses her supplementary materials – she avoids the use of song, music, dances and movies in her classes. She explains to her students that she does not use songs or music in class because of her faith. She uses real-life situation videos such as people talking in the street.

On the other hand, Salem uses songs a lot in his class because he has found that students love songs whatever their age. He uses songs to teach English – vocabulary and to practice listening – and to instill a value. He does not want to use songs merely for fun and to get students just to clap and dance. He uses technology as far as possible but he is very careful regarding images and photographs. He usually starts a Facebook page for each class he teaches and provides his students with links to materials that he feels would be useful for them.

Safaa attempts to stay away from controversial issues and always uses materials that have a moral lesson. She stated that she 'would never bring materials that are not usual or offbeat. I would not get a song that uses foul language or a movie that is explicit in a way or another. I would use songs for example that have a humane sort of concept.'

Sadek does not believe there are any taboos; if there is a controversial issue, he thinks that it should be discussed in class. He argues that Islam promotes critical thinking and students would know what is right and what is wrong.

Balance between integrating local and international culture

All teachers believed that both the local and the international culture should be integrated into the classroom effectively. The local culture is seen as motivating for students and adds to their experiences. Some teachers are selective regarding which aspects of international culture should be brought into the classroom.

Father Joseph believes that the local culture should be integrated in teaching because language is not a subject in itself but is a carrier of our culture, and he wants to meet the needs of his students. He cautions, though, that if the integration of local culture is exaggerated, then students make fun of this because they do not use the foreign language in these situations. He brings to class current events and refers to news headlines.

Salem integrates international culture in his classes as long as it is not offensive because there are some things that are acceptable in one culture and not acceptable in another. Safaa thinks that we should teach the good aspects of the foreign culture such as equality and fairness.

Rita integrates both international and local cultures. She notes that although as Eastern people we have a different culture, freedom of thought is important. Students should accept them the way they are and we have the right to reject the culture for ourselves. Similarly, Sadek thinks teaching cultural values that are not compatible with Islam is not a problem at all because Islam teaches Muslims not to take things for granted:

> We are encouraged in Islam to do talk about cultural issues. There is no fear in Islam that you question your religion. The Ayats (verses) in the Qur'an push Muslims to think critically. Our religion is strong and that's why we do not have to worry about critiquing and challenging certain rules. If you do not understand, you follow blindly and that's why we restrict Islam to rituals. A true Muslim has a role in life for humanity. (Sadek)

Importance of fairness and not cheating

All teachers stressed the importance of being fair in treating and assessing their students and not accepting any form of cheating in their classes. Salem notes that fairness is very important in the assessment of students' work because 'being fair is part of our religion' and 'God will ask me about this'. Eman states that 'We talk about honesty and no cheating … if you can't see Allah, Allah can see you'. Father Joseph tells his students that cheating is equal to stealing and as a teacher he is not supposed to teach thieves.

Both Rita and Safaa stressed the importance of being fair with students and having no biases. Rita described an experience she had a female student in her class wearing the niqab (face veil) who was very clever. She was very pleased when the student got an 'A' and told Rita that Rita was extremely fair.

Cheating is an issue for Rahma and fairness really concerns her when grading essays or giving grades. She sometimes agonizes about giving grades to be sure that she is being fair.

Mixed views regarding discussing religion explicitly in the classroom

Teachers had mixed views about discussing religion explicitly in their classes. There were no differences between Christian and Muslim teachers. Some teachers completely avoided religion even if it was raised by students in the classroom while others discussed it whenever the opportunity presented itself.

For Salem, one of the taboos is to discuss religion explicitly in the classroom. An example he gave was during an oral quiz, when one of his students tried to quote a saying of the Prophet Mohamed (pbuh) and the teacher stopped the student. He does this because he believes that it is hard to control discussions about this religion in class because 'we don't have this culture of disagreement, we don't have it in Egypt'.

For Rita, discussing religion is a taboo for her. Once a whole class was interested in knowing about the differences between Catholics, Protestants and Orthodox Christians. She explained that she did not like getting into such issues.

On the other hand, Rahma noted that religion can enter the class quite unexpectedly. She gave an example of an incident with a high school class where the brother of one of the students had been killed in the Portsaid (a city located in the northeast of Egypt) football match. There was an aura of sadness in the class and the students were asking questions about the purpose of life and what will happen when they go to paradise. Rahma then told them a story of Moses in the Qur'an and they discussed this, all in English.

John stated that, while he does not bring Christian topics into the curriculum or into the classroom, if they do come up he does not overlook them – for example, when they start asking questions about why people exchange gifts at Christmas. He did note that the taboo for him was talking about Islam.

Gender issues in the classroom

All eight teachers encouraged males and females to work together in groups. One teacher noted that he would never force students to do this if they were not comfortable. Another teacher noted that she encourages female students to mix with male students.

Most teachers would not be comfortable discussing sensitive gender-related topics such as female circumcision in mixed classes. This is not based on religious reasons – just out of social embarrassment. Only one teacher mentioned that she likes to talk about women and how they are represented in Islam. She said that she loves to clarify to students how some Islamic sheikhs deny the roles and importance of women and their rights.

Differences between devout teachers and teachers who do not observe religious practices

Six teachers agreed that there are differences between teachers who do and who do not observe religious practices. Father Joseph and Rita preferred to use the term conscientious teacher.

Father Joseph considers that a conscientious teacher is usually a religious teacher who does not waste class time. Both Father Joseph and John see giving a long break as stealing students' time. Both John and Father Joseph mentioned that they are very sensitive about how they handle the prayer time of their Muslim students during class and they had different approaches. Father Joseph said that 'even if the rule is not to give time for the students to pray, I had to wait for them'. John does not allow students to go out for prayers during exams. Rita views conscientious teachers as being punctual and fair.

Eman sees a difference between devout teachers and those who do not observe religious practices, stating that 'It is clear from the materials we use and jokes we tell for fun to our students, from the language we use'. Rahma stated that the difference is not in the way they teach but in how they deal with, talk to and engage with students. Salem believes that teachers who are not devout may not keep in mind being fair, being accurate about what they say or caring about students' learning.

RQ2: What, if any, is the relationship between religion and attitudes towards Arabic and English as perceived by Muslim and Christian English language teachers in Egypt?

The interviews with the eight teachers focused partly on their attitudes towards both Arabic and English. The analysis showed a number of themes emerging from the data as presented in the following part.

The importance of Arabic

Both groups agreed about the importance of Arabic at personal and professional levels. A common theme in the data that teachers continuously emphasized is the fact that Arabic is an essential part of their national identity. For example, Father Joseph argues that 'we cannot understand Egyptians, if we do not understand Arabic'. He adds: 'Copts are part of the Arab world; most of our literature is in Arabic, sermons are in Arabic. We read the Bible every day in Arabic. If I cannot read it correctly, I would convey the wrong message.' As shown in the previous quotation, Father Joseph uses Arabic to read the Bible and also to give sermons. He thinks that Arabic is one of the requirements for being part of the local and regional context. The Muslim group also stressed the importance of Arabic as the religious language of Islam since it is the language in which the Qur'an was originally revealed to the Prophet Mohamed. Many of the Muslim teachers repeatedly reported the use of Arabic to read the Qur'an on a daily basis. One of them actually took pride in Arabic being the language that will be used on Judgment Day.

Both groups indicated the importance of Arabic as a tool for daily communications since it is the national language in Egypt. For example, teachers mentioned the use of Arabic either to read or to write literature. Some of them reported the use of Arabic when translating from and to English – some of the participants work on translation tasks as part of their job responsibilities. Many of the Muslim teachers referred to the richness and beauty of the Arabic language as well. On a related note, many teachers believed that Arabic is important for them as English teachers. For example, Sadek argues that Arabic is a great asset for English teachers in Egypt:

> I think it is a good asset for English teachers if they have strong Arabic proficiency. It will be useful for them in class. It will open their minds to how to look at the meaning of words in both languages. So, it will help them when they design activities for their students and when they discuss vocabulary questions with them. (Sadek)

As Sadek says, having advanced proficiency in Arabic would help language teachers in their classes. According to some participants, Arabic could be used to save time when students cannot understand the meaning of a specific word in English. However, most teachers indicated that this strategy should be used as a last resort. Rahma reported using Arabic as a 'bonding' strategy with her students for the purpose of establishing rapport.

The importance of English

The interviewees from both groups equally agreed that they regularly use English to carry out different functions with family members, friends and students. Given the fact that English has become a lingua franca and the main international language, the teachers indicated that English is important for them and for their students as well. In a country like Egypt, where there are relatively few jobs, people tend to look for job opportunities elsewhere. For this reason, school students and fresh graduates attempt to improve their English in order to be able to compete in the international job market. Given this importance, many of the teachers reported using English heavily on a daily basis:

> I do use English in my daily life. It just happens. I mix a lot – ingrained, inherent words – 'sorry', 'hello'. English had a major influence on my life. I only read in English. The only book I read in Arabic is the bible, everything else I read in English. (John)

This quotation refers to another issue that emerged in the data, which has to do with code switching. The teachers indicated that they insert English words into their conversations with friends and family members. However, they stressed the fact that they do not do it to show off, as code switching usually comes naturally. However, one of the teachers (Sadek) indicated that he does not use English at all outside the classroom: 'I rarely speak English at home or with friends outside work. Even with those who insert English words in English, I speak in Arabic to them. I think it is related to religion, it is the language of the Qur'an.' This attitude probably reflects a stance that sees the use of English instead of Arabic as something harmful to the national identity, an issue that will be discussed in the next section.

English and the threat to national Identity

While both groups agreed that English is an important asset for all Egyptians, given the myriad benefits discussed in the previous section, there are some differences with regard to how the spread of English is perceived by both groups. The four Muslim teachers feel that this is a clear threat to their national identity. They mentioned a number of problems associated with the spread of English, the first of which is the negative impact on the Arabic language with the increasing role of English in their daily lives. Many of them alluded to the fact that many Egyptians nowadays are increasingly using English in their conversations. Others referred to the higher status English enjoys in certain contexts, with people using purely English or switching between Arabic and English to reflect prestige. One of the participants, Sadek, referred also to the status of English in the publishing world:

> If you are a researcher and you are doing research in any discipline, the books and the references are in English and the results will be produced in English even if the researcher is academically prepared in Arabic. Arabic should have the same importance and status even more. What is happening now as a Muslim, as an Egyptian, and as an Arab, we are killing the language one way or another. We are promoting research in English not in Arabic. I do believe with it comes culture and other things. (Sadek)

As stated in the quotation, this teacher complains about the deteriorating status of Arabic to the degree that he argues that we are killing Arabic by resorting to such practices. On the other side, the Christian teachers did not think that English negatively affects Arabic.

Another negative aspect for the spread of English has to do with changes in identity-related variables. When a language is taught, other byproducts come with it, especially the foreign culture. According to Eman, 'culture affects us both positively and negatively'. However, the Muslim teachers felt that the negative impact is more serious, as suggested by Salem:

> Yes, it has affected the identity of many people who would act like Americans or Europeans forgetting about our identity and this happens a lot ... Some of them copy not only the language after watching movies or listening to songs but also changing identity ... the way they are dressed, the way they talk and behave. (Salem)

Other Muslim teachers shared the same concerns as Salem, while three Christian teachers did not feel the same way. The only Christian teacher sharing these concerns is Rita, who argues the following:

> When it comes to culture and identity, some of them feel they are lost. They feel they do not belong any more to Egypt and they do not belong to Western societies. The problem is that they do not feel they are standing on a solid ground. Especially because of the way they are brought up; some people are just very keen to have rapid social mobility; they feel they want to get rid of their past, family ideas and doctrines. They just want to go to the other side hoping to receive acceptance from others ... I pity those. Some of them feel ashamed because they belong to the Egyptian society ... I saw it, I feel it and I know it because they want to immigrate ... they want to leave for economic reasons, but they are not proud to be Egyptians. This is pathetic. (Rita)

The other Christian teachers did not see the spread of English as a threat to national identity and emphasized the benefits that come with English and the doors that English opens for students. For example, Father Joseph indicated that national identity is not determined by language since language is just one component.

One of the Muslim teachers recommended taking a more proactive stance and not remaining on the defensive:

> It is risky because what is happening is that the West and English speaking community at large are doing every effort to promote the culture everywhere and putting a lot of money into it. The Arabs are not doing this at all. We are not promoting the language nor the culture coming with it. We are not even exerting 10% of the efforts and time they are giving. If you look at the English programs, whether funded by foreign aid or personally financed, I learn the language and culture. Our environment, mainly the education system, does not promote critical thinking and, many of them will say that the American or British culture is much better and we are bad and they start thinking of immigrating to these countries. (Sadek)

Sadek laments the missed opportunities related to empowering the Arabic language and reforming the educational system. By addressing these issues, he thinks that we can bring up generations that have confidence in their abilities and pride in their language and country.

Discussion

It is clear from the interviews that religious beliefs strongly impact and define the way the interviewees perceive themselves as teachers as being messengers or servant leaders or servant teachers. Religious beliefs have an impact on the values that teachers emphasize in class and the choice of materials to be used, topics to be discussed including religion and gender issues, and the integration of both local and international culture. Religious beliefs also have an impact on how these devout teachers perceive teachers who do not observe religious practices. This is in line with current research in the field. Pasquale (2013: 50) states that 'faith can have a direct influence on teaching (either positive or negative) and that a teacher's faith is integral to their identity'. As mentioned in our introduction, we are only beginning to explore this area in our context and far more research is needed to pursue this at a deeper level. As Smith (2013: 157) stated, 'some more unpacking will be needed in order to trace the role being played by faith'. Further in-depth interviews with other less devout Muslim and Christian teachers should be conducted, focusing explicitly on religious beliefs combined with classroom observations, as well as classroom artifacts such as lesson plans, handouts, assessments, etc.

Although there is a clear link between the spread of English, colonialism and the work of missionaries at several points in Egypt's history, this, as shown in the results, is no longer the case. Both Muslim and Christian teachers equally think that the demand for and importance of English is driven by pragmatic decisions and personal development. Because of the Egyptian education system and the need for English in the workplace, it is important to be proficient in English in order to achieve educational and socio-economic success (Gebril & Hozayin, 2014). Similar results were obtained with regard to the importance of Arabic. Both groups indicated that Arabic is essential for them at a personal and professional level. They cited a number of contexts in which they use Arabic. This result is surprising given the common assumption that Christians in Egypt do not pay enough attention to Arabic. On the other hand, this result makes sense given the fact that Egyptians use Arabic to fulfill their daily needs. As for Christians, while Coptic is restricted to church rituals, Arabic is used in all other religious ceremonies including reading the Bible.

There is a relatively striking difference between both groups regarding how the spread of English is perceived. While the four Muslim teachers indicated that this phenomenon is a serious threat to both the Arabic language and to national identity, three of the four Christian teachers did not believe so. In general, Muslims in the Middle East feel that some elements of Western culture, which are essentially Christian, are sometimes in contradiction with their belief systems. For this reason there is that sense of ambivalence when it comes to this issue. However, there is religion-related proximity between Egyptian Christians and elements of the Western culture. This proximity might be the reason behind these results.

Study Limitations

Readers should take into consideration the limitations of this study when interpreting the study results. This is a small-scale study that collected data from one instructional context at a private university in Egypt.

The participants in this study were purposively selected as being devout Muslims and Christians, and thus the results of the study may not be generalizable to other less devout Egyptian teachers. The researchers also collected self-reported data based on interviews. Future research investigating the relationship between religion and language teaching should use other tools, such as ethnography, which can allow in-depth understanding of different variables affecting this relationship.

Conclusion

This study is one of the very few that has focused on the relationship between religion and beliefs about language teaching in the Middle East, following a qualitative design in data collection using interviews to address these issues. The study showed a clear link between faith and instructional practices and beliefs. This result is not surprising in a society where religion for many people is a way of life. In general, faith motivates people and in this study it is clear that teachers are driven by their religion. Teachers derive a lot of satisfaction from intellectual and spiritual relationships with their students. The implication of this result is that faith can also be a motivational strategy for students. Teachers can and do use faith to support their students in handling their personal problems as well as guiding them in their learning. Faith can be a powerful source of motivation for both teacher and students, which is an area that should be further explored in this context.

Given the study limitations, there is a clear need for more research that goes beyond self-reported data and in other parts of Egypt. An interesting area where research is needed is the observation of actual teaching practices, with more in-depth interviews conducted to explore these beliefs and probe more deeply.

References

Altan, M.Z. (2012) Preservice EFL teachers' beliefs about foreign language learning. *European Journal of Teacher Education* 35 (4), 481–493.

Behnam, B. and Mozaheb, M.A. (2013) Identity, religion and new definition of inclusiveness in Iranian high school EFL textbooks. *Social and Behavioral Sciences* 70, 1099–1108.

Gabillon, Z. (2012) Revisiting foreign language teacher beliefs. *Frontiers of Language and Teaching* 3, 190–203.

Garrett, P. (2010) *Attitudes to Language: Key Topics in Sociolinguistics*. Cambridge: Cambridge University Press.

Gebril, A. and Hozayin, R. (2014) Assessing English in the Middle East and North Africa. In A. Kunnan (ed.) *The Companion to Language Assessment*. Malden, MA: Wiley-Blackwell.

Johnson, A.C. and Vishwanath, K.R. (2011) Servant professorship and its implications. *International Journal of Education Research* 6 (1), 135–146.

Lewko, A. (2012) Linguistic projection and the ownership of English: Solidarity and power with the English language in Egypt. Unpublished master's thesis, American University in Cairo.

Mansour, N. (2008) The experiences and personal religious beliefs of Egyptian science teachers as a framework for understanding the shaping and reshaping of their beliefs and practices about science-technology-society (STS). *International Journal of Science Education* 30 (12), 1605–1634.

Mansour, N. (2009) Science teachers' beliefs and practices: Issues, implications and research agenda. *International Journal of Environmental & Science Education* 4 (1), 25–48.

Mansour, N. (2011) Science teachers' views of science and religion vs. the Islamic perspective: Conflicting or compatible? *Science Education* 95 (2), 281–309.

Mansour, N. (2013) Modelling the sociocultural contexts of science education: The teachers' perspective. *Research in Science Education* 43 (1), 347–369.

Nguyen, S.T. (2013) *The Relations between Vietnamese EFL Students' and Teachers' Language Learning Beliefs*. Newcastle upon Tyne: Cambridge Scholars.

Pajares, M.F. (1992) Teachers' beliefs and education research: Cleaning up a messy construct. *Review of Educational Research* 62 (3), 307–332.

Pasquale, M. (2013) Folk linguistics, content-oriented discourse analysis, and language teacher beliefs. In M.S. Wong, C. Kristjánsson and Z. Dörnyei (eds) *Christian Faith and English Language Teaching and Learning: Research on the Interrelationship of Religion and ELT* (pp. 154–164). New York: Routledge.

Patterson, K. (2003) *Servant Leadership: A Theoretical Model*. Virginia Beach, VA: School of Leadership Studies, Regent University. See https://www.regent.edu/acad/global/publications/sl_proceedings/2003/patterson_servant_leadership.pdf (accessed 26 September 2017).

Ramaswami, S., Sarraf, I. and Haydon, J. (2012) *English Language Quantitative Indicators: Morocco, Algeria, Tunisia, Egypt, Jordan, Lebanon, Iraq and Yemen: A Custom Report Compiled by Euromonitor International for the British Council*. London: British Council. See https://www.teachingenglish.org.uk/sites/teacheng/files/Euromonitor%20report%20final%20July%202012.pdf (accessed 3 May 2018).

Rubenson, S. (1996) The transition from Coptic to Arabic. *Egypte/Monde Arabe* Series 1, 27–28, 77–92. See http://ema.revues.org/1920 (accessed 3 May 2018).

Saad, A.I. (2003) As of next year: English from first primary. *Al-Ahram*, 10 March, p. 3.

Sarnoff, I. (1970) Social attitudes and the resolution of motivational conflict. In M. Jahoda and N. Warren (eds) *Attitudes* (pp. 271–282). Harmondsworth: Penguin.

Shaaban, K. and Ghaith, G. (2003) Effect of religion, first foreign language, and gender on the perception of the utility of language. *Journal of Language, Identity, & Education* 2 (1), 53–77.

Sharkey, H. (2008) *American Evangelicals in Egypt*. Princeton, NJ: Princeton University Press.

Smith, D.I. (2013) Frameworks for investigating faith and ESL: A response to Snow, Lessard-Clouston and Baurain. In M.S. Wong, C. Kristjánsson, and Z. Dörnyei (eds) *Christian Faith and English Language Teaching and Learning: Research on the Interrelationship of Religion and ELT* (pp. 1–7). New York: Routledge.

Varghese, M.M. and Johnston, B. (2007) Evangelical Christians and English language teaching. *TESOL Quarterly* 41 (1), 5–31.

Wong, M.S. and Canagarajah, S. (eds) (2009) *Christian and Critical English Language Educators in Dialogue: Pedagogical and Ethical Dilemmas*. New York: Routledge.

Wong, M.S., Dörnyei, Z. and Kristjánsson, C. (2013) Introduction: The faithful fence. In M.S. Wong, C. Kristjánsson and Z. Dörnyei (eds) *Christian Faith and English Language Teaching and Learning: Research on the Interrelationship of Religion and ELT* (pp. 1–7). New York: Routledge.

World Factbook (2013–2014) *Egypt*. Washington, DC: Central Intelligence Agency. See https://www.cia.gov/library/publications/the-world-factbook/geos/eg.html (accessed 3 May 2018).

12 Church-sponsored English as a Second Language in Western Canada: Grassroots Expressions of Spiritual and Social Practice

Carolyn Kristjánsson

Introduction

Church-sponsored English as a second language (ESL) programs for newcomers have existed in Canada in one form or another for 150 years (Wang, 2006). Nevertheless, they are virtually invisible in the academic literature. To shed some light on these programs, in this chapter I investigate the perspectives of three directors and their reports of program practices.

Within a sociocultural paradigm, language learning cannot be fully understood apart from the relations between stakeholders and associated conditions in which learning occurs. It is a framework in which teaching and learning can be seen as social practice, a relational view of persons, their actions and the world (Lave & Wenger, 1991: 50). From this perspective, 'objective forms and systems of activity, on the one hand, and agents' subjective and intersubjective understandings of them on the other, mutually constitute both the world and its experienced forms' (Lave & Wenger, 1991: 51). This sociocultural understanding informs the task at hand. I begin by situating the study in the historical and contemporary Canadian context and then explore the construct of social practice and linked matters of agency and identity which guide the investigation. Based on an analysis of the interview accounts of program providers, I argue that the church-sponsored ESL programs under consideration can be best understood as mutually constituted expressions of social and spiritual practice. It is a position that challenges the limits of current sociocultural perspectives while opening up a view of the potential for interconnected understandings of social and spiritual agency (Dörnyei *et al.*, 2013).

The Canadian context

Immigration has a significant place in Canadian history and, although Canada has a mixed record in its treatment of newcomers (Avery, 1995), in 1971 it became the first country to adopt multiculturalism as an official policy (Citizenship and Immigration Canada, 2012). While this led to a national settlement program in 1974 and several diverse language instruction initiatives for newcomers, systematic provision of ESL programs for adults did not emerge until 1990, when the federal government established immigrant language training as a national priority (Fleming, 2007). Since then, as part of the broader scope of settlement assistance, government-funded programs have provided an average of 800–1300 hours of free language instruction, variously configured, to eligible newcomers across Canada. While helpful for those who qualify, even in this group many have found they still needed more instruction (Ricento *et al.*, 2008).

In addition to government-funded programs, Canada has a long tradition of settlement support provided by volunteers. These are rooted in two main movements, the 'self-help movement' (Bettencourt *et al.*, 2003: xiii), whereby newly arrived immigrants look to earlier arrivals for assistance, and the 'philanthropic voluntary action movement', consisting of help provided by 'philanthropic associations, many of them based on religious affiliation' (Bettencourt *et al.*, 2003: xiii). Language classes have often figured prominently in the latter, with early instances of classes for Chinese workers documented in the colony of British Columbia prior to the birth of Canada as a nation (Wang, 2006).

Today the number of church-sponsored language programs in Canada is undocumented; however, there is evidence to suggest a substantial presence. In 2003 an analysis of publicly listed ESL programs in the Vancouver metropolitan area of British Columbia indicated that 19% of all known non-government funded language programs were sponsored by Christian churches, a number accounting for 43% of community-based programs (Kristjánsson, 2003). More recently, in a national cross-denominational survey of 260 churches, two-thirds of respondents reported that they provide settlement and relief services for newcomers occasionally or always, with non-government funded language support services the most frequently named example (Janzen *et al.*, 2010). For their part, it is not uncommon for newcomers to Canada to look to religious institutions of various types for settlement help and language classes (Han, 2009; Handy *et al.*, 2005). While published studies of church ESL programs in the United States are beginning to emerge (e.g. Baurain, 2013; Chao & Kuntz,

2013), the known published literature pertaining to such programs in Canada is limited to one study of classroom interaction (Kristjánsson, 2013). The need for additional insight is put into perspective by Layder, who observes that 'macro phenomena make no sense unless they are related to the social activities of individuals who reproduce them over time. Conversely, micro phenomena ... have to be understood in relation to the institutions that provide their wider social context' (in Hall, 2002: 175). This type of relational insight is helpfully facilitated by an exploration of the construct of social practice and interconnected components of agency and identity, to which I now turn.

People in the world

Freire (1998) asserts that all educational practice implies a theoretical stance on the part of educators, a stance based on an interpretation of humans in the world. This position is consistent with that of Lave and Wenger (1991), and Wenger (1998: 149), who posits that 'our practices deal with the profound issue of how to be a human being'. From this perspective, humans are not merely biological or cognitive beings, they are also social beings, a starting point central to Wenger's understanding of learning as social participation, a process of 'being active participants in the practices of social communities and constructing identities in relation to those communities' (Wenger, 1998: 4). As such, practice in this sense is always social practice and, as in related sociodynamic paradigms, encompasses matters of agency and identity (Dörnyei & Ushioda, 2011; Lantolf & Thorne, 2006; Ushioda, 2009; Yang, 2013).

Agency, from a sociodynamic perspective, is understood as a person's capacity to act within the possibilities afforded by the social structures in which he or she is situated (Miller, 2010; van Lier, 2008) while not necessarily being determined by them (Gao, 2007; Kristjánsson, 2013). As a context-related capacity:

> Agency refers to people's ability to make choices, take control, self-regulate, and thereby pursue their goals as individuals leading, potentially, to personal or social transformation ... Agency can also enable people to actively resist certain behaviors, practices, or positionings, sometimes leading to oppositional stances and behaviors leading to other identities. (Duff, 2012: 417)

More than performance or doing, agency also encompasses the capability to ascribe significance to things and events, to attribute meanings and interpretations to activity (Lantolf & Thorne, 2006). In short, agency is the link between motivation and action, that which defines 'a myriad of paths taken' (Lantolf & Thorne, 2006: 239).

Seen from this vantage point, a focus on social practice is not only a functional perspective on human activities. 'It includes not just bodies ...

and not just brains ... but moreover that which gives *meaning* to the motions of bodies and the working of brains' (Wenger, 1998: 51, italics in the original), meaning that emerges from 'the dynamic relation of living in the world' (Wenger, 1998: 54) and encompasses the construction of identities through relations of engagement and participation (Noels, 2013; Norton, 2000; Wenger, 1998). It is through this lens of meaningful action (Arnold & Murphey, 2013) that I approach the investigation of church-sponsored ESL, framing it as a social practice. Since the meaning ascribed to practice cannot be free from the values and dispositions of participants (Canagarajah, 2013a), this involves exploring the perspectives of program directors along with related implications for localized program practices in an approach that recognizes a social practice, broadly defined, and its constitutive local practices as complexes of belief and action (Smith, 2013).

It is also an approach requiring a recognition of research practices as complexes of belief and action. Crookes (2009) observes that much Western philosophy, including philosophy of education, is secular, although this has only been the case for about a century, and that much philosophy in other parts of the world is more closely connected to its religious heritage (Crookes, 2009: 14). Nevertheless, the values of a secular philosophical outlook have permeated the academy such that the parameters of academic and scientific inquiry for most of the past century have privileged perspectives rooted in secular humanism and scientific behaviorism (Gross & Simmons, 2009) with implications for stakeholders in various quarters whose worldview differs (e.g. Canagarajah, 2009; Craft *et al.*, 2011; Karmani, 2005; Osborn, 2006; Stevick, 2009; Watson-Gegeo, 2004). Not insignificantly, the dominant perspective has itself been likened to a religious faith (e.g. Benne, in Gross & Simmons, 2009; Baer & Carper, 1998/1999; Stevick, 1990), a position Goheen (2009) clarifies:

> The religion of secular humanism domesticates traditional religions that offer another view of the world by limiting them to the private domain of life, to the 'spiritual' and 'moral' areas of life. The religion of secular humanism that has shaped the West, and that is now a major player in the global world, is a story that simply eliminates rival truth claims and competing visions of the world by finding a non-threatening place for those rival stories. (Goheen, 2009: 70)

From this perspective, it is not difficult to understand the challenge faced by those in the multifaceted group of stakeholders who seek to articulate or investigate potential influences of 'rival stories' and non-materialist positions from within the academy (e.g. Beauregard & O'Leary, 2007; Kristjánsson, 2007; MacKian, 2011; Nord, 2011; Schwartz & Begley, 2002).

With regard to English language teaching, Crookes (2009: 77) acknowledges that some stakeholders may have a spiritual position on their practice, thus adding this dimension to other positions of cognitive and socially oriented and embodied understandings of being in the world (e.g. Atkinson, 2011; Ortega, 2011; Zuengler & Miller, 2006). He also notes that investigations of teaching philosophies, or related areas such as values, beliefs and aims, have just begun (Crookes, 2010: 1129) and predicts that spiritually informed perspectives encompassing both religious and non-religious positions 'seem certain to form part of the research agenda' going forward (Crookes, 2010: 1133). From a complementary standpoint, Canagarajah (2013b) addresses the consequential matter of assumptions that researchers themselves might bring to such endeavors, highlighting the potential value of an 'insider perspective', including the possibility for insights that researchers from 'outside the faith' might not be able to offer (Canagarajah, 2013b: xxii). It is from such an insider perspective that I approach this study,[1] seeking to investigate the social practice of church-sponsored ESL in light of the following questions: (1) How do providers of church-sponsored ESL programs understand the relationship between themselves and newcomers to Canada? (2) What might be the implications for program practices?

The Study

This inquiry is based on interviews with the directors of three ESL programs studied in the final phase of a three-part investigation of church-sponsored ESL initiatives, conducted from May 2006 to December 2008 in British Columbia, Canada. Phases 1 and 2 consisted of a telephone survey and follow-up interviews with program directors, while Phase 3 involved on-site case studies. Participants were recruited by means of a purposive and emergent sampling strategy (Gall *et al.*, 2007) in the first phase and subsequently invited to participate in the second and third phases, respectively, with a maximum of five programs to be potentially included in the case study phase. Directors of 34 programs participated in Phase 1 while directors of 23 programs elected to participate in Phase 2, in both instances representing a combination of mainline, evangelical and non-denominational Christian persuasions. Service providers in three programs sponsored by diverse evangelical denominations volunteered for the final case study phase. This chapter draws on individual interviews with the directors of these programs. All were female and also taught a class in their respective programs. Two were Caucasian while one was a visible minority who had immigrated to Canada with her family as a child. One, identified here as Director1, represented a small, recently established program, ESL1, while the other two, Director2 and Director3, represented larger programs that had been established for approximately two decades at the time of data gathering, identified as ESL2 and ESL3, respectively. Program background information is seen in Table 12.1. All phases of the investigation and related procedures and documents underwent research ethics review.

Table 12.1 Program background

Program	Years of operation	Student population	Proficiency levels	Cost
ESL1	3	15	2	Free
ESL2	19	60–80	6	$1.25/hour + $30 books[a]
ESL3	20	120	7	$0.70/hour[b]

Notes: [a]Fees and book charges reduced or waived for refugee claimants. [b]Fees waived for students facing financial difficulties.

Interviews with program directors were based on a semi-structured format and included inquiries about program origins and whether there were any links to religious values, as well as questions about program features, perceptions of what motivated teacher and student involvement, and perceptions of program contributions to the community.[2] The interviews drawn on here lasted from 47 to 58 minutes and were fully transcribed.

Transcripts were examined by applying discourse analysis techniques coupled with constant comparative thematic analysis. According to Mohan (2011), a social practice as a unit of culture draws on the discourse of action and reflection in a practice–theory relation. Action discourse is the discourse of doing a social practice. Reflection discourse is the discourse of talking about the social practice and functions to construct and maintain knowledge about it. Reflection discourse can be further subdivided into the two categories applied to data analysis in this study: specific reflection and general reflection. The former addresses the events of practice and may be understood to provide accounts of agentive behavior, while the latter provides evidence of participants' beliefs or generalized knowledge about the practice as well as underlying values that give the action significance. To gain insight into themes that might be present in both dimensions, data were also analyzed using a constant comparative approach to identify, code and classify primary patterns (Merriam, 1998).

Results

Perspectives of program providers

How do providers of church-sponsored ESL programs understand the relationship between themselves and newcomers to Canada? An examination of participant accounts presents a picture of program providers who understand this relationship in terms of both social perspectives and perspectives linked to values rooted in Christian faith.

(a) Social perspectives

When asked how their programs began, all three directors responded with comments of specific reflection that constructed accounts of program inception with reference to changing social demographics in the broader Canadian context and their communities. These accounts included interrelated references to themes of reaching out and meeting the needs of newcomers.

The two largest programs, ESL2 and ESL3, began at a similar time with individual initiatives that led to social interaction with newcomers and subsequent collaborative efforts to teach English. In the case of ESL2, members of a Christian home group had been individually interacting with newcomers. As reported by Director2:

> It was a grassroots thing. A home group ... had a heart for reaching out to people who were newcomers to Canada ... At one point they said, 'Well, why don't we do something together and bring the people we're reaching out to together?' And so the first thing we actually had was international potluck dinners. One thing led to another. Mainly it was the needs of the people they were reaching out to. These people need to learn English. So why don't we teach them English? So that's how it started. (Director2)

The significance of the language need faced by many newcomers at this time was highlighted by Director3. Before becoming a church-sponsored effort, ESL3 had begun with the individual initiative of a church pastor and his wife in response to perceptions of pressing social need:

> Our pastor ran into some refugees who were coming from other countries who were not eligible for any kind of English classes at that time ... it could be a matter of up to two years at that time before they got their status for refugees and ... then they were eligible for government sponsored classes. There were very, very few English classes, probably there would have been one government class at that time and nothing else ... huge gap, huge gap. So that's when the pastor and his wife started it. ... There was really nothing else out there. (Director3)

The newest program, ESL1, also had links to individual initiatives on the part of established community members. Some years earlier, Director1 had been involved with newcomers from Honduras and, in response to their language needs, had been part of 'an impromptu English class' hosted with others from the church, a class which lasted until 'all learned to speak'. However, unlike the earlier impromptu initiative, the present program originated with an institutional initiative and subsequent responses from people in the community, which at that point included a large proportion of Asian immigrants. As Director1 described it:

> Our church had taken a survey of the neighborhood where we're located, and asking people what sort of things they would like to see us do ... we had about 40 households that wanted an ESL program. (Director1)

This program then differed from the others in that it came about in response to a request from people in the neighborhood, resulting from steps taken by the institution to ask community members how the church might best serve them.

(b) Underlying values

But what prompted the individual and institutional initiatives? Discourse elements of general reflection in participant comments point to the values underlying their linked understandings of reaching out and meeting needs, along with references to the related theme of friendship. For Director1, reaching out was expressly linked to the purpose of making friends:

> Our church is doing a lot of things, my [ESL] program is just one of them, to reach out and make friends in the neighborhood ... our idea is ... to reach out to the people that are with us, and whatever we're doing is to achieve that. (Director1)

For Director2, reaching out also encompassed the explicit intention of offering help in the context of friendship. This she framed as a practical expression of the faith-informed value of showing love, which she viewed as foundational to ESL2:

> from the very start it was because of the love of Jesus that they wanted to show these people. They thought, 'How can we practically show that to people? We need to help them with the needs they have.' And so, being a friend alongside to show the love of Christ to people was the very root of why things started here. (Director2)

The underlying values associated with reaching out and showing love were also noted in the comments made by Director3, who linked them to her understanding of Christian teachings regarding care for others, in particular for the marginalized of society, and made connections to individual and institutional enactment of those teachings:

> ... the Christian faith, you're going to reach out to your town and then broader around it and it keeps expanding until it becomes like world, caring for the world. And our church in particular is very much ... looking into the community and saying 'What are the needs of the community and how can we as Christians actually help those people?' And part of it is, of course, our Christian belief in that we want them to know about Jesus, but the other thing is that the teachings of Jesus are very much that you are going to be looking after the widows and the orphans ... our widows and orphans are not real orphans but their husbands are in their countries and they are lonely and they are really struggling. Or they are brand new immigrants with no language and can't fit into the job, you know, the employment market here in

> Canada ... to me these are the widows and the orphans ... the Christian faith tells us who we are to reach out to. So, not only as [individual] Christians but as a church organization, those values are very, very strong. (Director3)

Here Director3 begins her remarks by paraphrasing 'reaching out' with reference to the Biblical passage where Christ tells his followers to bear witness to him where they were located, the regions beyond and the world. She links this to the stance of her church, personifying the local institution to illustrate the collective practice of that particular faith community in response, also indicating the manner in which the church was relating to the larger local community by seeking to identify and meet needs. She goes on to explain the reasons for reaching out. The first is to bear witness to Christ by telling people about him. The second is to enact Christ's teachings, with the implication of bearing witness. Here she again draws on the discourse of Christian faith to elaborate, referring to 'widows and orphans', terms used in the Bible to denote the marginalized and economically disadvantaged of society. She then personalizes this by appropriating the scriptural terms to describe newcomers to Canada, denoting a faith-informed relationship between them and the church community of which she is a part, simultaneously assuming a position of responsibility by designating them 'our widows and orphans'. This is accompanied by further clarification of her understanding of their social and economic status and lack of access to support and resources. She ends her remarks by again expressing her understanding framed with reference to the discourse of Christian faith, and underscores the strong influence of faith values at both individual and institutional levels.

For her part, Director2 took a similar position, but went further in making connections to practical implications when describing what she hoped to accomplish through ESL2:

> We're wanting to show the love of Christ to people in a practical way. We want to help them in their lives, to adjust to life in Canada, to learn the skills they need to learn, and English is a really important one to be able to communicate ... to be able to find better work ... And helping them to network with resources that are there for them, because so many of them don't know about things. You know, having somebody who's a friend helping them know about how they can access different things. (Director2)

According to Director2, showing love meant helping newcomers adjust to life in Canada, which included not only helping them learn English, but also being a friend and facilitating access to resources in society. This relationship, while described with reference to current social realities, is represented as a faith-informed stance.

While these comments were made by Director2, they are congruent with the positions taken by Director1 and Director2. All three program providers viewed the relationship between newcomers to Canada and themselves and their church institutions not just in social terms, but 'through the eyes of faith', so to speak. Furthermore, they understood themselves to be representing faith-based values in their interactions with newcomers.

Program practices

What implications might this have for program practices? An examination of the data depicts program practices as the instantiation of program providers' understanding of themselves as insiders in Canadian society in faith-informed relationships with newcomers, seeking to facilitate their wellbeing and access to resources and opportunities.

Interpersonal relationships

When asked to describe their programs, all three directors began with comments of general reflection that foregrounded a relational component, including strategic attention to practices aimed at fostering networking and friendship among students as well as supporting strong interpersonal relationships between teachers and students.

Director1 highlighted the importance of friendship among students. In her view: 'friendship among the people that is the biggest thing ... they come and they make a friend, and especially for people who are brand new in the country, a friend is ... important.' This perspective was shared by Director3, who elaborated on the nature and significance of student friendships fostered at ESL3:

> a number of them that come here have no support networks when they get here and that's one of the things that our school does. ... It's a place where our students come in and develop relationships with their own language group and network through that and that's also a very positive thing ... they make friends, and get, you know, emotional support for what's happening in their lives. (Director3)

Each director also highlighted the value placed on strong interpersonal relationships between teachers and students and conditions that would facilitate such interaction if desired by students. In the view of Director2, ESL2, like other faith-based ESL programs, was distinguished by the nature of teacher–student relationships, a position indicated in comments of combined general and specific reflection:

> Probably for all faith-based ESL programs, I think that one of the things that makes us stand out from other ESL classes held in the community

> is that we do more than just teach English. So often when people go to class ... their teacher teaches them English, and she's paid to teach them English, and they come to the class and the class is finished, and then go home. And there's not a real connection with the teacher apart from that ... when people come to faith-based ESL programs, I think because people are there to show the love of Christ, we really try to do more. We really befriend them and their families ... help them in whatever way we can. And ... different social activities and stuff like that, we often do that. (Director2)

The comments of Director2 thus sketch an image of church-sponsored ESL program providers positioning newcomers not so much as language clients but as potential friends, people teachers are prepared to help beyond the classroom limits and with whom they interact socially. She attributes this view of teacher–student relationships to the core faith-informed value of showing love.

Curricular representation of faith values

It is also at the nexus of relationships that the curricular focus emerged, in a space constituted by program providers' understanding of the different types of relationship they and newcomers each had to Canadian society at large, coupled with a faith-informed understanding of their relationship to each other. Nevertheless, in spite of the shared faith dynamic, program providers did not take a uniform approach to curricula. Director2 and Director3 chose not to include explicit Christian content in the planned curriculum. Director1 did. However this did not mean a 'secular' versus 'Christian' approach. The understanding was more nuanced.

At ESL2, for example, the policy was to inform new students of the Christian orientation of the program while refraining from public prayer and the incorporation of explicit Christian content in the regular curriculum. Nevertheless, this did not preclude spontaneous in-class discussions of values and Christian perspectives, particularly around holidays of significance to Christians and in the context of teachers' and students' own life experiences. As Director2 described it:

> When people come to register ... we give them a welcome letter that says we're Christians and that we want to show God's love to you, and things like that. Some schools start with prayer. We don't ... we don't want to push anyone. ... [students] come from many backgrounds, Muslims, Buddhists, Hindus ... in class we'll often share about special holidays, so Christmas and Easter, just kind of a natural way to share about the meaning of Easter and the message of the Gospel through that. ... And often it will come up in class as we talk, we'll discuss values, our lives, you know. So often teachers share about their lives and students share about their lives as well. (Director2)

As for explicit use of the Bible, she went on to note:

> We don't in the regular classes. But the Friday night class which we offer for free to whoever wants to come, we tell them explicitly, we're using the Bible, we're talking about questions, you know, about the meaning of life, and things like that. So they know when they come. (Director2)

According to Director2, the policy at ESL2 was one of transparency. Yet, in spite of making the Christian orientation explicit and in spite of the practice of some other church-sponsored ESL programs, there was a decision to steer clear of programmatic elements that might cause students from different religious backgrounds to feel they were being forced to participate in Christian activities. Discussion of faith-informed beliefs and values was an accepted practice in the context of topics such as symbolically meaningful holidays and at the level of spontaneous interpersonal interaction. However, explicit and planned Bible use occurred in a separate class, not part of the regular ESL program, with the focus made known in advance, thus also realizing the commitment to transparency.

Director3 described a similar approach, in her case a decision informed by observations made before becoming director. As she explained it:

> Some church-based programs I know use the Bible or use Bible-based ESL. We tried that. ... under our first director it was tried and I felt at that time it wasn't effective. Many of the students stayed away those days. And so when I took over as director, I decided that our focus would be to be the very best English classes that you could have that would meet the needs of the students and that we would be the face of Jesus ... not preaching to them and not necessarily using the Bible. Using the Bible if it fits into our lesson plan, and being open to praying for students if they would ask or they desired that, but asking them not grabbing them. And so it's a very non-threatening kind of class ... we have Muslim students, we have Buddhist students ... lots of non-church people or very nominal Christian background who are very comfortable here. And they don't have to study the Bible. (Director3)

Like Director2, Director3 chose not to base any part of the planned curriculum in her program on the Bible. She also acknowledged that this differed from the practice of some other church-based ESL programs and also from that of her own program prior to her involvement as director. Her decision was grounded in observations of student absence when the curriculum was linked to Bible study. Consequently, her goal was to be 'the face of Jesus', an expression akin to 'showing God's love' (or variant) frequently used by Director2, denoting an embodied representation of faith. As in ESL2, in the ESL3 program this encompassed refraining from didactic exposition of Christian faith principles; however, it did not rule out use of the Bible when deemed relevant to the focus of a lesson.

Similarly, teachers did not dismiss the possibility of prayer; however, it was offered in response to requests or expressions of interest from students and based on permission from them rather than aggressive initiatives on the part of teachers. In the director's opinion, this contributed to an environment that was welcoming to people of many different faith persuasions. Studying the Bible was not a condition for participation in ESL classes.

In contrast, Director1 did incorporate explicit Christian content in the scheduled planned curriculum, using approximately one-quarter of available class time each week for this purpose. She described her practice:

> I use children's storybooks, about a Grade 2 level ... that seems to work really well. And then after we've read the children's storybook, I have a New Testament that has the Chinese in parallel with the English, and so we go around the circle and everybody reads from their New Testament. ... They like the parables that Jesus tells, and I have a book on Mary and Martha, Martha complaining that Mary wasn't helping her. That seems to appeal to them. I've got another book on the Good Samaritan ... that seems to relate to them, too. It's amazing how many of their values in terms of how people relate to each other are similar and they can understand and relate to. (Director1)

Director1, then, drew on a combination of reading material, including books for early readers in English and dual-language Bibles, using not only English but also students' first language when everyone in attendance was from the same language group. Her focus was on short, high-interest stories, choices she found students could relate to because the stories reflected many of their own values. Her expression of amazement at this suggests it challenged her initial assumptions, although she did not specify. Unlike Director3, she reported that the explicit presentation and discussion of Bible passages was not resisted by students and, on the contrary, she saw some as very interested in this along with related topics, noting:

> I haven't had anyone who's objected to the Christianity part of it ... Others that are very interested. One of them, we were talking about praying and talking to God, and she said, 'But, I'm not so sure that God speaks Chinese.' And I said, 'Why wouldn't he speak Chinese?' 'Well, maybe he doesn't know about us.' We had an interesting discussion about that. (Director1)

Director1 thus made space to explicitly address Christian beliefs and values, in other words to offer declarations of faith, through limited regularly scheduled use of Christian material alongside other material in the planned curriculum. Not only was the use of sacred text a valid part of the curriculum, but so was discussion of related matters such as prayer. Although English was the primary language through which these activities were mediated, Director1 also frames them as legitimately accessed through students' first language and values, indicating recognition of the linguistic and moral resources of students – an attitude which also informed related discussions.

Curriculum for life in Canada

Regardless of the stance taken towards representing Christian beliefs and values in embodied or declared form, the accounts of the directors indicated that curriculum content in all three programs was directed at facilitating access, adjustment and wellbeing within the Canadian environment. This included helping students develop communicative ability in English, understanding of culture, and connections to the community.

With regard to developing students' communicative ability, in comments of specific reflection, each director reported attending to various aspects of language, although oral abilities received the greatest overall emphasis. The accounts of all three also indicated a commitment to curricular practices intended to facilitate students' immediate engagement in the local community, and class content was not uncommonly influenced by direct input from students themselves.

Director1, for example, made specific connections between the priorities in her classroom and students' needs for English in daily life. She also noted how she approached student inquiries as an opportunity to draw on the experience and expertise of others in the class:

> Most of the students are dealing with the day-to-day life. They're dealing with the bank, dealing with shopping, dealing with doctor's appointments, dealing with neighborhood issues or strata council where they live or all of those things ... if something is brought up that someone's interested in, we'll deal with it ... I think it's important to be flexible. ... I usually deal with it right at the point and ask them questions about whatever it is and how they have solved it. We get input from the other people in the group. (Director1)

Director2 also highlighted aspects of class learning shaped by the needs of students, including employment needs and student reports of mistreatment:

> We make good use of the ESL Newspaper as well, often articles about employment or something like that. And we'll discuss it in class, and what are their rights ... because different ones have told us about how they were being taken advantage of. (Director2)

In combined comments of general and specific reflection, Director3 likewise reported curricular emphases and practices with reference to student needs, in particular her program's emphasis on conversation. An unusual feature of ESL3 was the advanced level conversation classes, geared for students who had a strong academic background in English but limited oral proficiency. As she explained, 'They don't want the academic English. They want conversational English.' She further emphasized the importance of combining conversation skills with a content focus that would facilitate participation in the community:

> If you're in McDonald's, working there, [you need] completely different skills than when you're discussing something that is like the news ... you have to have a much higher level of conversational English to be able to actually intelligently discuss something out of the newspaper. So our higher levels are like that, which is not really out there in other programs. ... my particular class is what's happening, I call it my current events [class] ... below that we do use a [published] curriculum, but again, the curriculum that we use is conversationally based and very much what's happening in society. (Director3)

This focus on language and content of relevance to students was complemented by attention to opportunities for enhanced cultural knowledge and experience. Comments by all three directors indicated that the primary focus on culture in the planned curriculum revolved around national holidays or cultural events and included information about origins and customs. Coffee breaks in ESL1 and ESL3 were regularly used as opportunities to foster such awareness, and an extended period of up to 30 minutes or more was allotted for this time, when students from all classes came together. Coffee breaks at ESL3 frequently incorporated a planned presentation as well. Director3 explained:

> So we do, like any kind of holiday ... We approach it from not just the Christian perspective, so Halloween, this is what you're going to expect, this is Canadian culture ... and some people might disagree ... but that's what's out there and what you need to know. ... Same as Christmas ... Easter ... we do make a lot of effort and that's both in our coffee break time, and in the class the teachers do that too ... Last week we had a segment of this. We have a significant percentage of our students who have elementary school kids ... and of course you have Valentine's parties and cards, like what is expected for the moms ... these things. So we really try to meet those needs of the students. (Director3)

Yet again this director framed her priorities in terms of meeting students' needs and providing information to help them navigate cultural practices in the broader Canadian context and in their personal spheres of interaction. She alluded to an awareness that some in the Christian community might view a holiday curriculum primarily as a carrier of Christian content. However, although she did include Christian perspectives, it was not to the exclusion of other cultural information she felt students needed.

The practice of extended coffee breaks and planned presentations in ESL3 was one of various practices that also served to foster specific connections between students and the community through invited presentations by guest speakers representing community agencies or organizations of significance to students. In addition, all three directors reported making available a diverse range of extracurricular opportunities that facilitated multifaceted connections. These activities included, but were not limited to, holiday events and all-school potluck meals as well as smaller class gatherings in the homes of teachers. The directors also reported passing on information about church groups and activities beyond the program, including those sponsored by ethnic congregations in the community. The accounts of program-sponsored extracurricular activities as well as other possibilities indicated that they were characterized by pronounced experiential and interpersonal components and, alongside the scheduled activities of program hours, created opportunities for networking among students, between teachers and students, and between students and people in the community.

In short, the accounts of program directors indicated that they understood both their interaction with newcomers and their local program practices to be informed by a social perspective rooted in faith values. These values were represented in the program in the form of embodied and declared expressions of faith. Embodied, that is demonstrated, expressions of faith were seen in approaches to language learning, cultural understanding and networking which would facilitate access to and well-being in Canadian society. This was the predominant focus in program implementation. However, there was also evidence of explicitly articulated, that is declared, expressions of faith. In ESL1 the planned curriculum included a regularly scheduled Christian content component. In ESL2 and ELS3 explicit discussions of beliefs and values were reported to occur in the context of spontaneous or serendipitous curriculum implementation, although it could be argued that the favorable disposition towards such inclusion constituted a plan nonetheless, albeit less structured. All programs also provided students with information about extracurricular options or church-sponsored groups where beliefs and values grounded in the Christian faith would be explicitly presented and discussed. However, the majority of contact time was allocated to emphases represented in terms of embodied expressions of faith.

Discussion

According to Wenger (1998: 51), a social practice is a way of being human in the world and is, above all, a process by which participants make meaning of their experience in it. Furthermore, meanings attributed to participation extend beyond the localized outworking of specific activities with specific people, drawing also on understandings located in the various communities to which participants belong. Participation in a social practice is thus the outworking, to a greater or lesser extent, of one's identity as a member in those communities. Moreover, since identities cannot be turned on and off, participation in social practice occurs at the nexus of multimembership where the forms of participation from different communities interact, influence each other and require coordination and reconciliation (Wenger, 1998: 159). In this study, the practice of church-sponsored ESL is represented in the accounts of program directors as a way in which they engage the world from their location as citizens and Christians in a country where interrelated government policies result in the presence of newcomers in their local communities. In their collective narrative, program directors position themselves as insiders in Canadian society, established members of their communities, people with resources and access to resources. Newcomers, in contrast, are positioned in terms of their less established, more peripheral social situation in Canada and characterized in terms of related needs, including the need for English as a key resource to becoming established in Canada. At the same time, the directors depict newcomers as being in social and relational proximity to themselves, representing them as members of the immediate community, neighbors and potential friends. Furthermore, they depict themselves as feeling a measure of responsibility for their wellbeing in the Canadian context, a perspective inextricably rooted in their understanding of themselves as Christians. It is this position which gives rise to the language programs, a means of practically addressing the needs of newcomers as well as an expression of faith values on the part of the program providers. While program providers do want people 'to know Jesus', to use the words of Director3, they do not view their programs as a cover for proselytizing, a position borne out by the focus of program practices in general and thought given to the nature and focus of Christian content in particular.

In his discussion of community membership and identity, Wenger (1998) introduces the term imagination as 'the process of expanding our self by transcending our time and space and creating new images of the world and ourselves' (Wenger, 1998: 176). He goes to some lengths to explain that this process does not produce a less real or less significant type of interaction than that based on mutual social engagement, but rather concerns views of self and the world that transcend such engagement. In this way, it is possible for people to locate themselves in broader connections and configurations. Ishiyama (1995) takes a similar position in his depiction of transpersonal self, the difference being that this dimension does not merely transcend mutual social engagement; it transcends the social to include a spiritual dimension of self and identity (see Kristjánsson, 2010, 2013). This is the perspective reflected in the accounts of the program providers, a perspective further explained by Volf (1996), a theologian, who argues that 'Christians inescapably inhabit two worlds – "they are in God" and "in the world" – the world of the biblical traditions and the world of their own culture' (Volf, 1996: 208). It is a position that affirms both a spiritual dimension of existence and the outworking of related relationships and commitments in culturally situated ways (Volf, 1996: 211).

In their accounts, the program directors in this study situate themselves in their local Christian communities and, by extension, the institutional denominations represented by the churches that sponsor their programs, but they also locate themselves in the world of Biblical scripture and Christian faith, drawing on a repertoire of linked images and concepts that reify aspects of Christian practice. In Wenger's (1998) paradigm, reification and participation are necessary to understand each other (Wenger, 1998: 62–71).[3] As such, this repertoire is significant in highlighting the way in which program providers construct their relationship to the world and, concomitantly, their relationship to newcomers to Canada, including how it is instantiated in the social practice of church-sponsored ESL. This is, then, not merely a social relationship or a social response. It is the response of people who understand their existence in spiritual as well as social terms, a point underscored by the director of ESL1 who, when reporting her discussion about prayer with a student, framed it as 'talking to God' (understood as communicating with a non-human being), a practice open to people regardless of their language or ethnicity. The understandings of program providers about themselves and their practice thus derive from forms of participation and related meanings originating in spiritual communities as well as social. As such, the practice of church-sponsored ESL, as they represent it, can best be understood as mutually constituted expressions of spiritual and social practice.

Given this understanding, the agency of program providers can also be seen to emerge at the nexus of multimembership (Wenger, 1998), encompassing belonging and participation in local communities and related broader constellations of Canadian society and Christian faith. It is from this location that program providers and the institutions they represent 'reach out' 'to show Christ's love', by 'being a friend' and 'meeting needs' to support and enable access to Canadian society. Taking a stance of door openers rather than gatekeepers, program providers position newcomers as legitimate participants in Canadian society and envision a trajectory of movement from a peripheral location to one affording greater possibilities. It is a trajectory they seek to facilitate in light of forms of social participation and understanding rooted in their spiritual community. It is a form of agency that constitutes collaborative relations of power (Cummins, 2000). However, recognizing that many newcomers claim belonging and forms of participation rooted in faith communities outside of Christianity, the directors of ESL2 and ESL3 also exercise agency by not incorporating into the curriculum scheduled prayer and Bible use, although this could be deemed a legitimate practice given that the programs are provided and operated by members of the Christian community on premises owned by them. The director of ESL3 also refrains from limiting her discussion of holidays to Christian emphases. For her part, the director of ESL1 is unaware of any tension generated by the use of Bible narratives, and she chooses to build on shared understandings while also validating students' first languages. It is noteworthy that, although program providers are members of a strongly individualistic culture where identity is largely construed in terms of 'I' rather than 'We' (Hofstede, 2001), the spiritual values of Christian faith foster a construal which prioritizes interconnected community and the use of agency and power to facilitate the same. Based on the significance program providers ascribe to their actions, the practice of church-sponsored ESL may arguably be understood as being generated by mutually constituted expressions of spiritual and social agency (Dörnyei *et al.*, 2013; Sims, 2013).

Conclusion

Church-sponsored ESL programs are not unique to Canada or the United States (e.g. Ou, 2014; Yu, 2007). Likewise, the interface of Christian faith values and practice is not unique to the experience of those in church-sponsored programs (e.g. Baurain, 2012; Smith & Osborn, 2007; Snow, 2001; Stevick, 1990; Wong & Canagarajah, 2009; Wong *et al.*, 2013), nor is the interrelation of faith and practice unique to Christians (e.g. Ali, 1999; Kubota, 2009; Mahboob, 2009). Why might this matter? An understanding of teaching and learning as a sociodynamic process cannot ignore the potential influence of faith-informed values on the part of teachers in the complex relationship between teacher and student motivation, agency, and related interactions with contextual processes and learning outcomes (see Dörnyei & Ushioda, 2011).

During the past century, understandings of language education have been influenced by assumptions of humans as biological beings (Chastain, 1972), cognitive beings (Doughty & Long, 2003) and social beings (Atkinson, 2011). By also seeing humans as spiritual beings (Crookes, 2010), we position ourselves to gain a much richer, and potentially more complete, understanding of our practices in the world, not least the practices of language teaching and learning.

Acknowledgments

I wish to thank the study participants for enriching my understanding of church-sponsored ESL, and Suresh Canagarajah and Bill Acton for conversations that helped me to clarify ideas expressed in this chapter. I am also indebted to Bill Acton, Mary Wong and Ahmar Mahboob for helpful comments on earlier drafts. Any faults are my own.

Notes

(1) I am a follower of Jesus Christ and have been enriched by extended participation in Christian communities in Canada, Brazil and Iceland, and through visiting participation in ethnic minority Christian communities in Canada, as well as Christian communities in Uruguay, Korea, Thailand, Mozambique, Zimbabwe, England, Scotland and the United States.

(2) The interview guide is available upon request.

(3) According to Wenger (1998: 58–59), reification refers to the process of giving form to an experience by producing a conceptual object or 'thing' which becomes a focal point around which to organize meaning.

References

Ali, H. (1999) Second language teaching and learning from an Islamic perspective. *Muslim Education Quarterly* 16 (2), 47–54.

Arnold, J. and Murphey, T. (2013) *Meaningful Action: Earl Stevick's Influence on Language Teaching*. New York: Cambridge University Press.

Atkinson, D. (ed.) (2011) *Alternative Approaches to Second Language Acquisition*. New York: Routledge.

Avery, D. (1995) *Reluctant Host: Canada's Response to Immigrant Workers, 1896–1994*. Toronto: McClelland & Stewart.

Baer, R. and Carper, J. (1998/1999) Spirituality and the public schools: An evangelical perspective. *Educational Leadership* 56 (4), 33–37.

Baurain, B. (2012) Beliefs into practice: A religious inquiry into teacher knowledge. *Journal of Language, Identity, & Education* 11 (5), 312–332.

Baurain, B. (2013) Putting beliefs into practice in a church-run adult ESOL ministry. In M.S. Wong, C. Kristjánsson and Z. Dörnyei (eds) *Christian Faith and English Language Teaching and Learning: Research on the Interrelationship of Religion and ELT* (pp. 136–153). New York: Routledge.

Beauregard, M. and O'Leary, D. (2007) *The Spiritual Brain: A Neuroscientist's Case for the Existence of the Soul*. New York: Harper Collins.

Bettencourt, E., Caranci, R., Hoo, S., Millard, J., O'Gorman, K. and Wilder, H. (eds) (2003) *Understanding LINC: Language Instruction for Newcomers to Canada*. Toronto: Citizenship and Immigration Canada.

Canagarajah, S. (2009) Introduction: New possibilities for the spiritual and the critical in pedagogy. In M.S. Wong and S. Canagarajah (eds) *Christian and Critical English Language Educators in Dialogue: Pedagogical and Ethical Dilemmas* (pp. 1–18). New York: Routledge.

Canagarajah, S. (2013a) *Translingual Practice: Global Englishes and Cosmopolitan Relations*. New York: Routledge.

Canagarajah, S. (2013b) Foreword. In M.S. Wong, C. Kristjánsson and Z. Dörnyei (eds) *Christian Faith and English Language Teaching and Learning: Research on the Interrelationship of Religion and ELT* (pp. xxi–xxiii). New York: Routledge.

Chao, X. and Kuntz, A. (2013) Church-based ESL program as a figured world: Immigrant adult learners, language, identity, power. *Linguistics and Education* 24 (4), 466–478.

Chastain, K. (1972) Behavioristic and cognitive approaches in programmed instruction. In H. Allen and R. Campbell (eds) *Teaching English as a Second Language: A Book of Readings* (2nd edn) (pp. 49–59). New York: McGraw-Hill.

Citizenship and Immigration Canada (2012) *Canadian Multiculturalism: An Inclusive Citizenship*. Ottawa: Citizenship and Immigration Canada.

Craft, C., Foubert, J. and Lane, J. (2011) Integrating religious and professional identities: Christian faculty at public institutions of higher education. *Religion & Education* 38 (2), 92–110.

Crookes, G. (2009) *Values, Philosophies, and Beliefs in TESOL*. New York: Cambridge University Press.

Crookes, G. (2010) Language teachers' philosophies of teaching: Bases for development and possible lines of investigation. *Language and Linguistics Compass* 4 (12), 1126–1136.

Cummins, J. (2000) *Language, Power and Pedagogy: Bilingual Children in the Crossfire*. North York, Ont.: Multilingual Matters.

Dörnyei, Z. and Ushioda, E. (2011) *Teaching and Researching Motivation* (2nd edn). Harlow: Pearson Education.

Dörnyei, Z., Wong, M.S. and Kristjánsson, C. (2013) Conclusion faith and SLA: An emerging area of inquiry. In M.S. Wong, C. Kristjánsson and Z. Dörnyei (eds) *Christian Faith and English Language Teaching and Learning: Research on the Interrelationship of Religion and ELT* (pp. 265–272). New York: Routledge.

Doughty, C. and Long, M. (eds) (2003) *Handbook of Second Language Acquisition*. Malden, MA: Blackwell.

Duff, P. (2012) Identity, agency, and second language acquisition. In S.M. Gass and A. Mackey (eds) *Handbook of Second Language Acquisition* (pp. 410–426). London: Routledge.

Fleming, D. (2007) Adult immigrant ESL programs in Canada: Emerging trends in the contexts of history, economics, and identity. In J. Cummins and C. Davison (eds) *International Handbook of Language Teaching, Vol. 1* (pp. 185–198). Norwell, MA: Springer.

Freire, P. (1998) The adult literacy process as cultural action for freedom. *Harvard Educational Review* 68 (4), 480–497.

Gall, M., Gall, J. and Borg, W. (2007) *Educational Research: An Introduction* (8th edn). New York: Pearson.

Gao, X. (2007) A tale of Blue Rain Café: A study on the online narrative construction about a community of English learners on the Chinese mainland. *System* 35 (2), 259–270.

Goheen, M. (2009) Probing the historical and religious roots of economic globalization. In M. Goheen and E. Glanville (eds) *The Gospel and Globalization* (pp. 69–90). Vancouver, BC: Regent College Publishing.

Hall, J. (2002) *Teaching and Researching Language and Culture*. London: Longman.

Han, H. (2009) Institutionalized inclusion: A case study on support for immigrants in English learning. *TESOL Quarterly* 43 (4), 643–668.

Handy, F., Anderson, L. and Diniz, L. (2005) *The Role of Ethnic Congregations in Volunteering: A Research Report*. Toronto: Imagine Canada – Knowledge Development Centre. See http://sectorsource.ca/resource/file/role-ethnic-congregations-volunteering-research-report (accessed 3 May, 2018).

Hofstede, G. (2001) *Culture's Consequences: Comparing Values, Behaviors, Institutions, and Organizations Across Nations* (2nd edn). Thousand Oaks, CA: Sage.

Ishiyama, F. (1995) Culturally dislocated clients: Self-validation and cultural conflict issues and counseling implications. *Canadian Journal of Counselling* 29 (3), 262–275.

Janzen, R., Dildar, Y. and Araujo, L. (2010) *Beyond the Welcome: Canadian Churches Responding to the Immigrant Reality in Canada*. Kitchener, Ont.: Centre for Community Based Research, in collaboration with World Vision Canada and TIM Centre

Karmani, S. (2005) TESOL in a time of terror: Towards an Islamic perspective on applied linguistics. *TESOL Quarterly* 39 (4), 738–744.

Kristjánsson, C. (2003) Whole-person perspectives on learning in community: Meaning and relationships in teaching English as a second language. Unpublished doctoral dissertation, University of British Columbia.

Kristjánsson, C. (2007) The word in the world: So to speak (a Freirean legacy). In D.I. Smith and T. Osborn (eds) *Spirituality, Social Justice and Language Learning* (pp. 133–153). Charlotte, NC: Information Age.

Kristjánsson, C. (2010) Collaborating with a (non)collaborator: Interpersonal dynamics and constructions of identity in graduate online learning. In J.R. Park and E. Abels (eds) *Interpersonal Relations and Social Patterns in Communication Technologies: Discourse Norms, Language Structures and Cultural Variables* (pp. 305–327). Hershey, PA: IGI Global.

Kristjánsson, C. (2013) Inside, between, and beyond: Agency and identity in language learning. In J. Arnold and T. Murphey (eds) *Meaningful Action: Earl Stevick's Influence on Language Teaching* (pp. 11–28). New York: Cambridge University Press.

Kubota, R. (2009) Spiritual dimensions in language teaching: A personal reflection. In M.S. Wong and S. Canagarajah (eds) *Christian and Critical English Language Educators in Dialogue: Pedagogical and Ethical Dilemmas* (pp. 225–234). New York: Routledge.

Lantolf, J. and Thorne, S. (2006) *Sociocultural Theory and the Genesis of Second Language Development*. Oxford: Oxford University Press.

Lave, J. and Wenger, E. (1991) *Situated Learning: Legitimate Peripheral Participation*. New York: Cambridge University Press.

MacKian, S. (2011) Crossing spiritual boundaries: Encountering, articulating and representing otherworlds. *Methodological Innovations Online* 6 (3), 61–73. See http://oro.open.ac.uk/30490/5/Crossing%20spiritual%20boundaries.pdf (accessed 3 May, 2018).

Mahboob, A. (2009) English as an Islamic language: A case study of Pakistani English. *World Englishes* 28 (2), 175–189.

Merriam, S.B. (1998) *Qualitative Research and Case Study: Applications in Education*. San Francisco, CA: Jossey-Bass.

Miller, E. (2010) Agency in the making: Adult immigrants' accounts of language learning and work. *TESOL Quarterly* 44 (3), 465–487.

Mohan, B. (2011) Social practice and register: Language as a means of learning. In E. Hinkel (ed.) *Handbook of Research in Second Language Teaching and Learning* (pp. 57–74). New York: Routledge.

Noels, K. (2013) Identity theory. In P. Robinson (ed.) *The Routledge Encyclopedia of Second Language Acquisition* (pp. 289–291). New York: Routledge.

Nord, W. (2011) Does God matter? Taking religion seriously in our schools and universities: An excerpt. *Religion & Education* 38 (1), 3–23.

Norton, B. (2000) *Identity and Language Learning*. Harlow: Longman.

Ortega, L. (2011) SLA after the social turn: Where cognitivism and its alternatives stand. In D. Atkinson (ed.) *Alternative Approaches to Second Language Acquisition* (pp. 167–180). New York: Routledge.

Osborn, T. (2006) *Teaching World Languages for Social Justice: A Sourcebook of Principles and Practices*. Mahwah, NJ: Lawrence Erlbaum.

Ou, S. (2014) Language & faith: A case study of church-sponsored EFL. Paper presented at CELT Christians in English Language Teaching Conference, Taipei, Taiwan.

Ricento, T, Cervatiuc, A., MacMillan, F. and Masoodi, S. (2008) *Insights into Funded ESL Programs: Report on the LINC Program*. Calgary: University of Calgary. See http://www.ucalgary.ca/tricento/files/tricento/lincreport.pdf (accessed 3 May, 2018).

Schwartz, J. and Begley, S. (2002) *The Mind and the Brain: Neuroplasticity and the Power of Mental Force*. New York: Harper Collins.

Sims, R. (2013) Discursive agency and collective action among Lubavitch Hasidic women. *Young Scholars in Writing* 10, 58–71.

Smith, D. (2013) Frameworks for investigating faith and ESL: A response to Snow, Lessard-Clouston, and Baurain. In M. Wong, C. Kristjánsson and Z. Dörnyei (eds)

Christian Faith and English Language Teaching and Learning: Research on the Interrelationship of Religion and ELT (pp. 154–164). New York: Routledge.
Smith, D. and Osborn, T. (2007) *Spirituality, Social Justice, and Language Learning*. Charlotte, NC: Information Age.
Snow, D. (2001) *English Teaching as Christian Mission: An Applied Theology*. Scottdale, PA: Herald Press.
Stevick, E. (1990) *Humanism in Language Teaching: A Critical Perspective*. Oxford: Oxford University Press.
Stevick, E., with Kristjánsson, C. (2009) Afterword: The dilemma. In M.S. Wong and S. Canagarajah (eds) *Christian and Critical English Language Educators in Dialogue: Pedagogical and Ethical Dilemmas* (pp. 292–297). New York: Routledge.
Ushioda, E. (2009) A person-in-context relational view of emergent motivation, self and identity. In Z. Dörnyei and E. Ushioda (eds) *Motivation, Language Identity, and the L2 Self* (pp. 215–228). Bristol: Multilingual Matters.
van Lier, L. (2008) Agency in the classroom. In J. Lantolf and M. Poehner (eds) *Sociocultural Theory and the Teaching of Second Languages* (pp. 163–186). London: Equinox.
Volf, M. (1996) *Exclusion and Embrace: A Theological Exploration of Identity, Otherness and Reconciliation*. Nashville, TN: Abingdon Press.
Wang, J. (2006) *'His Dominion' and 'The Yellow Peril': Protestant Missions to Chinese Immigrants in Canada, 1859–1967*. Waterloo, Ont.: Wilfrid Laurier University Press.
Watson-Gegeo, K. (2004) Mind, language, and epistemology: Toward a language socialization paradigm for SLA. *The Modern Language Journal* 88 (3), 231–250.
Wenger, E. (1998) *Communities of Practice: Learning, Meaning, and Identity*. Cambridge: Cambridge University Press.
Wong, M.S. and Canagarajah, S. (eds) (2009) *Christian and Critical English Language Educators in Dialogue: Pedagogical and Ethical Dilemmas*. New York: Routledge.
Wong, M., Kristjánsson, C. and Dörnyei, Z. (eds) (2013) *Christian Faith and English Language Teaching and Learning: Research on the Interrelationship of Religion and ELT*. New York: Routledge.
Yang, H. (2013) Activity theory and SLA. In P. Robinson (ed.) *The Routledge Encyclopedia of Second Language Acquisition* (pp. 8–10). New York: Routledge.
Yu, K. (2007) Christianity and English language teaching: A study of an English conversation class for Mainland Chinese scholars at an English-speaking church in Hong Kong. Unpublished Master's dissertation, University of Hong Kong.
Zuengler, J. and Miller, E.R. (2006) Cognitive and sociocultural perspectives: Two parallel SLA worlds? *TESOL Quarterly* 40 (1), 35–58.

13 Response to Part 3. Religious Faith and the Language Learning Context: Exploring the 'Interface'

Brian Morgan

Introduction

Three chapters comprise Part 3 of this book on spirituality and language teaching. They are Shabaan's chapter on 'Language and Religion in the Construction of Lebanese Identity', Boraie, Gebril and Gabriel's chapter on 'Teachers' Perceptions of the Interface between Religious Beliefs and Language Pedagogy in Egypt' and Kristjánsson's chapter on 'Church-sponsored English as a Second Language in Western Canada: Grassroot Expressions of Social and Spiritual Practice'. In seeking out thematic unity across these varied contributions, certain challenges arise. How does one examine or determine what are, strictly speaking, faith-based influences on language learning across three different settings and three different nation-states, each with their own unique sociopolitical conditions and histories, particularly with regard to the (relative) co-existence of spiritual and secular values? As is apparent from reading these chapters, the meanings and observances ascribed to particular religions (Christianity and Islam) are not uniform. The beliefs and communal practices that affirm the identity of a devout Maronite Catholic in Lebanon (cf. Shabaan) or a Coptic Orthodox Christian in Egypt (cf. Boraie *et al.*) would not necessarily signify and confer the same level of recognized adherence for an evangelical Christian in Western Canada (cf. Kristjánsson).

Islam, similarly, manifests complex intrareligious differences in these chapter settings. Adherence to the Five Pillars of Islam, common to all believers (Oxford Islamic Studies Online, 2016), would be juxtaposed by beliefs (e.g. succession of the Prophet, Quranic interpretation and law) that differentiate Sunni from Shiite as well as from Druze,

Maronite and Orthodox Christian denominations in Lebanon (Shabaan). Indeed, these positioning practices (cf. Harré & van Langenhove, 1999; Pavlenko & Blackledge, 2004) as they relate to religious identity would be subject to consolidation and overt strengthening, particularly by groups who perceive their faith-based communities to be under threat. Following Shabaan's utilization of core values theory (cf. Smolicz, 1992), such differentiating and identity-maintaining values/practices might be 'hyperbolized' (Fader, 2006) in one setting – i.e. made *more* 'core' – while understated in another. In the chapter from Egypt (Boraie *et al.*), for example, where Sunnis constitute a vast demographic majority (87% of the Muslim population; Black, 2015), Sunni–Shia sectarian issues are not mentioned, since the primary source of religious identification differentiation in Egypt is between Muslim and Christian, a process of identification that also involves alignments (i.e. Islam with Arabic; Christianity with English) around values perceived by many to be intrinsic to English and a potential threat to Egyptian traditions and Islamic sensibilities.

Such differences cannot be attributed solely to the scriptural or doctrinal disputes that have marked the great schisms of the world's major religions. Clearly, as these authors detail, religious faith is neither insular nor autonomous. Intensification or diminution of religious observance – even the recourse or withdrawal into so-called fundamentalist beliefs (Castells, 2004) – reflect worldly externalities and draw attention to what Boraie *et al.* aptly describe as an 'interface' of sacred and secular activities, specifically the ways in which religious beliefs shape language teaching and influence the identities of language teachers and students. Kristjánsson's chapter appropriately conceptualizes this interrelationship via sociocultural theory (Lave & Wenger, 1991; Wenger, 1998), a theoretical orientation that foregrounds the mutual or bidirectional constitution of social and spiritual domains as well as unique forms of agency that potentially transform the language learning context.

Religion and Language Learning: From Micro to Macro Contexts

In regard to complex and multilayered interfaces, the notion of a language learning context itself poses many conceptual challenges for thematic and analytical unity. To what extent is the context of language learning and teaching *intra-personal*, involving deeply felt and internalized emotions that arise from one's personal relationship with God/Allah/Yahweh? This intimate level of context comes through more clearly in the chapters that foreground interview data with participating teachers: the eight teachers at the American University of Cairo (AUC) (Boraie *et al.*) and the three program directors of church-sponsored English as a second language (ESL) in Kristjánsson's chapter. Regarding the latter, it is important to consider what Johnston (2017) describes as a key tenet of evangelical faith, the belief in 'crucicentrism: the centrality of Jesus Christ, and the importance of developing a "personal relationship" with Christ and of emulating him in every possible aspect of life' (Johnston, 2017: 12), in some cases through bearing witness to one's *personal* faith through the outward service of ESL teaching. Faith, although communal and social in respect of ritualized observance, is still deeply affective, invoking strong passions and structures of feeling that shape pedagogical practices in ways both anticipated and not.[1]

The fact that participants in both the Kristjánsson and Boraie *et al.* chapters often negotiated their religious identities and professional roles in varying ways (e.g. in determining taboo subjects, cf. Boraie *et al.*; in how one realizes or manifests a love of God, cf. Kristjánsson) perhaps speaks to the complex emotional underpinnings that shape both teacher and student identities and define the *inter-personal* context of learning, where both collaborative and coercive relations of power (cf. Cummins, 2001) can arise via curricular content and the communication of values both spiritual and secular. Of course, these interactions take place in *classrooms* and *schools*, contexts of learning that potentially afford a great deal of curricular autonomy for faith-based content in language learning (e.g. church-sponsored adult ESL programs, Kristjánsson) or, conversely, limit the ways in which faith can inform or complement institutional goals such as the development of English for specific purposes (ESP) at a major university (cf. Boraie *et al.*).

The larger context of *community* is also worth noting, again in reference to Kristjánsson's chapter and her utilization of a community of practice framework (COP; Wenger, 1998), in which particular practices constitute and/or revitalize community boundaries and cohesion. When the COP is constituted by evangelical Christian values, it highlights core practices by which the faith-based community is (re-)created and unified. Along with the tenets of crucicentrism, witnessing and conversion, Johnston (2017) states the core importance of Biblicism for evangelical communities – the belief in an inerrant Bible, revealing the true words of God.[2] Within this specific community/COP, and the language learning context created for ESL classes, the pressure/desire to utilize the Bible as language learning content would be amplified, whereas the openness to critique or reinterpret this content in ways that challenged core beliefs would be less welcome, a point I develop later in this chapter. Given the relative powerlessness of the students – particularly of vulnerable migrants and refugees – as well as their justifiable gratitude and desire to reciprocate the generosity provided, the likelihood of students questioning the appropriateness of faith-based materials and practices is miniscule, and their silence should not necessarily be considered as consent or genuine inquisitiveness, as suggested by some of the participating ESL program directors in Kristjánsson's study.

Beyond community, larger contexts such as *city, region* and *nation-state* determine the top-down development of language in education policies, as well as the provision/regulation of public versus private education, all of which will have critical implications for religious influence on schooling and curricula. In this regard, tensions between the local and national – between faith-based community, language use and the imagined nation-state – are most apparent in multi-faith, multilingual Lebanon and its consociational political system, which has been based on proportional representation of its various religious communities. Given its history of conflict, as Shabaan notes, 'Sectarianism permeates every aspect of the lives of the Lebanese people' (this volume, p. 139), including languages spoken, taught and learned, reinforcing loyalties to religious communities (Shia, Sunni, Druze and Christian) that hinder efforts to develop a cohesive and secularized nation-state identity. In Shabaan's words, the situation can be characterized as 'religion-and-language-in-the-service-of-politics' (this volume, p. 142), where 'private, religion-based schools hold the upper hand in terms of quality and number of students [which] helps perpetuate sectarian autonomy as a primary tool in shaping people's identities and feeding prejudices towards other sects' (this volume, p. 139). Interestingly, Shabaan points to multilingualism as a unifying dimension of a nation-state identity, in which a common language, Arabic, is augmented by a variety of foreign languages through which the political and economic aspirations and alignments of its religious communities can be pursued.

The identity politics of the nation-state – its relative religiosity and/or secularism – are also important contextual features of language learning in the other two chapters in this section. In the case of Egypt, Boraie *et al.* describe Egypt as a religious society 'since antiquity', but with a complex legal arrangement by which Sharia law serves as the main source of legislation, while at the same time allowing for the coexistence of an 'interreligious law' by which 'Muslims, Christians and Jews are governed by the personal status laws of their respective communities' (Berger, 2005: 25).[3] This inter-faith coexistence is reflected in Boraie *et al.*'s introductory comments, in which the authors (two Muslims and one Christian Copt) note the centrality of religion in their lives but one that was rarely discussed between Muslims and Christians, that is, until the election of the Muslim Brotherhood and its leader, Mohammad Morsi in 2012, who was subsequently overthrown by the Egyptian military in 2013. Not unlike Lebanon's modern history, these turbulent transitions in Egypt's politics have amplified religious tensions and divisions and, for the authors of this chapter, raised previously unexamined issues regarding the interface of religion and language pedagogy in their place of work, the American University of Cairo (AUC), but also in the current debates/disputes regarding the political and economic future of Egypt within a globalizing world. As the authors' interview data show, both Muslim and Christian educators recognize the educational and socio-economic advantages that come from learning English at AUC. Yet, the four Muslim English teachers in the study also see English as a threat to the Arabic language and to Egypt's national identity, particularly in the perceived alignment of English as a language invariably carrying Christian values which potentially threaten Egypt's Islamic cultural and religious traditions.

The Egyptian example, as well, serves to illustrate the multiplicity of overlapping and often contradictory boundaries and contexts through which religious identities and corresponding language practices are negotiated. At the nation-state level, the Muslim teachers at AUC are part of a dominant religious majority (90% of the population compared to the 10% Christian population, according to the authors). Yet, within the context of transnationalism and globalization, self-perceived or emic vulnerabilities arise whereby the same 'majority' simultaneously becomes a minority, precipitating and justifying closer attention to and regulation of Arabic as a marker of an authentic Egyptian identity. The Muslim English teacher Sadek, for example, consciously limits his use of English at home or with friends, preferring Arabic as he sees it as being closely related to religious identity. He is also worried about the deteriorating status of Arabic as a language of research or as a language amenable to critical thinking. Salem, a Muslim colleague in the English teaching program at AUC, bemoans the 'by-products' of English and the allure of its popular culture, resulting in 'people who would act like Americans or Europeans forgetting about our identity' (this volume, p. 167).

Clearly, the contextualization and performativity of a minority religious identity can be a source of collective anxiety but also a rationale for the (hyper-)regulation of identificatory practices by which particular borders and boundaries are sustained (cf. Fader, 2006). Such identity performances can also serve to justify language practices that might otherwise be questioned or challenged on pedagogical and possible ethical grounds.

A Focus on Church-based English as a Second Language in British Columbia, Canada: Insider/Outsider Positionings

Similar to the participants in the Egyptian study, Kristjánsson's chapter shows both the author and her research participants alternately positioning themselves as insiders and outsiders in relation to nation-state values and their roles as English teachers. For church-based ESL, the status of being a minority outsider arises through the depiction of a monolithic insider, the Western nation-state and its hegemonic academies, disseminating secular humanist and scientific behaviorist norms inimical to spiritual values. This positioning is extended and hyperbolized, via a quote from Goheen (cited in Kristjánsson), which critiques the prevailing 'religion of secular humanism [that] domesticates traditional religions ... limiting them to the private domain of life, to the "spiritual" and "moral" areas of life ... a major player in the global world ... that simply eliminates rival truth claims and competing visions of the world by finding a non-threatening place for those rival stories' (this volume, p. 175).

This quote from Goheen invites critical evaluation on several grounds. First, the rhetorical conflation of science and secularism with religious faith – i.e. as 'rival truth claims' – exaggerates degrees of commonality and equivalence where in fact a more fundamental incommensurability exists, starting with the rigorous terms of inquiry, critique and revision that underpin all scientific 'truths' in the academy. No academic theory or methodology would ever claim to be 'inerrant' (cf. evangelical Biblicism; Johnston, 2017) or permanently closed to question and qualification. Perhaps such conditions constitute a relativistic and/or pluralistic version of truth(s), but hardly one that 'rivals' or 'competes with' the interpretive orthodoxy, suspension of doubt and submission to faith that religion requires of its devotees.

Secondly, the claim that secular humanism has 'domesticated' traditional religions, consigning them to private, non-threatening spheres of life, seems surprising in the context of Canada, a nation-state whose constitutional Charter of Rights and Freedoms begins with the following preamble: 'Whereas Canada is founded upon principles that *recognize the supremacy of God* and the rule of law ...' (Government of Canada, 1982, emphasis added). Canada also has three provinces (Ontario, Alberta and Saskatchewan) that have publically funded Catholic school systems with faith-based curricula. In the province of British Columbia, where Kristjánsson's study takes place, charter rights protect freedom of religion, resulting in numerous cases of public consultation and educational compromise between religious sensibilities and secular principles (see, for example, 'Walking the line: Secularism and religious freedom', in Stryker *et al.*, 2013: 19–22). Claims of religious 'domestication' are further countered if we examine the litany of devout clergy and religious figures that emerged from 'non-threatening spheres of life' to challenge social power relations through a politics informed by religious beliefs and values. The 'father' of publicly funded, universal health care, Premier Tommy Douglas of Saskatchewan, was also a Baptist minister (Shackleton, 1975). The first leader of the socialist Cooperative Commonwealth Federation (later to become the New Democratic Party) in the Canadian federal parliament, J.S. Woodsworth, was also a Methodist minister. Other notables include William 'Bible Bill' Aberhardt, a radio evangelist prior to becoming Premier of Alberta (1935–1943), as well as Quebec Premier Maurice Duplessis, who 'declared Quebec a Catholic province and actively promoted the Church's welfare' (Seljak, 1996: 109). Irrespective of their political affiliations – left and right – these were public figures and policy makers who exemplify the 'interconnected understandings of social and spiritual agency' which Kristjánsson (this volume, p. 173) advances in her chapter and which many see as foundational to Canadian values such as liberal multiculturalism, and our imagined nation-state identity as global peace keepers and a welcoming sanctuary and home for refugees – as generously demonstrated by the church-based ESL programs described in this chapter.

In sum, the Canadian secular humanist threat that Kristjánsson advances is, in historical fact, rife with religious underpinning and accommodation, and in the context of her chapter serves rhetorically to position church-based ESL as a minority 'outsider' activity, whose values/rights are endangered by a secular majority and whose (pedagogical) vigilance must be mobilized as a corrective to the spiritual void of mainstream ESL programming. Moreover, by framing secular humanism as 'religion' rather than 'ideology', Kristjánsson's discussion shifts the connotational and moral terrain towards what philosopher Charles Taylor (1994) has termed the 'politics of recognition', ironically a cornerstone of Canadian liberal multiculturalism, by which the nation-state is deemed responsible for supporting and protecting the collective rights of all ethno-linguistic/religious minorities, particularly those elements of collective identity most necessary for their long-term flourishing. In this scenario (i.e. Taylor's politics of recognition), a more openly religious ESL curriculum – conceptualized 'through the eyes of faith' (this volume, p. 181) – would be easily justified, as it would constitute core identity values of the evangelical 'minority' offering language instruction to newcomers. In effect, the boundary between sound pedagogy and soft proselytization becomes blurred and possibly erased, a condition reflected in Director3's teaching strategy of 'using the Bible if it fits into our lesson plan, and being open to praying for students if they would ask or they desired that, but asking them not grabbing them' (this volume, p. 183). In short, we have a language learning context worthy of a tightrope walker.[4]

The interview data from Kristjánsson's ESL Directors also clearly show that the 'program directors position themselves as insiders in Canadian society, established members of their communities, people with resources and access to resources' (this volume, p. 188). As 'insiders', they are able to teach the kinds of sociocultural skills and second/additional language practices that will 'facilitate access to and wellbeing in Canadian society' (this volume, p. 187). Of course, a key difference, in comparison to the Egyptian and Lebanese chapters where English serves more specialized purposes, is the functional importance/necessity of English for all aspects daily life in Canada.[5] Kristjánsson's section on 'Curriculum for life in Canada' demonstrates the responsible and relevant design of these ESL programs in terms of covering cultural content and employment-related materials. At the same time, one comment by Director3 regarding her conversation class on current events caught my attention. In discussing this higher level class, the director foregrounds the priority she places on intelligent conversation, while suggesting the relative uniqueness of this class: 'So our higher levels are like that, *which is not really out there in other programs*' (this volume, p. 186, my emphasis).

I may be extrapolating too much and unwisely from this comment, but it seems again to suggest the issue of overlapping or hybrid identities (of insider/outsider, minority/majority) which I have applied to both the Egyptian and Canadian chapters in respect to the interface of religion and language teaching. My initial response in reading Director3's comment was, 'Great class! I'm sure the students really enjoy it.' My second response was, 'Why would she think that this is not really out there in other programs?' My own experiences as a community-based adult ESL instructor, language teacher educator and adult ESL curriculum consultant have shown me that this type of current events conversation class is quite common, especially for content-based language instruction (Brinton, 2013; Stoller, 2004) and programs with continuous intake and multilevel classes – conditions of ESL teaching that have been partially addressed through the thematic organization of Language Instruction for New Canadians (LINC) curricular documents in Canada (see, for example, Hajer, 1999).

I do not want to imply that Director3 has been professionally negligent (there may indeed not be any other classes in her immediate social context that utilize a conversational, current events approach); instead, I would like to suggest or speculate that she has been 'preoccupied', a condition that may very well be common to all of the religiously devout teachers whose voices and values illuminate these three chapters. In common, the devotion to faith (the intra-personal, emotional context) experienced by these teachers requires/demands an ongoing self-engagement in finding a balance between one's spiritual and professional identity and in struggling to achieve that balance on a day-to-day basis. It may leave little time or motivation for further inquiry; that is, what none of these chapters seems to address is the inevitable displacement of alternatives (pedagogical, ideological) that this intense and all-encompassing aspect of identity negotiation requires. Moreover, this intensity is compounded by membership in one's faith-based community, adding conceptual insularity to how one balances the complexities of an insider/outsider identity.

What might be some of the pedagogical effects that potentially arise from this all-encompassing, hybrid dimension of a religious/professional identity? Returning again to the Kristjánsson chapter and how the ESL directors facilitate student integration into Canadian society, one of the impressions I have is that there might be an underlying deficit orientation that may inhibit the good intentions and hard work behind these church-based initiatives. In this regard, Director3's Biblical reference to 'our widows and orphans' in describing her students is telling. This Biblical association may indicate teacher perceptions that exaggerate student helplessness, which can lead to pity while promoting passivity in the classroom and beyond. As well, this type of Bible-inspired positioning can be seen as reinforcing a one-dimensional stereotype of newcomers that fails to address their intersectional complexity, in which identity issues of race, class, gender and sexuality contribute to the barriers that newcomers experience and for which spiritual guidance may be of limited efficacy in addressing the social power relations that marginalize newcomers (see, for example, Darvin & Norton, 2014; Motha, 2014; Nelson, 2009; Vandrick, 2011). We might also consider the forms of agency that frame this study as similarly one-dimensional, prone towards the recognition and utilization of *affordances*[6] (e.g. Morgan & Martin, 2014; van Lier, 2004) that reiterate – rather than reinvigorate or transform – prior religious belief regarding how we should relate/submit to power and authority in this world in light of the eternal salvation offered after. Indeed, this may be a core challenge for all devoutly religious language teachers in negotiating their professional identities and their relationships with students.

Conclusion

I have greatly appreciated the opportunity to learn about, discuss and debate the ideas presented in this section on 'Religious Faith and the Language Learning Context'. As noted in the title of this response chapter, my observations and comments are 'exploratory', reflecting my own 'outsider' status and lack of familiarity with the contexts described, especially Egypt and Lebanon, whose complex and fluid sociopolitical and ethnolinguistic environments, I imagine, would make any religiously devout language teacher carefully consider the ramifications of faith-based English language teaching (ELT). Compared to these two Middle Eastern contexts, church-based ESL in British Columbia would appear to be an oasis of calm, albeit with other external pressures (i.e. the societal dominance of secular humanism) concerning the ethical and pedagogical parameters of a more openly religious curriculum, one that is central to the identity negotiation of the ESL professionals who generously offer their time and support for newcomers to Canada. I come as an outsider to this latter setting on different terms, i.e. as an ELT professional whose own personal religious beliefs are ambivalent – a non-observant, minority cultural Jew, with agnostic and Gaia-informed possibilities – definitely lacking the devoutness and intensity of commitment revealed in the participants' interview data. My own secularized, interpretive biases should thus be judged with this experiential point in mind.

As I mentioned in my introduction, one of the key challenges in writing this response has been the development of thematic unity across these chapters on religious faith and the language teaching context. In researching this spiritual/secular interface, a newspaper article written by a regular columnist with the *Toronto Star* newspaper, Rabbi Emeritus Dow Marmur, caught my attention. In his article, Marmur (2015) discusses a 2015 report by the Sustainable Development Solutions Network (SDSN), and provides what seems to be a surprising comment given his previous religious occupation:

> Having observed contemporary congregations from the pulpit for some 40 years and experienced them in the pews for the past 15, I've come to believe that people find happiness more in being with each other than in communing with God. That's probably why recent liturgical reforms seem to be more sociological than theological. (Marmur, 2015: A11)

Marmur's comments come in response to the SDSN report and the value it attributes to countries' having 'strong social institutional capital' not only to 'support greater well being' but also as a source of 'resilien[ce] to social and economic crises' (Helliwell, cited in Marmur, 2015: A11). Marmur's comparative observation regarding happiness may be subject to debate, but the social importance – i.e. resilience in the face of worldly crises – in being part of a religious community is a theme that resonates across these three insightful and thought-provoking chapters. In a profession with limited material rewards and social recognition, those whose religious convictions motivate and sustain their dedication to language teaching and the building of community should be commended for the resilience they provide students at the spiritual/secular interface.

Notes

(1) This intra-personal 'level' of faith as the language learning context also suggests possible complementarity to recent research in psychoanalytic theories and emotional domains in ELT and SLA (e.g. Benesch, 2012; Morgan & Clarke, 2011; Motha & Lin, 2013).

(2) Johnston (2017: 12) describes conversionism as the 'experience of being born again or "saved"'. Of note, and in contrast to others who have raised ethical concerns regarding evangelical Christian educators in ELT (see, for example, Wong & Canagarajah, 2009), Johnston does not see the tenet of bearing witness as 'necessarily equated with the need to evangelize – that is, attempt to bring others into the church' (Johnston, 2017: 12).

(3) From both a legal and religious rights perspective, Berger (2005: 25) notes, 'Islamic law recognises other monotheistic religions and has institutionalised a level of coexistence and freedom of religious practice never attained in Christian canonical law'. In Egyptian legal literature, this recognition is reflected in the extension of the term Sharia for not only Muslims, but also Christians and Jews in respect to family law (Berger, 2005: 25). Of course, coexistence has its limits. If a dispute arises between Muslim and non-Muslim (e.g. a mixed marriage or divorce), intra-faith personal status laws no longer apply, and Islamic law is accorded pre-eminence (Berger, 2005: 26).

(4) To Director3's credit, she seeks a more balanced and 'transparent' approach to church-based ESL: 'our focus would be to be the very best English classes that you could have that would meet the needs of the students' (Director3, p. 14). Director1 seems to have few if any reservations in proffering a sustained and explicitly religious program, one that risks infantilizing adult students through materials choices such as Grade 2 children's storybooks.

(5) It is worth qualifying the claim of functional necessity in light of current research on metrolingualism (Pennycook & Otsuji, 2015) and superdiversity (Blommaert, 2013)

in major urban centers. My own case study of a community-based ESL program in Toronto (Morgan, 2002) similarly notes the high level of bi/multilingualism in major urban centers, hence challenging the notion of a one-size-fits-all, national ESL curriculum in which 'survival English' is a presumed priority.

(6) I refer here to Kristjánsson's discussion of agency as including 'a person's capacity to act within the possibilities *afforded* by the social structures in which he or she is situated' (this volume, p. 174, emphasis mine). In this quote, Kristjánsson cites van Lier, whose eco-semiotic perspective on affordances is worth considering: van Lier (2004: Ch. 4) emphasizes that affordances are not intrinsic properties of objects or things; they are instead relationships between participant/actor and environment, which he equates with the Hallidayan notion of 'meaning potential'. The full potential afforded, I argue, can only be realized when core values (cf. Smolicz, in Shaaban, this volume, Chapter 10) are also opened to scrutiny and reconsideration. I explore these types of issues in greater detail in Morgan (2009), particularly in my discussion of interactional versus transactional dialogue, as informed by the ethical work of the philosopher Emmanuel Levinas.

References

Benesch, S. (2012) *Considering Emotions in Critical English Language Teaching*. New York: Routledge.

Berger, M.S. (2005) Sharia and public policy in Egyptian family law. PhD thesis, Amsterdam School for Cultural Analysis (ASCA), University of Amsterdam. See http://hdl.handle.net/11245/1.241521 (accessed 26 April, 2018).

Black, I. (2015) Sunni versus Shia: Why the conflict is more political than religious. *The Guardian Online*, 5 April. See https://www.theguardian.com/world/2015/apr/05/sunni-shia-why-conflict-more-political-than-religious-sectarian-middle-east (accessed 26 April, 2018).

Blommaert, J. (2013) *Ethnography, Superdiversity and Linguistic Landscapes: Chronicles of Complexity*. Bristol: Multilingual Matters.

Brinton, D. (2013) Content-based instruction in English for specific purposes. In C. Chapelle (ed.) *The Encyclopedia of Applied Linguistics*. New York: Blackwell.

Castells, M. (2004) *The Power of Identity. Vol. 2: The Information Age: Economy, Society and Culture* (2nd edn). Malden, MA: Blackwell.

Cummins, J. (2001) *Negotiating Identities: Education for Empowerment in a Diverse Society* (2nd edn). Ontario, CA: California Association for Bilingual Education.

Darvin, R. and Norton, B. (2014) Social class, identity, and migrant students. *Journal of Language, Identity, & Education* 13, 111–117.

Fader, A. (2006) Learning faith: Language socialization in a community of Hassidic Jews. *Language in Society* 35, 205–229.

Government of Canada (1982) *Canadian Charter of Rights and Freedoms*. Justice Laws Website. See http://laws-lois.justice.gc.ca/eng/const/page-15.html (accessed 26 April, 2018).

Hajer, A. (1999) *LINC 4 & 5 Curriculum Guidelines: A Computer Integrated Curriculum Based on Canadian Language Benchmarks 4–6*. Toronto Catholic District School Board. Toronto: Citizenship and Immigration Canada.

Harré, R. and van Langenhove, L. (1999) *Positioning Theory: Moral Contexts of Intentional Action*. Oxford: Blackwell.

Johnston, B. (2017) *English Teaching and Evangelical Mission: The Case of Lighthouse School*. Bristol: Multilingual Matters.

Lave, J. and Wenger, E. (1991) *Situated Learning: Legitimate Peripheral Participation*. New York: Cambridge University Press.

Marmur, D. (2015) Social networks key to happiness. *Toronto Star Newspaper*, 4 August, p. A11.

Morgan, B. (2002) Critical practice in community-based ESL programs: A Canadian perspective. *Journal of Language, Identity, & Education* 1, 141–162.

Morgan, B. (2009) The pedagogical dilemmas of faith in English language teaching: A dialogical response. In M.S. Wong and S. Canagarajah (eds) *Christian and Critical English Language Educators in Dialogue: Pedagogical and Ethical Dilemmas* (pp. 193–204). New York: Routledge.

Morgan, B. and Clarke, M. (2011) Identity in second language teaching and learning. In E. Hinkel (ed.) *Handbook of Research in Second Language Teaching and Learning* (2nd edn) (pp. 817–836). New York: Routledge.

Morgan, B. and Martin, I. (2014) Towards a research agenda for classroom-as-ecosystem. *The Modern Language Journal* 98 (2), 667–670.

Motha, S. (2014) *Race, Empire, and English Language Teaching: Creating Responsible and Ethical Anti-racist Practice.* New York: Teachers College Press.

Motha, S. and Lin, A. (2013) 'Non-coercive rearrangements': Theorizing desire in TESOL. *TESOL Quarterly* 48 (2), 331–359.

Nelson, C. (2009) *Sexual Identities in English Language Education.* New York: Routledge.

Oxford Islamic Studies Online (2016) *Pillars of Islam.* See http://www.oxfordislamicstudies.com/article/opr/t125/e1859?_hi=17&_pos=3 (accessed 26 April, 2018).

Pavlenko, A. and Blackledge, A. (2004) New theoretical approaches to the study of negotiation of identity in multilingual contexts. In A. Pavlenko and A. Blackledge (eds) *Negotiation of Identities in Multilingual Contexts* (pp. 1–33). Clevedon: Multilingual Matters.

Pennycook, A. and Otsuji, E. (2015) *Metrolingualism: Language in the City.* New York: Routledge.

Seljak, D. (1996) Why the Quiet Revolution was 'quiet': The Catholic Church's reaction to the secularization of nationalism in Quebec after 1960. *CCHA, Historical Studies* 62, 109–124. See http://umanitoba.ca/colleges/st_pauls/ccha/Back%20Issues/CCHA1996/Seljak.pdf (accessed 26 April, 2018).

Shackleton, D.F. (1975) *Tommy Douglas.* Toronto: McClelland & Stewart.

Smolicz, J.J. (1992) Minority languages as core values of ethnic cultures: A study of maintenance and erosion of Polish, Welsh, and Chinese languages in Australia. In W. Fase, K. Jaspaert and S. Kroon (eds) *Maintenance and Loss of Minority Language* (pp. 277–305). Amsterdam: John Benjamins.

Stoller, F.L. (2004) Content-based instruction: Perspectives on curriculum planning. *Annual Review of Applied Linguistics* 24, 261–283.

Stryker, A., with Crestohl, L., Sull, M. and Vander Ende, D. (2013) *Rights Talk: Students and Civil Liberties at School.* Toronto: BC Civil Liberties Association. See https://bccla.org/wp-content/uploads/2013/11/2013-Handbook-Rights-Talk.pdf (accessed 26 April, 2018).

Taylor, C. (1994) The politics of recognition. In A. Gutman (ed.) *Multiculturalism: Examining the Politics of Recognition* (pp. 25–73). Princeton, NJ: Princeton University Press.

Vandrick, S. (2011) Students of the new global elite. *TESOL Quarterly* 45, 160–169.

van Lier, L. (2004) *The Ecology and Semiotics of Language Learning: A Sociocultural Perspective.* Boston, MA: Kluwer Academic.

Wenger, E. (1998) *Communities of Practice: Learning, Meaning, and Identity.* Cambridge: Cambridge University Press.

Wong, M.S. and Canagarajah, S. (eds) (2009) *Christian and Critical English Language Educators in Dialogue: Pedagogical and Ethical Dilemmas.* New York: Routledge.

14 Spirituality and English Language Teaching: Moving Forward

Ahmar Mahboob and Eve Courtney

Introduction

While professional and academic literature on English language teaching (ELT) continues to grow, questions about if and how teachers' spiritual and religious beliefs impact their professional practice are often left out of the discussions. This is an odd gap given the centrality of spiritual and religious beliefs in our everyday lives, society and politics. When the literature in ELT does engage with these issues, it mostly explores or questions links between Christianity and ELT. The relationship between other belief systems and English language education remains underexamined. This volume was designed to explore this relationship by inviting contributions from a range of religious and spiritual backgrounds. The individual contributions to the volume provide convincing evidence that teachers' and teacher educators' beliefs can and do influence their practice. Together, the chapters illustrate that religious and/or spiritual beliefs do not remain outside the door when we walk into our professional contexts, but rather they influence our professional identity, our pedagogical practices and the context in which we teach/learn languages. In this concluding chapter of the volume, we will first revisit the questions that were set out in organizing this volume. We will then conclude the chapter by looking at some possible future directions and implications of this volume.

Returning to the Questions

As pointed out in the Introduction, this volume was conceptualized in order to explore five broad questions. As we conclude this volume, we would like to briefly respond to these questions based on what we learned from our contributors and respondents.

(1) How do teachers' faith beliefs impact their identities, i.e. how do language teachers view themselves and how are they are viewed by others?

The contributions to this volume address this first question of teacher identity in a number of ways. One of the key themes that emerged in this volume is that teachers found satisfaction in teaching in a way that aligns with their spiritual identity. For example, Wong describes the 'delights' – gratification and joy – which result when teachers have a sense of the purpose behind their teaching, in addition to a sense that their actions 'align with [their] spiritual identity' (this volume, p. 23). Similarly, Vandrick's participants conveyed a sense of peace and meaning in their work which encompasses 'caring for their students not only regarding their education but regarding their wellbeing in a much wider sense' (this volume, p. 113). Smith, reflecting on Brown and Vandrick, comments that spiritual identity can help prevent burnout in a profession that 'can be peculiarly draining and challenging to one's sense of self' (this volume, p. 121).

A second theme that ran across the volume was related to levels of attachment and shifts in spiritual identity. For example, Kubota states that, unlike some/many other identities, religious identities are often chosen with 'conscious investment', leading to a strong attachment to associated ideas (like Christison, this volume). Kubota argues that teachers have 'emotional attachment to a certain belief or view, which may conflict with the beliefs and views of others' (this volume, p. 63). Nazari shares a similar perspective (however, from the viewpoint of a religion from childhood) and states: 'Sometimes accepting new ideas, thoughts or beliefs feels like denying our being, since we might be unable to separate our beliefs from our "selves" due to the critical time they were molded in us in our childhood. Therefore, we might prefer to let the self be as it is – secure and protected' (this volume, p. 60). In addition, a number of chapters in the volume discussed how religious and/or spiritual identities are not uniform, and are difficult to separate from culture and other influences. Smith, in responding to Sharma's contribution, notes 'The difficulty that the essay faces of tracing the entangled contours of the religious, the cultural, the philosophical and the historical helpfully points to the complexity of the actual landscape' (this volume, p. 123). Smith also notes that religious identity is not neatly tied to 'geographical and cultural locations'.

(2) What common values and practice do teachers from different religious backgrounds share and what can they learn from each other?

The contributions to the volume share a number of common values and practices from different backgrounds. Some of these include:

- critical pedagogy and strong values related to peace, the environment, justice, etc.;

- high level of importance placed on reflecting on one's identity and practice;
- the need to be aware of contextual factors in relation to content, pedagogy and students' backgrounds;
- the need to recognize and not gloss over difference; to seek comfort with uncertainty and ambiguity;
- motivation and a sense of purpose focused on the good of the student; this is defined as something wider than simply language learning, usually including the ability to think critically, but in many cases also including students' general and spiritual wellbeing;
- wariness towards the power of English.

The contributors also identify a range of values and practices that we can learn from one another. For example, the duoethnographic approach adopted in Heng Hartse and Nazari presents a method of interfaith dialogue through which teachers from different religious backgrounds can learn from and seek to understand each other (as individuals rather than as representatives of an entire faith) as they juxtapose their differences and shared experiences. Examples and suggestions of practices presented from one faith may be adapted and/or used for discussion and teaching in other contexts, which could enhance cross-cultural communication.

(3) What does faith have to do with teachers' pedagogy and interactions with students in the various contexts in which they teach?

Contributors to the volume discuss necessary mindsets/awareness of issues related to spirituality and ELT. For example, Wong (like Kubota) notes the need for awareness of power imbalances in the classroom, and the need to base interactions with students on the Belmont principles of respect (interest in and concern for their identities and backgrounds), beneficence (avoiding harm through not 'imposing' the teacher's faith or 'denigrating' the students') and justice (treating spiritual subject matter fairly and impartially and creating legitimate avenues for students to engage with it). Vandrick also highlights the need for teachers to be aware of the influence of their strong beliefs, religious or not. At the same time, she suggests that such teachers may actually have more awareness and sensitivity to different perspectives and identities as a result of their experience reflecting on these issues.

A number of contributors discuss teachers' motivation and sustenance of the teacher's 'spirit'. As Smith observes in his response, both Brown and Vandrick (but also Wong, Shabaan and Christison) underscore how spirituality can empower teachers to continue in the face of a role which Smith describes as 'peculiarly draining and challenging to one's sense of self' (this volume, p. 121). This has implications for their interactions with students. Morgan makes a similar observation regarding the way in which such sustenance can provide students with resilience at the 'spiritual/secular interface'.

Contributors to the volume also discuss wider pedagogical commitments that relate to spirituality in ELT. Brown expresses a powerful sense of personal duty (echoing the more theoretical discussions of Wong and Kubota) to 'help students develop the skills, perspectives and values necessary to discern and solve world problems' (this volume, p. 75) and 'assist ... in cultivating and communicating respect and curiosity and seeking fairness as they speak across religious divides and take stands in a religiously pluralistic world' (this volume, p. 79). This commitment shapes her pedagogy and interactions with students in a way that is different to her previous approach, which excluded any inclusion of personal views in classroom discussion.

Finally, the many contributors to the volume discussed the intersections between prevailing secular pedagogy and faith/culture-informed pedagogy. Wong argues that teachers may feel confused and conflicted about how to develop a pedagogy that is 'informed' by their faith (consistent with the identity issue of 'alignment' between faith and practice) yet will not cause conflict within their institutions or their own sense of ethical behavior as language teaching professionals. Sharma recounts embracing and internalizing modern, Western-originating and secular ideas through his teacher education courses in Nepal, which viewed local, traditional educational practices as 'unworthy' of attention 'due to the spiritual and religious values that undergirded any vestiges of those educational practices' (this volume, p. 86). However, his exploration of these historical Hindu practices produces a conflict with this dominant viewpoint, as he found many pedagogical similarities, particularly with regard to values of 'learner centeredness, teacher and student autonomy, discussion and argument-based classroom participation, and transformative pedagogy'. Sharma suggests that '[i]nstead of looking up to Western-originated philosophical and pedagogical traditions for their professional development, English teachers in the periphery can reflect on their own philosophical and spiritual background if such background is an important part of their teaching life' (this volume, p. 86). He argues that spiritual sources are useful in providing 'alternative perspectives' which are often relevant to our present context. Similarly, Smith observes that language teaching literature is negatively affected by a lack of interaction with and consideration of other areas of scholarship which more closely examine the relationship between spiritual perspectives and education (such as those related to religious education, children's spirituality, philosophy of religion and the theology and philosophy of education).

(4) In what ways do religion, faith and other belief systems enter the language classroom and what roles do they play in teaching and learning?

The contributors respond to this question in a number of ways. Wong argues that strong beliefs and values can enter the curriculum. She notes the possibility of 'overzealous' teachers prioritizing their 'agenda' over learning outcomes, but also suggests (with Kubota) that religion and values discussion can have useful role in learning as it helps connect with the lives, cultures and identities of students. Wong further argues that native-speaker quasi-teachers could negatively affect students' learning through 'lack of skills, knowledge and awareness' (this volume, p. 24).

A number of authors discuss the cultural context of ELT. For example, Nazari points out the importance of cultural context when making decisions about bringing spirituality into the classroom; in Iran, he felt free to begin lessons with a phrase written on the whiteboard acknowledging what followed to be in the name of God (and thus contextualizing the entirety of the lesson as a spiritual act). He remembers this creating 'a pleasant spiritual feeling' for himself and the students. However, in Canada he feels anxious about, and compelled to avoid, 'practical representations' of his faith in the classroom (something which Heng Hartse experiences to a lesser degree, although he feels able to discuss matters of belief in the classroom if the topic is initiated by a student).

Authors note the influence of prevailing religious ideologies on ELT. Nazari refers to his experience as a student in a public school system whose curriculum he describes as 'heavily loaded with ideology' as having impacted his 'subjectivity'. He highlights the circular, self-reinforcing relationship between institutional power and absolute religious ideology and the way this robs students of their ability to see from varied perspectives. Shaaban states that the majority of quality educational institutions in Lebanon are private, religion-affiliated schools, which are concerned with influencing students' moral development and values in addition to being concerned with general education.

(5) What connections do language teachers with religious convictions make between their faith beliefs and language policies?

Several connections and potential conflicts were found between a teacher's faith and policies of the school and state. In Part 1, Wong and Heng Hartse discuss and critique Christians who see English teaching (state encouraged as a result of language policies) as an opportunity to proselytize. Vandrick (and her participants) also cite these criticisms, including that 'some scholars have felt that spreading English throughout the world, even without an explicitly Christian focus, is a kind of imperialist spreading of Western and Christian values and culture'.

In Part 2, Sharma notes that in Nepal the English language teacher education field has embraced 'Western', 'modern' philosophy of education and pedagogies, leading to a dismissal of traditional Hindu (in the broader sense which encompasses religion, culture, spirituality, philosophy, history, pedagogy, etc.) approaches which offer demonstrable value. This also leads to culturally/religiously/spiritually inappropriate/irrelevant content. Sharma as a Hindu English language teacher feels conflicted due to the positionings as both Hindu/Nepalese and an educated language professional. Sharma suggests looking to the way in which traditional methods resonate with modern approaches (such as critical pedagogy, especially in relation to the environment, as well as learner centeredness and teacher and student autonomy, discussion and argument-based participation and transformative pedagogy).

And, in Part 3, Shaaban discusses the consociationalist system of government in Lebanon and the accompanying sectarianism of the society along religious and linguistic lines (language being used to reinforce exclusive group identity), and the consequent embrace of multilingualism as a defining characteristic of Lebanon. The various political groups/forces use language and language education to 'perpetuate sectarian autonomy' through 'shaping identities' (as noted by Morgan). Accordingly, the teachers displayed varying stances towards the teaching of English due to the way it fit or did not fit with their community (religious) alignment. Boraie, Gebril and Gabriel shared similar viewpoints from their participants: some of the Muslim teachers were hesitant to embrace English in areas outside of the professional due to the way it aligns them with a Western/Christian identity, even though the Egyptian government (like the Lebanese) prioritizes the teaching of English (a compulsory subject in public and private education, and the language of instruction in many Egyptian universities) for its importance to its citizens' global economic participation (although in both cases Arabic is the official language, and in Lebanon is the shared language across the multilingual communities). Finally, Kristjánsson notes how the official language of English in BC, Canada, and the monolingualism of most fields of social participation lead the program directors and teachers to endeavor to include newcomers in society through English instruction, as an embodiment of their faith ('showing love') – this is particularly to fill a gap in the government systematic provision of language education for 'eligible newcomers' which Kristjánsson states is sometimes insufficient or unavailable to some who need it.

Future Directions and Implications

The contributions to this volume highlight how identity and religious and/or spiritual ideology influence teacher beliefs and practices, which in turn may influence learner beliefs and identities. While some of the contributors (e.g. Nazari and Shabaan) point out the relationship between dominant religious beliefs in a community and ELT, how this may influence students is not fully explored in this volume. As discussed in Mahboob (2015), language in educational contexts can play a role in 'identity management'. Identity management, as defined in Mahboob (2015: 156), is 'any institutionalized or localized effort to shape or direct individual or group identities'. In this work, Mahboob argues that an individual's identity and sociocultural positioning can be influenced through discourse either locally (micro-level), by individuals or groups of people that a person interacts with, or through institutionalized (macro-level) processes. These processes can promote either norm-conforming or norm-contesting positions. The identity management framework, presented in Figure 14.1, posits that the individual identities can potentially be influenced into four types of discursive positioning: macro-conforming, micro-conforming, macro-contesting and micro-contesting. The differences between these four types of identity management are based on whether identity management is organized institutionally (macro) or if it is done through small-scale or individual (micro) initiatives, and whether the identity being promoted is in sync with the majority or dominant perspectives (conforming) or if it is contesting or alternative to the dominant perspectives. The contributors to this volume clearly demonstrate how teachers' religious and/or spiritual identities influence their professional actions and practices and how some of them might have experienced identity management. Although a few of the contributors refer to the influence of ELT on students, this is not fully explored. A follow-up question would

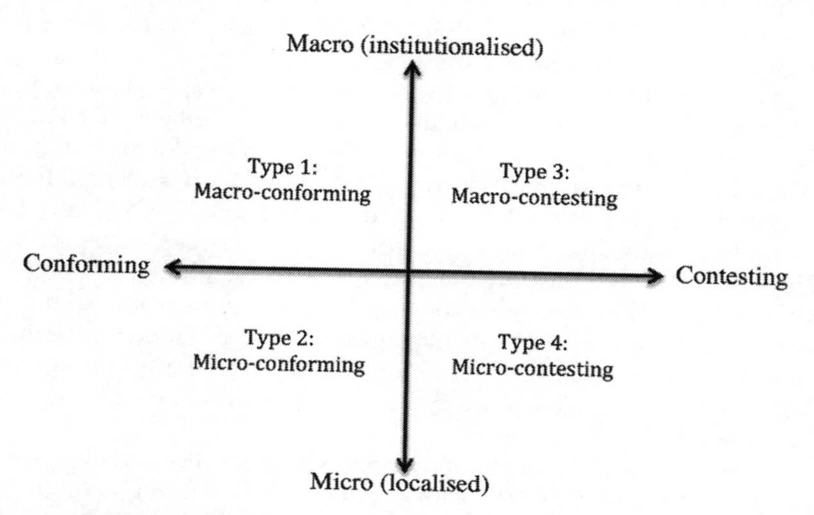

Figure 14.1 Identity management framework
Source: Adapted from Mahboob (2015).

be if and how these practices influence students. Furthermore, what kind of identities do they encourage, either directly or indirectly? Do they promote the dominant beliefs of the community (conforming), or do they encourage alternative ways of thinking and being (contesting)? These questions are yet to be explored, but the chapters in this volume separately and together suggest that identity management likely does happen in classrooms. We hope that this volume will generate an interest in researching these questions further.

In addition to raising questions about identity management, the chapters in this volume have a number of other implications. We will consider three of these here. First, the volume moves the debate beyond Christian evangelism and ELT to a range of belief systems. Previous research, as well as a number of contributors to this volume (e.g. Wong, Heng Hartse and Kristjánsson), explores the link between Christianity and ELT. However, as the contributions by Christison, Nazari, Brown, Sharma and Vandrick document, other religious and spiritual traditions also influence the ELT profession and professionals. There is little current research that explores these questions in depth and we believe that one implication of this volume will be to encourage research in this area.

A second implication, one that extends the point above, is that we now know that belief systems, regardless of what these are, influence professionals and their professional space (for example, see the chapters by Shaaban and Boraie, Gebril and Gabriel) and actions. Ignoring or rejecting this relationship does not make it go away; instead, we need to engage with these issues more deeply. Most current literature on English language teaching and teacher education does not discuss issues about religion and/or spirituality. This implies that discussions on these issues, if they do take place, are often done without reference to or informed by a research-based literature.

The third implication that we will consider here is again based on the collective findings of this volume that belief systems influence ELT. This implies that we need to consider this dimension in developing and using ELT material and resources. Currently, much of the research on religion and/or spirituality and ELT, including chapters in this volume, has focused on individual and/or group beliefs, practices and behaviors. There is only limited research (e.g. Cruz, 2016; Mahboob, 2009, 2015, Mahboob & Elyas, 2014) that looks at how teaching resources such as textbooks play a role in identity management. We need more research on this and to consider how material writers and curriculum planners, as well as authors of language teacher education material, need to address these issue in their domains.

In conclusion, the contributions to this volume, collected from people in different parts of the world, with different beliefs, drawing on a variety of data sources and adopting a range of research methods and approaches, provide evidence that spiritual and religious beliefs can and do influence

ELT practices. The volume thus underscores the importance of exploring the relationship between spirituality and ELT more deeply. The contributions to the volume provide examples of how spiritual and religious beliefs are intertwined with other beliefs (e.g. professional beliefs) in shaping ELT policy and practice. However, as pointed out above, there a number of aspects of this relationship that remain under-studied. We hope that this volume will generate a greater interest in exploring these questions and contribute to a knowledge base that acknowledges and considers the role of faith in ELT rather than ignoring it.

References

Cruz, P. (2016) Construing axiology: A study of identity management in English language teaching textbooks in the Philippines. Unpublished doctoral dissertation, Ateneo de Manila University.

Mahboob, A. (2009) English as an Islamic language. *World Englishes* 28 (2), 175–189.

Mahboob, A. (2015) Identity management, language variation, and English language textbooks. In D. Djenar, A. Mahboob and K. Cruickshank (eds) *Language and Identity Across Modes of Communication* (pp. 153–177). Boston, MA: Mouton de Gruyter.

Mahboob, A. and Elyas, T. (2014) English in the Kingdom of Saudi Arabia. *World Englishes* 33 (1), 128–142.

Afterword: Spirituality in Language Teaching

H.G. Widdowson

What I find so interesting about the contributions to this book is not only the insights they provide about how individual teachers relate their religious experience to their teaching, but also how, in different ways, these contributions raise fundamental questions about the very nature of religious belief and spirituality and how the two are related in general, and in the pedagogy of language teaching in particular. What I want to do here is to briefly, and speculatively, explore these questions from my own, admittedly agnostic, point of view.

The way language teachers teach is bound to be informed by beliefs of one kind or another about their subject: what it is appropriate for learners to learn and how they can best be induced to learn it. These may be beliefs that are based on their own learning experience or transmitted as received wisdom by seasoned fellow teachers, both of which are naturally informed by the sociocultural habitus of the communities they live in. Or they may be imported beliefs which teachers are persuaded to adopt on 'expert' authority in their pre- or in-service training. The history of English language teaching, for example, is a succession of such imported beliefs, which take the form of tenets of different pedagogic approaches – the structural, the communicative, the lexical, the task-based and so on, with each one making claims to be more valid than the other.

Imported beliefs are, of course, likely to be at variance with the ways of thinking to which teachers have been accustomed, and quite naturally give rise to resistance. Usually the proponents of a new approach see it as their task to break down this resistance as an impediment to progress. What they encounter, however, is not just a different pedagogic culture rooted in local tradition but a complex web of ideas and assumptions of individual teachers – what has been referred to as teacher cognition. Teachers do not think and act by simply conforming to an orthodoxy, whether traditional or imported, but by reference to their own cognition, their own interpretation of experience. This cognition has been subjected to a good deal of research and discussed in a number of publications (e.g. Barnard & Burns, 2012; Borg, 2009). This research has to do with a range of factors that (to quote from the title of an early review) influence 'what teachers know, think, believe and do' (Borg, 2003).

Although no reference is made to this research, this present book is also centrally concerned with such teacher cognition and extends the scope of its study by focusing on the influence of spirituality and religious faith on 'what teachers know, think, believe and do' – an influence that research on teacher cognition seems hitherto not to have taken into explicit account. This, on the face of it, is a rather surprising omission since, as the contributions in this book, and especially those in the first two parts, make convincingly clear, teachers of a religious conviction see their faith as crucial in defining their identity and in influencing how they go about their teaching. But, insightful though this perspective on language pedagogy may be, the absence of any direct connection with existing research on teacher cognition raises an intriguing question: How far does religious faith interact with other kinds of belief in shaping the way teachers teach?

This question raises a number of basic issues that I think call for inquiry. To begin with, we need to ask what, if anything, distinguishes a religious belief from any other. I assume that if you have religious belief you believe in a particular religion, and that what that means is that you subscribe to its particular version of reality. Religions, although based on divine revelation enshrined in sacred texts, are not, of course, made in heaven but designed and (in both senses of the word) authorized by human agency. In this respect, one might argue, a religion is a theory, and as such not essentially different from any other in that it seeks to provide explanations of phenomena which would otherwise be puzzling, and does so by abstracting underlying causes from the actual appearance of things. Like religions, other theories too have their prophets and reformers – such figures, for example, as Darwin, Marx and indeed Chomsky. And these theories too have their canonical texts, their disciples, their converts and their sectarian variants. So how is belief in a religion different from a belief in an evolutionary or political or linguistic theory? How is the belief of a Marxist, for example, different from that of a Christian? One obvious difference is that religious theory presupposes the existence and intervention of divinities of one kind or another as the ultimate explanation of phenomena, which puts the explanation beyond the reach of proof, either by rational argument or empirical evidence. Religions are based on interpretations that are endorsed without having to be verified: sanctioned – indeed sanctified – by institutional authority. Believers in a religious theory can only take it on trust. Belief indeed is a matter of faith.

But how do believers act on their beliefs? The tenets of a religion are, after all, not only philosophical abstractions but are also intended as prescribed maxims for actual behavior. And it is this relationship between belief and behavior that is explored by the chapters in this book. As previously pointed out, they can be seen as contributing to the existing inquiry into language teacher cognition. But there is a significant difference. This previous inquiry focused attention on the teachers' beliefs about language and language learning, how these relate to explicitly formulated theories and how these inform, and are informed, by actual teaching experience. In this sense, this inquiry is all about applied linguistics. What the contributions in this book are concerned with, however, is not applied linguistics but what we might call applied religious belief.

This perspective yields new insights into what influences how language teachers teach. But it also raises familiar problems about the relationship between theory and practice. A point frequently made about what I referred to earlier as imported theory, and one that is repeatedly made in the teacher cognition literature, is that it is often imposed unilaterally and without due consideration of the local context. Where this context is unfavorable to the acceptance or implementation of a new way of thinking, it is usually seen as a rather tiresome constraint that needs to be overcome rather than a necessary condition that needs to be taken into account. Thus, all too often, the proponents of a pedagogic belief, typically supported by an institutional authority of one kind or another, will tend to be intolerant of opposition and to think of themselves as on a mission to convert teachers to a more enlightened pedagogy in the name of progress.

The proponents of a religious belief can also, of course, be prone to the same intolerant proselytizing tendency. History is full of efforts to convert pagans and infidels, by coercion or persuasion, to what is believed to be the true faith. And what is taken as true is the specific formulation of belief enshrined in a particular sectarian dogma, so it is not only pagans and infidels but dissenters and heretics too that need to be shown the error of their ways. But belief in a religion is an abstraction that only has an effect when it is realized in actual behavior, and this is influenced by all manner of sociocultural, economic and political factors – factors that influence the institutional formulation of the religion in the first place. It is not the differences of religious belief in themselves but the different ways they are acted upon in combination with these other factors that give rise to confrontation and conflict.

So it is, historically, that although conflicts may be in the name of religion, it is generally not just religion that it is the driving force behind them. The priests who followed on the heels of the conquistadores may have believed in their mission to save souls but they were also complicit in colonial conquest, which was motivated by very different aspirations. And the same can be said, and has been said, of pedagogic missionaries spreading belief in new ways of language teaching. And new ways of believing may themselves be motivated by factors which are far from holy. In 1521, to give one example, Pope Leo X bestowed on Henry VIII the title of 'Defender of the Faith.' The faith referred to was orthodox Catholicism, a creed that the king found later to be inconvenient for his domestic affairs and which he found reasons in the scripture to replace with an alternative version. He was subsequently excommunicated but he kept the title, even though he ceased to defend the faith it referred to. This is, of course, not the only case where the principles of a belief are expeditiously interpreted to suit requirements. Consider, for example, how democracy as a political belief has been exploited in our contemporary world in its current interpretation as necessarily bound up with capitalism and Western values. As in the past, latter-day crusaders and conquistadores are on a mission to impose, by conversion or conquest, that version of a faith that is to their own political or economic advantage.

The point I would want to make is that the actualization as behavior of an abstract belief in a theory, religious or otherwise, must necessarily be conditioned by all manner of sociocultural, economic and political factors. And this applies to the belief in a particular approach to language pedagogy, however theoretically or empirically well-grounded it may claim to be. As mentioned earlier, the tendency in the past has been to disregard or gloss over such factors, both as they motivate the promotion of the approach and as they constrain how it is put into practice.

The question then arises as to how far a belief can survive the process of its practical implementation. If in order to accommodate local contextual factors, you modify, or even dispense with, tenets of your belief, how far can you go without undermining the very dogma of the belief that these tenets define? On the other hand, if you persist in maintaining the integrity of your belief, and graft it on the local context by conversion, it may well be counter to local teacher cognition and the likelihood is that it will not take. As the history of English language teaching shows quite clearly, this often, if not usually, happens with different approaches informed by applied linguistic beliefs of one kind or another. As a result, so-called developments in language teaching are for the most part largely academic and in practice confined to certain privileged educational contexts.

What then if your pedagogy is informed by religious conviction? I believe the same problem arises. To teach in accordance with the dogma that defines a particular religious belief may well be quite inappropriate in that it does not take local factors into account and so constitutes an exercise in conversion. As a number of contributors have made clear, this is not at all the kind of religious influence they have in mind. Rather, it is that their religious faith has led them to an awareness of the significance of certain general humanistic precepts such as a consideration for others, a tolerance of cultural diversity, respect for individual identity and so on. But these precepts of benevolent behavior are not specific to religious faith. Indeed it is a notorious fact that religious faiths of different kinds have in the past brutally violated them, and still do. The contributors in Part 2 of this volume provide an account of the doctrinal dogma of different institutionalized faiths before going on to discuss how the precepts that they, as individuals, have derived from them have influenced the way they teach. This is a kind of applied belief, but it is these derived individual precepts that are applied, not the tenets of institutionalized faiths.

These precepts can be derived from a religious faith, but do not have to be. They represent values, visions of an ideal ineffable world that human beings seem to instinctively recognize if they do not always respect, a sense of some other elusive reality that exists in a different dimension from that of immediate experience and which resists conventional categorization. It is this sense of a transcendent plane of being that we can call spirituality and it is this that motivates the making of religions in the first place. So it is spirituality that gives rise to religion and not the other way round.

So, to return to the question that prompted this discussion: How far does religious faith interact with other kinds of belief in shaping the way teachers teach?

As is pointed out in the introductory chapter of this book, spirituality is not the same as religious faith, although they are somehow related. According to its title, the book is about spirituality, but the different parts of the book, according to *their* titles, are about religious faith. This would appear to presuppose that there is some converse implicational relationship between them – that if you are spiritual this implies that you are religious and vice versa. But I would argue that in a sense the relationship is one of contradiction. The term 'teaching' is conventionally used to refer to the tenets of a particular doctrine, as in the teachings of Islam or Catholicism. I take it that to have religious faith is to subscribe to the teaching in this sense of a particular institutionalized religion and to act on this faith is to conform to its doctrine. I assume spirituality, on the other hand, to be an individual awareness of the kind of transcendental values I mentioned earlier – an awareness of the other, of dimensions of human experience that are superordinate to any specific formulation as a religious faith. To act on this awareness is to follow certain humanistic precepts of tolerance and empathy which will naturally incline you to understand and respect the otherness of people rather than to convert them.

A way of language teaching that is spiritual in this sense is indeed the very opposite of one that conforms to the teaching of an orthodox pedagogic doctrine but one, on the contrary, that seeks to resist dogmatism and to accommodate to other ways of thinking and believing. Spirituality can thus be seen as an essential influence on a teacher's assumptions and attitudes and so is integrally related to the teacher cognition referred to earlier, providing, we might say, an added dimension to these that is not only cognitive. As such they allow for the variable local adaptation of pedagogic ideas and serve as a corrective against indoctrination and the too-ready adoption of the dogma of imported beliefs.

What for me is so significant and timely about this book is that in exploring the influence of spirituality and religious faith on language teaching it raises critical issues which are directly relevant to how programs in language teacher education have been, and still are, designed and implemented. But more than that, it seems to me to point to the need in all human affairs for institutionalized beliefs, whether they be religious, political or whatever, to be interpreted in appropriately spiritual ways.

References

Barnard, R. and Burns, A. (2012) *Researching Language Teacher Cognition and Practice*. Bristol: Multilingual Matters.

Borg, S. (2003) Teacher cognition in language teaching: A review of what teachers think, know, believe and do. *Language Teaching* 36 (2), 81–109.

Borg, S. (2009) Language teacher cognition. In A. Burns and J.C. Richards (eds) *The Cambridge Guide to Language Teacher Education* (pp. 163–171). Cambridge: Cambridge University Press.

Index

Note: n refers to notes